Decision-making in Humanitarian Operations

Sebastián Villa • Gloria Urrea
Jaime Andrés Castañeda • Erik R. Larsen
Editors

Decision-making in Humanitarian Operations

Strategy, Behavior and Dynamics

palgrave
macmillan

Editors
Sebastián Villa
School of Management
Universidad de los Andes
Bogotá, Colombia

Jaime Andrés Castañeda
School of Management
Universidad del Rosario
Bogotá, Colombia

Gloria Urrea
Kelley School of Business
Indiana University
Bloomington, USA

Erik R. Larsen
Aarhus University
Aarhus, Denmark

ISBN 978-3-319-91508-1   ISBN 978-3-319-91509-8   (eBook)
https://doi.org/10.1007/978-3-319-91509-8

Library of Congress Control Number: 2018949164

© The Editor(s) (if applicable) and The Author(s), under exclusive licence to Springer International Publishing AG, part of Springer Nature 2019
This work is subject to copyright. All rights are solely and exclusively licensed by the Publisher, whether the whole or part of the material is concerned, specifically the rights of translation, reprinting, reuse of illustrations, recitation, broadcasting, reproduction on microfilms or in any other physical way, and transmission or information storage and retrieval, electronic adaptation, computer software, or by similar or dissimilar methodology now known or hereafter developed.
The use of general descriptive names, registered names, trademarks, service marks, etc. in this publication does not imply, even in the absence of a specific statement, that such names are exempt from the relevant protective laws and regulations and therefore free for general use.
The publisher, the authors and the editors are safe to assume that the advice and information in this book are believed to be true and accurate at the date of publication. Neither the publisher nor the authors or the editors give a warranty, express or implied, with respect to the material contained herein or for any errors or omissions that may have been made. The publisher remains neutral with regard to jurisdictional claims in published maps and institutional affiliations.

This Palgrave Macmillan imprint is published by the registered company Springer Nature Switzerland AG
The registered company address is: Gewerbestrasse 11, 6330 Cham, Switzerland

Preface

This book brings together research in three different streams: humanitarian operations, behavioral operations and dynamic simulation. This combination is distinctive because it allows readers interested in the humanitarian sector to receive a holistic vision of the different challenges involved in the decision-making process of humanitarian organizations. In addition, it allows scholars studying humanitarian operations to learn from different methodological applications in order to study this sector.

Why do we study the humanitarian sector? Humanitarian disasters have increased in frequency and impact during the last decades, and estimates indicate that they will continue increasing in number and severity. Humanitarian actors and the wider community have designed and implemented programs to mitigate the damage caused by disasters and improve society's quality of life. However, this is not an easy task for humanitarian organizations due to the large number of actors, time pressures, delays, feedback loops and uncertainties surrounding their operations. Interactions among different actors create inefficiencies in their performance, caused in turn by factors such as competition for media attention and funding, lack of coordination, and high turnover rates. All these circumstances pose important challenges for humanitarian organizations in (i) planning and implementing their operations and (ii) managing the pressure to be efficient and make the right decisions. In this book, we propose that scholars can understand those challenges better and find potential ways to mitigate them by using other methodological approaches, such as behavioral operations and simulation.

Behavioral operations emphasize the use of experiments to allow a better understanding of the factors that affect performance in real operations. Common results show that people are prone to decision-making biases and, consequently, display poor performance, even when they have the opportunity to identify and correct errors. People's bounded rationality explains biases, which are related to deficiencies in our mental models. Traditional models in humanitarian operations assume unbounded rationality, while behavioral models of bounded rationality propose heuristics, rules and norms to explain and understand people's behavior. Such understanding can be used within a humanitarian setting to improve decision-making.

Research into humanitarian operations has increased during the last 10 years and is one of the hottest topics in the operations management field. Similarly, from the behavioral perspective, there is a growing body of literature trying to understand human behavior in operations. We provide here an opportunity to study human behavior in the humanitarian context. There has been limited research analyzing humanitarian operations systematically, including their dynamics and behavioral aspects. This book provides a novel and provocative approach by integrating the humanitarian operations field with the typical strategic decisions and operational biases faced by people when making their decisions in different contexts. The book also proposes new avenues for future research that can become building blocks for the creation of future publications in top academic journals. Moreover, as courses in humanitarian logistics continue to capture the attention of many universities and humanitarian organizations around the world, this book provides novel and up-to-date teaching material for these kinds of introductory courses and training programs.

Overview of the Book

The book is organized into three parts according to the three research streams. The first part introduces the main concepts involved in the humanitarian operations field and discusses the main strategic challenges faced by different humanitarian actors. The second part of the book introduces the main behavioral issues that people face when making operational decisions, with special attention to discussing behavioral biases in humanitarian operations. Finally, the third part of the book builds on the concepts discussed in the previous sections and introduces the use of simulation techniques to analyze important misperceptions of dynamics in the humanitarian setting.

Part I: Strategy

The first part provides an introduction of the humanitarian sector, outlining the main characteristics and strategic challenges of humanitarian organizations. The topics covered in this part include preparedness, donations, knowledge management, climate change and issues related to refugees and social inclusion.

The chapter "Logistics Preparedness and Response: A Case of Strategic Change", by Jahre and Jahre, deals with the first stage of the disaster management cycle: preparedness. This chapter builds on a comprehensive literature review and case studies to explain how humanitarian organizations can better prepare to respond to disasters. It includes an example of the strategic changes that the International Federation of Red Cross and Red Crescent Societies (IFRC) followed to improve preparedness for their operations.

The next chapter, "Private Donations for Humanitarian Operations", by Urrea and Pedraza-Martinez tackles another fundamental issue for humanitarian organizations: funding. The authors conduct a review of the literature on private donations and propose avenues for future research by exploring the relationship of private donations of cash, time and in-kind items with humanitarian operations.

The chapter on "Strategy and Knowledge Management in Humanitarian Organizations", by Cruz and Schmitt, looks at how humanitarian organizations can better manage the knowledge of their various employees dispersed around the world. The authors propose that the social capital that individuals have in their networks can serve as a means for knowledge creation, sharing and retention. They analyze the case of the World

Health Organization (WHO) and provide three initiatives for knowledge exploitation and exploration.

The chapter "Innovating Short-Term Preparedness Actions Using Climate Information", by Urrea and Bailey, discusses how humanitarian organizations and climate scientists can contribute to the reduction of a major global issue, the impact of climate change. The authors propose that a better integration of climate information systems and humanitarian actors can improve the planning and implementation of long- and short-term actions to protect the most vulnerable. They give practical examples of the innovative approach of forecast-based preparedness actions in two countries: Bangladesh and Mongolia.

The final chapter in the first section, "Refugees and Social Inclusion: The Role of Humanitarian Information Technologies", by Camacho, Herrera and Barrios deals with one of the most important issues related to violent conflicts: forced displacement. The authors provide some applied examples of how proper information technologies can be used to collect, process and analyze information that may contribute to improve the livelihoods of refugees. They extend the analysis by discussing the use of information technology within the four steps of the refugee pathway: displacement, journey, temporary settlement and permanent settlement.

Part II: Behavior

The second part of the book introduces several behavioral aspects that impact operational decision-making, extending the same line of thought to explore behavioral biases in humanitarian operations. It introduces behavioral operations and experiments by discussing single and multi-agent operational problems, followed by additional applications such as quantal theory and the framing effect.

The chapter on "Behavioral Experiments in Single-Agent Operational Problems", by Castañeda, introduces behavioral experiments to study operational decision-making, followed by a discussion of decision-making biases in single-agent problems and several implications for humanitarian operations.

The chapter on "Behavioral Operations in Multi-Agent Settings and Humanitarian Operations", by Villa, extends the previous chapter by taking a look at the multi-agent setting. In a humanitarian setting, the operational performance is strongly conditioned by the behavior of decision-makers and their interactions with other agents. This chapter provides an approach by which to extend traditional multi-agent behavioral results to the humanitarian sector.

Chen and Song discuss the role of bounded rationality in operations in the chapter "Quantal Theory in Operations Management". The authors introduce quantal theory to consider bounded rationality in analyzing operational decisions based on the assumption that decision-makers make mistakes in calculating payoffs. They review the applications of quantal theory in operations management and discuss how to accommodate bounded rationality into humanitarian operations.

The last chapter in the second part, "The Framing Effect in Humanitarian Operations", by Castañeda deals with how the framing of operational decisions impacts operational performance, discussing several potential applications of framing research to humanitarian operations.

Part III: Dynamics

The third and final part of the book introduces system dynamics and agent-based modeling and discusses how these modeling techniques can be used to study dynamics and decision-making in humanitarian operations. The chapters in this part explain the system dynamics methodology and apply it to collaboration and relief distribution. The book finishes with an introduction to agent-based modeling and a final application of both simulation methods in a context with heterogeneous decision-makers.

The chapter "Modeling Disaster Operations Management Problems with System Dynamics", by Delgado-Álvarez and Olaya, discusses how system dynamics can be used as a tool to study humanitarian operations problems. The authors introduce the main concepts of the system dynamics methodology and illustrate its application to humanitarian operations through a model of water supply after a disaster.

The chapter on "Collaborative Strategies for Humanitarian Logistics with System Dynamics and Project Management", by Guzmán Cortés, González Rodríguez and Franco, shows how humanitarian operations can be approached as a project, and models collaboration through system dynamics. They integrate both approaches and show how planning and collaboration impact response times and inventories when multiple stakeholders respond to a disaster.

The chapter "Agent-Based Modeling in Humanitarian Operations", by Díez-Echavarría, Sankaranarayanan and Villa, discusses how agent-based modeling can be used as a tool to study decision-making in humanitarian operations. The authors discuss the main concepts of agent-based modeling, its advantages and disadvantages and the process of building an agent-based model. They use four examples to provide initial research ideas to scholars who would like to delve into the use of this methodology within the humanitarian sector.

The final chapter, "Effects of Wholesale Competition in Supply Chains: An Analysis with Heterogeneous Decision-Makers", by Arboleda and Arango-Aramburo, builds on the concept of the bullwhip effect when competition is included at a wholesale level. The authors use agent-based modeling together with system dynamics to simulate the impact of the heterogeneity on decision rules. In addition, they run a behavioral experiment to understand and capture the behavior of the agents in a supply chain and to test the results obtained with the system dynamics model. Finally, the authors provide some suggestions to capture the rationality of decision-making in a humanitarian context.

Bogotá, Colombia	Sebastián Villa
Bloomington, USA	Gloria Urrea
Bogotá, Colombia	Jaime Andrés Castañeda
Aarhus, Denmark	Erik R. Larsen

Acknowledgements

We would like to express our gratitude for the support we receive from our sponsors and institutions. The research for this book was supported by (i) the Swiss National Science Foundation (SNF), Doctoral Mobility Fellowship program, grant numbers P1TIP1_171887 and P1TIP1_178664, (ii) the School of Management at Universidad de los Andes, FAPA Project number P17.100322.016, and (iii) Universidad del Rosario, Small Grants research fund, grant number PR-N/A 064.

We thank all our contributors. Their commitment, and critical and constructive views have significantly improved the quality of the book and its potential impact on researchers and practitioners interested in the fields of humanitarian logistics and behavioral operations.

Special mentions must go to Professor Rico Maggi of Università della Svizzera italiana (USI), Professor Alfonso Pedraza-Martinez and the Operations and Decision Technologies (ODT) department at Indiana University, Elena Katok and her team at University of Texas at Dallas, and to our colleagues at the Department of Management at Aarhus University. Thank you all for your support and guidance. It has been fantastic to have had the opportunity to collaborate with and learn from all of you.

We also thank Tatiana García, and all our families and friends for giving us unconditional support and continuous encouragement. This project would not have been possible without them.

Finally, we gratefully acknowledge the constructive comments from the Palgrave editorial team and their guidance through this process.

Sebastián Villa
Gloria Urrea
Jaime Andrés Castañeda
Erik R. Larsen

Contents

Part I Strategy   1

1 Logistics Preparedness and Response: A Case of Strategic Change   3
  Marianne Jahre and Martine Jahre

2 Private Donations for Humanitarian Operations   31
  Gloria Urrea and Alfonso J. Pedraza-Martinez

3 Strategy and Knowledge Management in Humanitarian Organizations   55
  Margarita Cruz and Achim Schmitt

4 Innovating Short-Term Preparedness Actions Using Climate Information   77
  Gloria Urrea and Meghan Bailey

5 Refugees and Social Inclusion: The Role of Humanitarian Information Technologies   99
  Sonia Camacho, Andrea Herrera, and Andrés Barrios

Part II Behavior 125

6 Behavioral Experiments in Single-Agent Operational Problems 127
Jaime Andrés Castañeda

7 Behavioral Operations in Multi-agent Settings and Humanitarian Operations 147
Sebastián Villa

8 Quantal Theory in Operations Management 169
Yefen Chen and Yanan Song

9 The Framing Effect In Humanitarian Operations 193
Jaime Andrés Castañeda

Part III Dynamics 221

10 Modeling Disaster Operations Management Problems with System Dynamics 223
Carlos A. Delgado-Álvarez and Yris Olaya-Morales

11 Collaborative Strategies for Humanitarian Logistics with System Dynamics and Project Management 249
Diana Carolina Guzmán Cortés, Leonardo José González Rodríguez, and Carlos Franco

12 **Agent-Based Modeling in Humanitarian Operations** 275
   Luisa Díez-Echavarría, Karthik Sankaranarayanan, and Sebastián Villa

13 **Effects of Wholesale Competition in Supply Chains: An Analysis with Heterogeneous Decision-Makers** 291
   Yuly Arboleda and Santiago Arango-Aramburo

Index 313

Notes on Contributors

Santiago Arango-Aramburo is Full Professor, Associated Dean for Research and Director of the Decision Sciences Group at the Universidad Nacional de Colombia, Faculty of Mines. His research focuses on energy planning and dynamic complex systems through simulation and experimental economics. His papers have been published in *Energy Economics, Energy Policy, European Journal of Operational Research*, and the *Journal of Economic Behaviour and Organizations*, among many others.

Yuly Arboleda is an industrial engineer with a Masters in Operation Research from the Universidad Nacional de Colombia. She is currently an expert on complex project management, with experience in facilitating group decisions. Currently, she is a researcher associated to the Decision Sciences research group. She has experience consulting with both national and international organizations in simulations, scenario planning, and decision-making experiments.

Meghan Bailey is a technical adviser at the Red Cross Red Crescent Climate Centre, specializing in forecast-based financing and adaptive social protection. She received her doctorate from Oxford University, exploring the socially differentiated adaptation and coping strategies of food-insecure populations experiencing environmental change. She also holds a Masters degree in Environmental Change and Management from Oxford University and a Bachelor of Public Affairs and Policy Management from Arthur Kroeger College at Carleton University (Canada). She has worked for more than 10 years in the humanitarian and development sectors.

Andrés Barrios is an Associate Professor of Marketing at the School of Management, Universidad de los Andes (Bogotá, Colombia). His research analyzes marketing strategies for addressing the intersection between development, poverty and social conflict. Dr. Barrios' work has been published in several outlets including *Journal of Service Research*, *Journal of Business Research*, and *Journal of Public Policy and Marketing*. He is also a board member of the International Society of Markets and Development.

Sonia Camacho is an Assistant Professor at the School of Management, Universidad de los Andes (Bogotá, Colombia). Her area of research involves human-computer interaction. Her research interests include the dark side of information technology usage, e-commerce, and technology adoption. Dr. Camacho has served as a reviewer for Information Systems conferences (e.g., Americas Conference on Information Systems—AMCIS, and International Conference on Information Systems—ICIS) and journals (e.g., Journal of Management Information Systems—JMIS). She was also the recipient of the "Best Reviewer" award at the Pre-ICIS Workshop on Human-Computer Interaction Research in Management Information Systems in 2014 and 2015.

Jaime Andrés Castañeda is Principal Professor in the School of Management at the Universidad del Rosario, Colombia. He teaches operations management topics at both the undergraduate and graduate level. He studies decision-making biases in operations management using behavioral experiments, econometrics and simulation. He has published scientific articles in journals like *European Journal of Operational Research*, *International Journal of Production Economics*, *System Dynamics Review* and *Energy Economics*, and chapters in handbooks on behavioral operations and humanitarian logistics.

Yefen Chen is a senior algorithm engineer at Cainiao Smart Logistics Network located in Hangzhou, China. Her research interests focus on understanding consumer behavior in retailing, applying big data to improve supply chain performance, designing market mechanisms, and developing green supply chain management. She received a doctorate from Tsinghua University in 2014, and her research on behavioral operations management has been published in *Management Science, Production and Operations Management*, and other academic journals. Chen also co-authored a chapter in *The Handbook on Behavioral Operations* and has received several grants from various funding agencies including the Chinese National Natural Foundation.

Margarita Cruz is an Assistant Professor of Strategic Management and Entrepreneurship at Ecole hôtelière de Lausanne, HES-SO//University of Applied Sciences Western Switzerland. In her research, Margarita explores the role of authenticity in influencing strategic and entrepreneurial attempts such as entry of new organizations and product diversification strategies. Margarita holds a doctorate in Economics from the Università della Svizzera italiana (University of Lugano, Switzerland) and has also visited Robert H. Smith Business School, University of Maryland (USA) as visiting PhD student. Margarita's research has been published in journals such as *Organization Studies*.

Carlos A. Delgado-Álvarez is an Associate Professor at the Faculty of Business of Politécnico Colombiano Jaime Isaza Cadavid, Medellín, Colombia. He teaches undergraduate and graduate courses on operations research and system dynamics. His research focuses on applying simulation methodologies such as system dynamics and agent-based simulation along with experimental economics to study the behavior of complex social systems. He holds a PhD in Information Systems from the School of Business and Economics, University of Lausanne, Switzerland, and a Masters in Systems Engineering and a B.Eng. in Industrial Engineering from the Faculty of Mines, National University of Colombia.

Luisa Díez-Echavarría has a Bachelor's degree in management engineering and a Master's degree in systems engineering. She is currently a systems engineering doctoral student at Universidad Nacional de Colombia and a professor at Instituto Tecnológico Metropolitano ITM. Her research interests include agent-based modeling, discrete event simulation and system dynamics simulation in ecological, social and economic areas.

Carlos Franco is Auxiliary Professor at School of Management of Universidad del Rosario, Bogotá, Colombia. He holds a Bachelor's degree in Industrial Engineering from Universidad Distrital Francisco José de Caldas, and a Master's in Industrial Engineering with a major in Operations Research from Universidad de los Andes, Bogotá Colombia. He is currently pursuing a doctoral degree in Logistics and Supply Chain Management at Universidad de La Sabana, Chía, Colombia. His main research interests include the development and application of optimization techniques to healthcare and transportation systems.

Leonardo José González Rodríguez is a professor at Universidad de La Sabana, Chía, Colombia. He holds a Bachelor Degree in Industrial Engineering from Universidad Distrital Francisco José de Caldas, Bogotá, Colombia, and a

Masters in Industrial Engineering from Universidad de los Andes, Bogotá, Colombia. He currently is pursuing a doctoral degree in Logistics and Supply Chain Management at Universidad de La Sabana, Chía, Colombia. His main research interests include project management, mathematical modeling and humanitarian logistics.

Diana Carolina Guzmán Cortés holds a Bachelor's degree in Industrial Engineering from Universidad Distrital Francisco José de Caldas, Bogotá—Colombia, and an M.Sc. in Design and Process Management with a major in Logistics Systems from Universidad de La Sabana, Chía, Colombia. She is pursuing a doctoral degree in Logistics and Supply Chain Management at Universidad de La Sabana, Chía, Colombia. Her main research interest includes humanitarian logistics and supply chain management.

Andrea Herrera is an Assistant Professor at the Department of Systems and Computing Engineering, School of Engineering, Universidad de los Andes, Bogotá, Colombia. Her research focuses on how information and communication technologies (ICT) can make people, organizations and supply chains more resilient. Dr. Herrera has served as a reviewer for Information Systems conferences (e.g., AMCIS, and PACIS) and she is a keen follower of the use of ICT, mainly social media for emergency management and analysis of big data.

Marianne Jahre is Professor of Logistics at Lund University and BI Norwegian Business School. She has been a visiting professor at MIT (2014–15), at INSEAD (2018), and at Université de la Méditerranée in France for 7 years since 2003. She has co-edited and co-authored several books and published articles among others in *Journal of Operations Management* (JOM), *International Journal of Physical Distribution & Logistics Management* (IJPDLM), *Journal of Humanitarian Logistics and Supply Chain Management* (JHLSCM), *International Journal of Logistics: Research and Applications* and *International Journal of Logistics Management*. Jahre is a member of the editorial review board of JOM and the editorial advisory board of JHLSCM and IJPDLM. Jahre has been working with disaster relief logistics research and teaching since 2007, heading projects and supervising students in cooperation with IFRC, UNHCR, UNFPA, UNICEF, Norwegian Red Cross and the Norwegian Refugee Council. She is an international delegate to the Norwegian Red Cross, and undertook projects on health supply chains in Uganda for UNICEF and went to the Philippines to study the IFRC response after Typhoon Yolanda.

Martine Jahre is an MSc student of Security Risk Management in the Department of Political Science at the University of Copenhagen, where she focuses on political risk analysis and disaster risk management. After completing a B.A. in Political Science in 2015, she was vice-president of a Norwegian NGO before interning with the Norwegian Ministry of Foreign Affairs in Ethiopia.

Erik R. Larsen is a Full Professor at the Department of Management of the School of Business and Social Sciences at Aarhus University, Denmark. His research focuses on organizational theory, operations management and electricity markets. Dr. Larsen has published in leading academic journals such as *Management Science*, *Organization Science*, *European Journal of Operational Research (EJOR)*, *Omega,* and *Energy Policy*.

Yris Olaya-Morales is an Associate Professor at the Computing and Decision Sciences Department of the Universidad Nacional de Colombia, Medellín, Colombia. She teaches graduate and undergraduate courses on Systems Simulation, Strategy and Energy Policy. Her research focuses on developing optimization and simulation models that support planning, decision-making and policy analysis in the natural gas, power generation and mining sectors. She holds a Bachelor's degree in Petroleum Engineering and a Master's in Systems Engineering from Universidad Nacional de Colombia, as well as a doctorate in Mineral Economics from Colorado School of Mines.

Alfonso J. Pedraza-Martinez is an Associate Professor of Operations Management and Grainger Faculty Fellow at Kelley School of Business, Indiana University, USA. He is president-elect of the Humanitarian Operations and Crisis Management College, Production and Operations Management Society. His award-winning research has informed practitioners in humanitarian organizations. Dr. Pedraza-Martinez has published in leading academic journals such as *Journal of Operations Management (JOM)*, *Production and Operations Management (POM)*, and *Disasters*. He serves as senior editor at *POM*. He has co-edited special issues at *JOM* and the *European Journal of Operational Research*. Dr. Pedraza-Martinez holds a doctorate in Operations Management from INSEAD, France.

Karthik Sankaranarayanan is Assistant Professor of Operations Management at the University of Ontario Institute of Technology, Canada. Prof. Sankaranarayanan received his Ph.D. in Management majoring in Operations Management from the Università della Svizzera italiana (USI), Switzerland in 2011 and was visiting researcher at the New England Complex Systems Institute, Cambridge, MA. His research encompasses the study of complex adaptive systems using agent-based modeling, experimental design and other computational tools. His primary research is in the area of behavioral operations management and currently explores the application of different methodological tools to study behavior in humanitarian operations. Prof. Sankaranarayanan also uses machine-learning algorithms to analyze human decision-making in order to build better decision-aid models.

Achim Schmitt is Associate Dean, Graduate Studies and Associate Professor of Strategic Management at Ecole hôtelière de Lausanne, HES-SO//University of Applied Sciences Western Switzerland. Apart from several years in strategy consulting, Dr. Schmitt has academic experience at the University of Geneva (Switzerland), Columbia Business School (USA), Universidad de los Andes (Colombia) and Audencia Business School (France). He holds a PhD from the University of Geneva and obtained his Habilitation at the University of Paris-Dauphine (France). Dr. Schmitt's research focuses on organizational decline, corporate turnarounds and strategic management. He currently serves on the Editorial Board at *Long Range Planning*

Yanan Song is currently a postdoctoral fellow in the Academy of Mathematics and System Sciences at Chinese Academy of Sciences. She is interested in the behavior of strategic customers, the decisions and mechanism design of retailers, and competition among retailers facing strategic customers. She received her doctorate from Tsinghua University in 2017, and her research about behavioral operations management has been published in *International Journal of Production Economics*, *International Journal of Production Research*, and other journals. Dr. Yanan Song has received several grants from the China Postdoctoral Science Foundation and one of her ongoing works is under review by *Production and Operations Management*.

Gloria Urrea is a visiting researcher at the Kelley School of Business, Indiana University, USA. She holds a Ph.D. from the Università della Svizzera italiana (USI), Switzerland. She holds a Master's in Economics with major in Management, and another Master's in Humanitarian Logistics and Management, both from USI. Urrea studies humanitarian organizations and has collaborated in applied projects with UNICEF and the Red Cross Movement. She has published in journals such as *Socio-Economic Planning Sciences (SEPS)*. Gloria also worked for several years in the private sector, both as an entrepreneur and for a multinational company in Colombia.

Sebastián Villa is Assistant Professor in the School of Management at the Universidad de los Andes, Colombia. Sebastián holds a doctorate in Economics from the Università della Svizzera italiana and he is also a visiting scholar at the Jindal School of Management, University of Texas at Dallas. Sebastián's research has been published in journals such as *European Journal of Operational Research (EJOR)*, *Socio-Economic Planning Sciences (SEPS)*, *Journal of Humanitarian Logistics and Supply Chain Management (JHLSCM)* and *System Dynamics Review*.

List of Figures

Fig. 1.1	Key logistics activities in a humanitarian supply chain	7
Fig. 3.1	Antecedents of knowledge exploration, exploitation, and retention at the WHO	68
Fig. 4.1	Ideal use of climate information services	83
Fig. 5.1	Refugee pathway (Source: Schultz et al., forthcoming)	102
Fig. 5.2	A refugee's journey walking from Syria to Serbia (Source: Huber, 2016)	110
Fig. 6.1	*SL* emphasis impact on behavioral newsvendors and forecasters	137
Fig. 7.1	Interactions and flows of a humanitarian supply chain	151
Fig. 8.1	Demand and order quantity in newsvendor experiment	175
Fig. 8.2	Experimental data vs. quantal response equilibrium predictions in a high-cost condition	178
Fig. 8.3	Comparison among the experimental data, Nash predictions and quantal response equilibrium predictions	183
Fig. 9.1	Prospect theory's (a) value and (b) weighting functions. Source: adapted from Slovenia Hotel (http://sloveniahotel.info/)	196
Fig. 10.1	Stock and flow diagram for water delivery after a disaster	237
Fig. 10.2	Base case simulation results	241
Fig. 10.3	Policy analysis results	242
Fig. 11.1	Conceptual model of the humanitarian logistics system	261
Fig. 11.2	Network of activities	263

Fig. 11.3	Causal loop diagram of the base strategy	264
Fig. 11.4	Causal loop diagram of the proposed collaborative strategy	265
Fig. 11.5	Results of response times	267
Fig. 12.1	General steps in building an AMB [Authors, based on Macal and North (2006)]	280
Fig. 13.1	Simulation results. In T1 all wholesale customers follow the decision rule T1; and the same applies to T2 and T3, respectively. T4 is an interaction of decision rules where wholesale customers 1 and 2 follow T1; wholesale customers 3 and 4 follow T2, and wholesale customer 5 follows T3. Wholesale customer's behavior (left) and supplier's behavior (right)	301
Fig. 13.2	Economic experiment results. In T1 all wholesale customers follow the decision rule T1; and the same applies to T2 and T3, respectively. T4 is an interaction of decision rules where wholesale customers 1 and 2 follow T1; wholesale customers 3 and 4 follow T2, and wholesale customer 5 follows T3. Treatments of the laboratory experiment (right) and the average orders (left)	307

List of Tables

Table 1.1	Essential definitions	10
Table 1.2	Comparison of three operations (Jahre, 2015; Jahre & Heigh, 2008)	17
Table 2.1	Research on the link between private donations and humanitarian operations	38
Table 2.2	Summary table of research questions	48
Table 3.1	WHO initiatives for knowledge exploration, exploitation, and retention	65
Table 4.1	Summary of the case studies	91
Table 5.1	Overview of examples of IT usage along the refugee pathway	107
Table 8.1	Comparison between the experimental data and Nash predictions	182
Table 9.1	Summary of framing effects research in operations management	206
Table 9.2	Framing shortages under lives saved/lives lost frames	211
Table 9.3	Summary of applications of framing effects research in humanitarian operations	215
Table 10.1	Applications of system dynamics and systems thinking to HOM	229
Table 10.2	Parameters for model formalization	240
Table 11.1	Identification of the common elements of a humanitarian logistics project	259

Part I

Strategy

1

Logistics Preparedness and Response: A Case of Strategic Change

Marianne Jahre and Martine Jahre

1.1 Introduction

At 08:50 on the morning of the 9th of October, 2005, an earthquake measuring 7.6 on the Richter scale struck Pakistan. The affected area was almost 30,000 square kilometers, nearly was the size of Belgium, with tremors felt from Kabul to Delhi. In Pakistan, 73,000 people were killed, and more than 120,000 people injured. Approximately 3.5 million people were left homeless.

When a disaster occurs, it is up to the country's government to decide if international assistance is needed. In order for the International Red Cross and Red Crescent Movement to step in, the country's government and its Red Cross / Red Crescent National Society (NS) must ask for assistance. Following the 2005 earthquake, it was immediately clear that

---

M. Jahre (✉)
BI Norwegian Business School, Oslo, Norway

M. Jahre
Department of Political Science, University of Copenhagen, Copenhagen, Denmark

© The Author(s) 2019
S. Villa et al. (eds.), *Decision-making in Humanitarian Operations*,
https://doi.org/10.1007/978-3-319-91509-8_1

the Pakistan Red Crescent Society (PRCS) would require both regional and international assistance. The situation was complicated because half the affected population was in the disputed territory of Kashmir and the other half in the North West Frontier Province. By their mandate, the response had to be conducted by the International Committee of the Red Cross (ICRC) and International Federation of Red Cross and Red Crescent Societies (IFRC), respectively, for each of these areas.

PRCS staff responded immediately, providing rescue and first aid support. Within 24 hours an IFRC logistician was on the ground, later joined by other specialists (water sanitation, health, relief, etc.) to form a Field Assessment Coordination Team (FACT). The ICRC and the IFRC jointly deployed a four-man logistics Emergency Response Unit (ERU) from the Danish and British NS. The ERU team and the IFRC logistics coordinator worked with PRCS members to set up and assess main supply routes into the country, the logistics infrastructure, and available suppliers of transport and warehousing services. The findings of this assessment were combined with assessments of initial relief needs, mainly shelter and medical assistance. The logistics team then published a list of initial needs (called a mobilization table) for NS and other donors to pledge against. It was agreed at this point that one main supply route would be set up for all entities, with IFRC responsible for all goods received in Islamabad, and ICRC responsible for transport and storage to a break-bulk point at Mansehra, from which goods moved to their respective operational areas.

With the logistics personnel in the Geneva Headquarters (GVA HQ) managing pledges and procurement, the logistics team in Pakistan started receiving, storing, and forwarding the items for distribution to the affected population from day three after the event. This was done in coordination with the other major players on the ground. At the same time, IFRC mobilized a number of regional logisticians to complete the logistics team and identified the number of support resources such as vehicles and generators that would be required.

In spite of the immense effort by all involved, the operation had a number of challenges. First, there were multiple rounds of distribution. The procurement process for some items that were not pre-positioned, and were not on the original purchase order, did not allow for a compete package of items to be distributed at once and therefore slowed down the process. The costs of extra rounds of distribution were high, particularly since the distribution was in remote areas lacking infrastructure and transportation. Beneficiaries had to wait a very long time for some items. The process was further delayed by a lack of detailed specifications regarding needs. There was a lack of emergency procurement procedures locally and few existing local supplier relationships were in place. Pre-positioned stocks were located far away, which meant that the total distance traveled by goods in some instances was very high.

A second challenge was that communication with donors was difficult, partly due to the time difference between Pakistan, Geneva, and donor countries. This caused delays in activating the supply chain even after the mobilization table had been compiled, resulting in an average of 10 days between mobilization and purchasing an order. Only 38 percent of the goods were delivered within two months. One particular problem was the complexity of getting donors to allow the transfer of excess stock from the 2004 tsunami operation to the 2005 earthquake in Pakistan.

Third, delivery costs were difficult to calculate due to a lack of systematic information on transport costs for purchased items as well as in-kind donations. However, the multiple rounds of distribution, high transport distances, lack of information on exact needs, and poor communication between GVA HQ and the field suggest that the delivery cost per family was too high and could have been improved.

The experience from this operation and from the response to the 2004 Asia-Pacific tsunami led IFRC logistics personnel to embark on a major strategic change project to improve their logistics preparedness (Jahre & Heigh, 2008):

After the Indonesian tsunami in December 2004, it was an eye-opener. We realized we were using ocean shipping to move items from Asia to Europe and North America—and then flying them back to Indonesia. It was a 13,000 kilometer supply chain. (Stalder-Olsen, 2011)

This chapter discusses the strategic change project with the purpose of providing a better understanding of the concept of logistics preparedness and its effect on response. Based on Marianne Jahre's research in humanitarian operations over a decade, this chapter combines results from literature reviews with secondary data (Jahre, 2017; Jahre, Pazirandeh, & Van Wassenhove, 2016) and three case studies of IFRC logistics preparedness and response (Jahre, 2008, 2015; Jahre & Fabbe-Costes, 2015; Jahre & Heigh, 2008). Details regarding the research design are provided in the appendix.

Starting with an overview of the humanitarian supply network, the chapter continues by defining logistics preparedness and discussing some core challenges, followed by how IFRC tried to solve these challenges through their strategic change project. The chapter concludes with a discussion of future challenges, suggesting further research topics on logistics preparedness.

1.2 The Humanitarian Supply Network

The humanitarian sector has been through many major changes since businessman Henry Dunant founded the Red Cross in 1863 after he saw injured soldiers left on the ground to die after a bloody battle in Solferino, Italy. Several humanitarian organizations were established after World War II, but it was not until the 1990s, with an increasing number of complicated crises and people wanting to help, that the need to professionalize the industry was recognized. Especially after the 1994 genocide in Rwanda and the establishment of a refugee camp in Zaire (now the Democratic Republic of Congo) where tens of thousands of people died every day due to poor sanitation, standards and principles for better and equally distributed help were established. The Sphere standards came into place in 1997 to ensure that everyone has the right to help if they need it, and to ensure the quality of assistance and the accountability of organizations. Standards were established for what is required by organizations involved in a disaster response, such as how much food or water a person should receive per day (Sphere Project, 2016).

1.2.1 Key Actors

Humanitarian organizations are but one group of actors involved in assistance (GHA, 2015; Kovács & Spens, 2007). Others are the affected themselves; donors, including governments, philanthropists, businesses, and individuals; national and international militaries; the affected countries' own governments and the departments within them tasked with providing assistance; the International Red Cross and Red Crescent Movement; NGOs at the local, national, and international levels; the United Nations (UN) system; civil society institutions, such as police and fire departments; and private companies providing goods and services. Together these groups form a complex and varied supply network of funding, materials, information, and service flows (Jahre, Pazirandeh, et al., 2016).

1.2.2 Key Activities and Resources

Figure 1.1 depicts key logistics activities using the IFRC supply chain as an example (Jahre, 2008).

When a disaster has occurred and IFRC responds, this is what happens:

1. Experts map the needs of the affected population, while logisticians map logistical needs as well as the available capacity in terms of infrastructure, other organizations and actors involved, and access to transportation, airports, ports, warehousing facilities, etc.

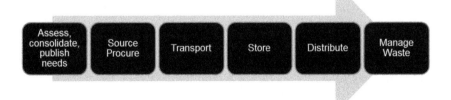

Fig. 1.1 Key logistics activities in a humanitarian supply chain

2. IFRC staff compile the needs and release the mobilization table, providing a basis for budgeting, appeals for funding, and other types of assistance. Compiled reports describe the logistical capacity and logistics needs in the affected area.
3. The mobilization table is the basis for determining what items need to be delivered in order to mobilize and set up the supply chain. The assistance can be in the form of physical items provided by donors (in-kind), goods from the stockpile (pre-positioned), or goods that are purchased locally or globally through framework agreements. The table is updated continuously as goods arrive and needs change.
4. The logisticians are responsible for international and domestic transportation, including contracts with service providers, planning, maintenance and procurement, customs clearance, and insurance.
5. Inventory management in temporary as well as permanent warehousing facilities includes goods reception and registration, storage, distribution, securing the warehouse, personnel, insurance, and reporting. The goods are stored until they are distributed by another group of experts called "relief" (see further explanation below).
6. While providing sanitation and access to clean water has been important relief for many years, waste management has not traditionally been a defined part of the supply chain. However, this area is now getting more attention. Facilities for management of waste such as solid waste and packaging, and equipment for handling hazardous waste such as syringes and medicines must be available.

Like other humanitarian organizations, the Movement uses a set of global tools, as shown in the Pakistan response described in the introduction. First, ERUs are teams of trained specialists who normally have other jobs in their home countries, but who are available for a short periods of time (four to six weeks). In addition to personnel, the ERUs have prepackaged sets of standardized equipment for immediate use. Their guidelines state that they shall be operational within one week, be self-sufficient for one month, and within four months have trained new, local personnel and transferred equipment and the responsibility for services to them. The NS from various countries make their ERUs available when needed. Six different types of ERU correspond to the sectors according to which relief is generally organized: water and sanitation, relief, health, and support functions of IT, logistics, and "basecamp" (Jahre & Fabbe-Costes, 2015).

Second, a Red Cross FACT consists of experienced specialists from the IFRC and NS who can be operational within 12 to 24 hours, anywhere in the world. Together with corresponding expert teams from local governments, the UN system, and other organizations, they make the first assessment of the situation, asking for ERUs when needed and coordinating these ERUs as well as providing personnel and material. FACTs try increasingly to integrate local and regional Red Cross personnel in their activities.

Third, like most other large organizations, such as World Food Program and the United Nations High Commissioner for Refugees, IFRC has a fleet of over a thousand 4×4 vehicles for use by its own workers.

Fourth, they have compiled a catalog of emergency supplies, and other products and equipment that they use. This "emergency items catalogue" gives a detailed description of everything from mosquito nets, blankets, and hygiene kits to kitchen equipment, with specifications important for planning logistics, such as weight, volume, and price (http://itemscatalogue.redcross.int).

Fifth, frame agreements with suppliers which in principle guarantee delivery when needed; that is, when disaster occurs. Last but not least, as other organizations do, the IFRC pre-positions vital resources such as blankets, tents, and other basic relief items (Jahre, 2008).

1.2.3 The Needs

The humanitarian supply network bridges supply and demand. Demand derives from the needs occurring after a disaster. The needs depend not only on the nature of the disaster itself, but also on the community's ability to respond. We all remember the Haiti earthquake in January 2010, while few recall that a much larger earthquake hit Chile six weeks later. Why? Chile had better buildings and infrastructure and was generally better prepared for earthquakes than Haiti, and thus had greater capacity to handle such an event. Accordingly, very few people were affected in

Table 1.1 Essential definitions

Disaster = (vulnerability + risk)/capacity	
Disaster	A disaster is a major upheaval, accident, or destructive event that involves many people at the same time, and that causes great consequences for the population and society. "Disaster" also refers to events that the community and its regular support services are unable handle. A disaster can lead to rapid changes or slower destruction. (Directorate for Security and Preparedness [DSB], 2014, p. 14)
Vulnerability	Vulnerability is an expression of the problems a system may encounter when the system is exposed to an unwanted event, as well as the problems the system encounters when trying to resume its operations after the event has occurred. (NOU, 2000, p. 24)
Risk, Hazard	Risk or hazard is a dangerous phenomenon, substance, human activity, or condition that could result in loss of or damage to life, other health effects, loss of livelihoods and services, property and infrastructure damage, or other social, economic and environmental damage. (The United Nations Office for Disaster Risk Reduction [UNISDR], 2016)
Capacity	Capacity is the combination of all the strengths, features, and resources available in a community, society, or organization that can be used to reach the goals that have been agreed upon. (UNISDR, 2016)

Chile, unlike in Haiti. This example illustrates that an earthquake or other hazardous event does not necessarily constitute a disaster. A society's vulnerability, its ability to handle the event (capacity), and the scale of the event (risk) are the deciding factors, as shown in Table 1.1.

Logistics preparedness is a key aspect of a community's capacity and is also important to other actors involved in disaster preparedness and response (Jahre, Pazirandeh, et al., 2016).

1.3 Logistics Preparedness and Important Challenges

As in disaster management in general (Coppola, 2015), it is common to divide disaster relief logistics, often called humanitarian logistics, into three phases: before (preparedness), during (response), and after (recovery/reconstruction and development; Kovács & Spens, 2007). Often seen as part of a circle, the "after" phase should help to prevent and prepare society better for the next time a disaster strikes.

A widely used statistic is that 1 USD invested in disaster preparedness can save 7 USD in the aftermath (ACF, 2017; UNDP, 2015). In other words, not being prepared is expensive. Why is logistics so important? Logistics accounts for approximately 60–80 percent of the costs associated with international assistance (ACF, 2017; Van Wassenhove, 2006). If we can streamline and improve logistics by making the right investments in logistics preparedness, we can get much more relief out of the available funds.

Research on logistics preparedness is characterized by a strong focus on pre-positioning in terms of the location of warehouses and what to stock in them (Kunz, Reiner, & Gold, 2014). The same goes for practice: organizations present stockpiles as one of the most important, sometimes the only, element in their logistics preparedness. There is little agreement between international organizations about what logistics preparedness entails, what its purpose is, and how it differs from general preparedness (Jahre, Pazirandeh, et al., 2016).

The most recent attempt to define the term in the academic literature says logistics preparedness is "the implementation of processes, structures and systems that connect local, national and international actors through design, planning and training for rapid, cost-effective and appropriate mobilization of material, financial, human and information resources when needed. This includes a variety of activities including needs assessment, acquisition, warehousing, transport, distribution and waste management as well as monitoring (measurement) for the purpose of relieving vulnerable people's suffering" (Jahre, Pazirandeh, et al., 2016). The resources referred to in the definition include the following:

- Emergency services such as shelter and equipment (buckets, blankets, etc.), food, water, and sanitary and health items
- Facilities and infrastructure for warehousing, administration, communication, transportation, etc.
- Personnel available for mobilization (the "roster"), and exercises and trainings for these personnel

- Systems and tools like IT, procedures, manuals, standards, and plans
- Relationships between actors; for example, contracts, agreements, and cooperation

The big question is how much of these resources can and will be put into preparedness compared to what is provided after a disaster has already occurred. This question relates to key challenges with logistics preparedness, which we discuss in the following sections. The challenges were first identified in discussions with practitioners in 2007 (Heigh et al., 2007).

1.3.1 The Challenge of Funding

Only one percent of total international humanitarian assistance is allocated to minimizing and preventing the consequences of disasters (UNDP, 2015); that is, for preparedness. This means there is a lack of stable, long-term funding. A lack of funds ahead of a disaster, as well as the use of earmarked funds for special operations, areas, and/or goods and services, creates problems in developing appropriate logistics preparedness (ACF, 2017; Aflaki & Pedraza-Martinez, 2016; Besiou, Pedraza-Martinez, & Van Wassenhove, 2014; Jahre, Pazirandeh, et al., 2016; Natarajan & Swaminathan, 2014; Van Wassenhove, 2006). Evidence on the effect that logistics preparedness has on response is needed to improve the availability of funding for preparedness investment.

Another challenge is that goods in kind, and particularly unsolicited donations, create problems in supplying what is really needed, especially when there is limited capacity in the recipient systems, such as at airports and in the vehicles for transport to warehouses and distribution points. It is problematic and often expensive to get rid of items that cannot be used, such as out-of-date items, clothing that is unfit for the climate, and hygiene articles that are not used in certain cultures (Jahre, 2015).

1.3.2 The Challenge of Assessing Demand and Supply

Any supply system must know what is needed, where to acquire it, and how to move it to those who need it. In humanitarian operations, obtaining such information can be problematic. With disasters, future needs are uncertain because no one knows when and where the next disaster will hit (Duran, Gutierrez, & Keskinocak, 2011; Rennemo, Fougner Rø, Hvattum, & Tirado, 2014; Salmerón & Apte, 2010). In addition, it is also challenging to get an overview of the infrastructure after a disaster. This applies to roads, ports, aircraft capacity, available vehicles, and storage space, as well as to communications and funding. Keeping track of the supplies coming in is also challenging. This makes it difficult to plan efficient distribution to the areas that need assistance (McCoy & Brandeau, 2011).

Unpredictable demand makes it impossible to plan and prepare for everything. It is simply too risky (items can be in the wrong place, and/or expire) and costly as disasters occur at other places and other times than predicted (Jahre, 2015). The solution, therefore, is to find the right level of investment in preparedness, such as how much of specific items to pre-position and where. This level of investment depends on a number of factors including the type of operation (Jahre, Kembro, et al., 2016), type of disaster anticipated (Kovács & Spens, 2007), and disaster location. For example, different types of tents are needed after an earthquake in Pakistan during the winter than after a flood in the Philippines.

Repeated floods and droughts in specific areas are easier to predict and allow for more planning and forecasting (Chang, Tseng, & Chen, 2007) than do less predictable crises, for which organizations have to make assumptions about future needs as a starting point for pre-positioning (Jahre & Heigh, 2008). The potential for damage to infrastructure, such as transport, energy, and/or communications systems determines what type of equipment is needed (Barbarosoğlu, Özdamar, & Cevik, 2002). This potential relates to how developed the region was before the disaster occurred (Wisner, Blaikie, Cannon, & Davis, 2003). As these factors affect how the logistics response will need to be set up, they must also be taken into account when preparedness is established. More systematic knowledge about what type of logistics preparedness is required in different situations is needed.

1.3.3 The Challenge of Coordination

Especially in major disasters, there are many actors who want to join the operation. After the earthquake in Haiti, for example, over 1,000 organizations participated (GPPI, 2010). Some are local organizations who know the conditions. Some are large, professional organizations experienced in providing international assistance. Others are small organizations established in the aftermath of specific disasters, and many of them lack sufficient resources and expertise to work independently (Elsharkawi, 2010).

It is very challenging to reach the necessary level of cooperation and coordination among so many actors (ACF, 2017; Altay & Naktim, 2014; Balcik, Beamon, Krejki, Muramatsu, & Ramirez, 2010; Jahre & Jensen, 2010). For example, after the 2004 tsunami, 72 coordination meetings were held every week in Banda Aceh during the first phase of the operation (Fritz Institute, 2005). Flows of funds, information, goods, and services should be coordinated to avoid gaps and overlap; this coordination can be very challenging in a chaotic situation. It may even be difficult for organizations to coordinate internally.

Much has been done to improve coordination in recent years, including the development of clusters, where organizations working in the same sector, such as health or education or logistics, exchange information, agree on their respective roles, and take overall responsibility only when there is no one else who can do it (UNOCHA, 2016). Cooperation before the disaster occurs is required so that the actors can develop common preparedness (Jahre & Jensen, 2010). More knowledge is needed on how the humanitarian community can establish coordination in the preparedness phase so that the right resource mix can be mobilized to set up response supply chains.

1.3.4 The Challenge of Measurement and Evaluation

Traditionally, evaluation has been done after an operation has ended, which is useful only for future operations and for reporting to donors how their funds were used. Real-time evaluation and measuring of how well logistics works during an operation, so that improvements can be made, have been gradually increasing (Blecken, Hellingrath, Dangelmaier, & Schulz, 2009). The selection of key performance indicators is important for making the right decisions. These indicators evaluate productivity, efficiency, flexibility, accountability, and sustainability (Haavisto & Goentzel, 2015). However, systems and data to conduct evaluations systematically are lacking (Santarelli, Abidi, Klumpp, & Regatteri, 2015). To get more funding, estimate future demand, and improve the supply network, actors must measure the progress of operations, both during and after, to be able to adjust.

1.4 At the Right Time in the Right Place: The IFRC Case

Based on their experiences in 2004 and 2005, and to cope with the challenges discussed above, the IFRC developed a new logistics strategy in 2006 (Heigh, 2006; Jahre, 2008; Jahre & Heigh, 2008).

1.4.1 Developing Regional Logistics Preparedness

Until 2006, IFRC's logistics preparedness had consisted of loosely coordinated stocks owned by NSs and framework contracts with suppliers coordinated through the GVA HQ. For each new disaster, the field delegations set up a new supply chain. As illustrated in the Pakistan operation described above, this resulted in slow and expensive responses.

The new strategy established Regional Logistics Units (RLUs), with their own physical stockpiles of key relief items, based in Kuala Lumpur, Dubai, and Panama. The RLUs enabled IFRC logistics to better allocate responsibilities between GVA HQ and the field. As a result of regionalizing responsibility regional competence and framework agreements with regional suppliers were developed. GVA HQ, on the other hand, got more time to develop the global logistics strategy, standardize specifications for products and services, and establish processes for the activities illustrated in Fig. 1.1, including procurement, transportation, and warehousing. It can also assist the RLUs in developing logistics preparedness resources (see Sect. 3) such as expertise, IT systems, and measurement and reporting systems.

The new purchasing approach comprised four essential elements: frame agreements, more decentralized purchasing based on new limits for sign-offs, standardization of procurement processes, and standard specifications of items. The regional pre- positioning improved logistics preparedness with an ability to respond faster and at lower transport costs. The regionalization could not have been undertaken without appropriate information systems and support. A humanitarian logistics software (HLS) was implemented by the RLUs. IFRC received funding specifically for putting in place the regional units and pre-positioned goods.

Through the changes, IFRC attempted to solve the four challenges discussed above. *Coordination* improved between their different units: GVA HQ, the RLUs, and the NS. They analyzed previous operations to get a better overview of needs in the different regions with the purpose of *improving future demand estimates*, thus knowing what to pre-position in the RLUs. They conducted case studies to compare operations before and after the strategic change and developed performance indicators to allow for a more *systematic evaluation of ongoing operations*. Finally, the case studies provided evidence of the effect of a response from improved regional preparedness, resulting in better *arguments for more long-term funding*. The changes resulted in better, cheaper, and faster responses, as illustrated in the Yogyakarta operation, as compared to Pakistan (see Table 1.2 in the following section). IFRC therefore continued using this strategy to achieve further improvements.

Table 1.2 Comparison of three operations (Jahre, 2015; Jahre & Heigh, 2008)

Months 1 and 2	Pakistan 2005	Yogyakarta 2006	Philippines 2013
Average distance goods to population (km)	2,962	1,671	4,063
Goods delivered from Asia-Pacific region (percentage by volume)	68%	100%	75%
No. of families receiving partial relief package	36,083	0	62,331
No. of families receiving complete relief package	0	42,911	0
Average number of families reached per day	555	613	1,005
Time taken to activate supply chain (days)	10	3	3
Supply chain rate (tonnes/day)	73	36	38
Percentage of emergency relief items available for distribution at 2 months	38%	74%	65%
Total families assisted at 2 months	36,083	42,911	62,331
Logistic costs as a percentage of total operational costs at 2 months	90%	87%	73%
Logistics costs per family assisted at 2 months (excluding tents)	824	142	77

1.4.2 Further Logistics Preparedness Expansion

After the initial strategy implementation from 2006 to 2010, IFRC's Global Logistics Services (GLS) undertook case studies to document effects, showing major improvements in costs and response times (Gatignon, Van Wassenhove, & Charles, 2010; Heigh, 2006; IFRC, 2008; Jahre, 2008; Jahre & Heigh, 2008), but also highlighting future challenges in the regional concept, such as more complex coordination, high resource demands, uncertainty over consistency in support, and the fact that regional units were still not close enough to the disaster areas (Jahre, 2008). Hence, an analysis of the future context for disaster relief logistics was conducted (Heigh & Leonard, 2009; Majewski, Navangul, & Heigh, 2010), followed by GLS suggesting an expanded regional logistics preparedness structure in their LOG2015, that is, their new logistics strategy (IFRC, 2010).

A process for establishing future demand forecasts (Jahre, Navangul, et al., 2011) was combined with an optimization model to support decisions regarding location and inventory levels of sub-regional warehouses (Jahre & Grønland, 2014). GLS established additional logistics units with pre-positioning in Nairobi and Beirut. GLS began offering logistics services to other organizations and established a structure to secure sustainable funding through cost recovery; that is, charging service fees for the support provided. A case study of the IFRC logistics response to Typhoon Haiyan in the Philippines in 2013 was conducted to observe the effects on response of the logistics preparedness expansion (Jahre, 2015).

In the autumn of 2013, Typhoon Haiyan hit the Philippines, directly affecting more than 16 milllion people. Over 6000 people died and nearly 30,000 were injured. Four million people had to leave their homes, and there was extensive damage to crops, forests, and buildings. Many islands were hit. Transportation complications and a lack of infrastructure posed logistical challenges for the responders.

Nonetheless, the Movement, in cooperation with other organizations, not least the Filipinos themselves, managed to provide assistance to a large number of people in a fairly short time. Included was the largest cash transfer program by the IFRC after an emergency (IFRC, 2014). Table 1.2 compares the operation after the earthquake in Pakistan in 2005 with those in Yogyakarta in 2006 and the Philippines in 2013, both of which came after the initial strategic change in 2006.

The operation in the Philippines continued the positive development from Yogyakarta with regards to the number of families assisted during the first two months, the cost per family, the time it took to activate the supply chain, the response time, and the total number of tons of relief materials shipped per day. Stockpiles in Kuala Lumpur and Dubai along with additional personnel from Dubai and Geneva made a quick response possible. The regional office in Kuala Lumpur had an overview of where goods should be bought, despite challenges with regard to capacity and expertise on the purchasing side. Local suppliers were used when available.

Local logistics capacity was a problem in terms of both physical and human resources. One problem that delayed the response was procurement of sleeping pads and blankets. The original plan of buying locally was abandoned due to lack of availability, but local size standards differed from the IFRC's global standards, making global sourcing difficult. Another problem was that hygiene articles for the relief package were not available until more than two months into the operation, which was why nobody received a full package in the Haiyan case. Due to recent previous operations, the PRC did not have any locally pre-positioned items, making for high transport distances. Local suppliers, market knowledge, and purchasing competence were lacking. A shortage of agreements with transport providers was another problem. There was also a lack of warehousing capacity, packaging materials, and pallets.

Lack of coordination within the IFRC created further challenges, as did large volumes of unsolicited donations, showing that improvement is required in coordination and need-based restrictions regarding donations. The biggest challenge identified through the case study was cost recovery; that is, the fact that NSs have to pay GVA HQ and regional units for the logistics support provided. The study found sustainable funding for continued regional expansion would be very difficult, if not impossible (Jahre, 2015).

1.5   Conclusions and Future Research

The case study of the Haiyan operation and a comparison with the challenges identified in 2006 revealed the following:

1. *Lack of sustainable funding for logistics preparedness*, particularly regional pre-positioning: The 2013 case demonstrated the effect improved logistics preparedness can have on response, but funding is still hard to find, suggesting that pre-positioning must be complemented with other, less costly aspects of logistics preparedness.
2. *Lack of local capacity and competence* in logistics, market knowledge, and procurement: The 2013 case demonstrated the need for local logistics preparedness, but did not yield details on the type of preparedness required in specific situations or regions.

3. *Lack of coordination*, particularly in assessments: While there has been some improvement here, more is needed, especially in coordination across organizations.

These challenges suggest the need for further research on the following aspects of logistics preparedness. With regard to point 1, the opportunities for and effects of developing other types of logistics preparedness (other than physical storage in separate facilities) constitute an interesting area for future research. Alternatives to pre-positioning are necessary to reduce cost and increase flexibility. These include vendor-managed inventories and other use of commercial services (Van Wassenhove & Pedraza-Martinez, 2012), transfer between programs (Bhattacharya, Hasija, & Van Wassenhove, 2014), and the integration of supply chains for different types of operations (Jahre, Kembro, et al., 2016; Stauffer, Pedraza-Martinez, & Van Wassenhove, 2015) and organizations (Aćimović & Goentzel, 2016). More research into which exercises or trainings work best to develop human resources is also required (Harteveld & Suarez, 2015). In particular, there must be a greater focus on developing local resources (Sheppard, Tatham, Fisher, & Gapp, 2013).

Regarding point 2, there is a need for more research into local logistics preparedness in general and procurement in particular. This includes preparedness necessary for successful cash programming. Despite the fact that procurement constitutes up to 65 percent of costs (Schulz, 2008), there seems to be little study of systematic improvements that can be made to the process. Uncertainties regarding funding and unpredictable demand, as well as strict regulations, including tedious tendering processes, has resulted in bureaucracy and lack of innovative and strategic thinking in humanitarian organizations' purchasing processes. More modern approaches to procurement focused on greater cooperation with suppliers and other organizations (Bealt, Barrera, & Mansouri, 2016; Pazirandeh & Herlin, 2014), use of e-commerce, and various types of contracting are areas of great potential, both for testing in practice and documenting through research.

Regarding point 3, tools and concepts for assessing and predicting future needs must be developed, including scenario planning (Chang et al., 2007; Jahre, Kembro, et al., 2016) and forecasting (Jahre, Navangul, et al., 2011). Simultaneously, technologies such as social media and drones can be used to improve needs assessment in the early stages of a response (Holguín-Veras, Jaller, Van Wassenhove, Pérez, & Wachtendorf, 2012; Meier, 2014). However, research is needed to document experiences with these technologies, and how the whole supply system adheres to the stated needs, whether they come from forecasts, needs assessments, or both.

Appendix: Research Designs

The following presents an overview of the research designs of the studies and papers referred to above. More details and references to the research literature are provided in the reference list.

Jahre (2008) and Jahre and Heigh (2008): Explorative Case Study of IFRC Strategic Logistics Change

The case study is based on a multitude of sources, including technical artifacts (that is, physical structures, product catalogs, and informantion and communication technology systems), systematic interviews, documents, and archival material. We used a pre-structured case outline for data analysis to maintain construct validity. In order to ensure reliability, a case study protocol guide was developed. Interview guides were developed and refined during the process, depending on the interviewees. The questions concerned (1) a description of logistics systems, processes, and structures before and after the 2006 change; (2) the interviewee's views on the change—advantages and disadvantages, main challenges, and implications for funding, assessment, coordination and measurement; and (3) consequences of the change. More than 30 semi-structured interviews with IFRC staffers were undertaken between June 2007 and February 2008. Interviews were taped and transcribed, and important elements related to the pre-structured case outline were chosen. Artifacts were used to confirm facts emerging from the interviews. The resulting descriptions were sent to the respective interviewees so they could check for any possible misinterpretations. The head of logistics and the project manager also checked the entire case study. A case study database that included notes from each interview, detailed write-ups of aspects of the case, and other documentation was created.

Jahre (2015): Case Study of IFRC's Philippines Haiyan Operation in 2013 with a Focus on Logistics

Secondary and primary data were collected in 2015 and analyzed based partly on a theoretical framework, and partly on frameworks developed in previous case studies. The research journal included the case study protocol and data collection instruments for continuous collection of secondary material, such as—reports and other documents. Information was triangulated and comprised primary data interviews, site visits and field trips; system data; and secondary data from reports and operational updates. The analysis was conducted as follows:

1. Establish timeline for the response based on appeal updates and other reports.
2. Collect relevant information to fill the "skeleton" timeline (relevant for logistics, the specific events taking place, changes of importance and quantified data).
3. Use the initial reflection note (made immediately after the field trip and interviews) to make a structure for conclusions.
4. Triangulate with secondary information (real-time evaluation and other documentation) and primary information (interviews and extracts from the Humanitarian Logistics System).
5. Analyze 35 interviews by transcribing the main points from each interview, coding according to themes, and then consolidating/sorting all data in accordance with the themes, finally resulting in the case structure.
6. Document the performance improvements/changes in costs and service, comparing this response with previous ones, using similar key performance indicators.

7. Check case description with respondents to exclude misunderstandings and incorrect facts.

Jahre and Fabbe-Costes (2015): Longitudinal Case Study of IFRC's ERU Concept

Based on a conceptual framework and a systematic literature review, we conducted a longitudinal, exploratory, abductive case study of the ERU concept, focusing particularly on the Health ERU in the Norwegian Red Cross. In addition to the two previous case studies (Jahre, 2008, 2015), data specifically on the ERU was collected in 2008–2009 through interviews and participation in training courses, and then again with semi-structured interviews in May 2015 using an interview guide developed based on the initial analysis and literature review. Data was triangulated with technical artifacts (for example, physical structures and product catalogs), systematic interviews, documents, and archival material. The final structure of the case study emerged through many iterations of data analysis, using color-coding for recurrent themes and contrasting views, followed by sorting and categorizing emerging elements under subtitles and bullet points. We created a case study database in which we included guides, tapes and notes from each interview, summaries of all evaluation reports, and other documentation. Interviewees representing both the IFRC and Norwegian Red Cross examined the case report. Interviewees for the final round were selected using the snowball technique.

Jahre, Pazirandeh, et al. (2016): Literature Review and Secondary Data Analysis on Logistics Preparedness

The literature review used key search terms including logistics, preparedness, humanitarian and operations, and focused on logistics, operations, and supply chain management journals. The systematic review to map logistics preparedness efforts of humanitarian organizations started with outlining the review protocol and criteria for inclusion or exclusion, and mapping publicly available information on the Internet by accessing, retrieving, and judging the quality and relevance of the organizations and the retrieved information. An initial set of organizations was selected by scanning titles of Google search hits based on a set of predetermined criteria. We identified and extracted the data from relevant documents (webpages and publicly available online reports discussing preparedness) for each organization using a five-stage keyword search. We excluded reports related to specific missions or regions, and continued until we reached saturation. Extracted data was inductively analyzed, coded, and reduced to map definitions of logistics preparedness and then to map logistics preparedness efforts. The content analysis revealed two aspects discussed in all definitions, which we compared across organizations: Preparedness level (for example, organization, network, or community) and preparedness goal. Following Seuring and Müller's (2008) approach, we inductively coded and categorized logistics preparedness efforts before listing them in tabular form, then we regrouped them to develop mutually exclusive categories. The frequency of efforts among organizations was re-stated and discussed based on the observations. Finally, we compared the identified categories of effort with those identified in the literature.

Jahre (2017): Systematic Literature Review and Review/Classification of Published Case Studies

We conducted a systematic review and identified numerous supply chain strategy (SCS) frameworks in supply chain risk management. We defined the constructs and operationalizations and developed a framework for SCS in the humanitarian context, which we then used to classify published case studies. Four databases—Business Source Complete, Emerald, Science Direct, and Wiley—were selected to cover all articles published by June 2016 in internationally refereed logistics, supply chain, and operations management journals.

References

ACF. (2017, November). *Supply chain expenditure & investment opportunities in the humanitarian context*. Action Contre la Faim.

Aćimović, J., & Goentzel, J. (2016). Models and metrics to assess humanitarian response capacity. *Journal of Operations Management, 45*, 11–29.

Aflaki, A., & Pedraza-Martinez, A. J. (2016). Humanitarian funding in a multi-donor market with donation uncertainty. *Production and Operations Management, 25*(7), 1274–1291.

Altay, N., & Naktim, P. (2014). Information diffusion among agents: Implications for humanitarian operations. *Production and Operations Management, 23*(6), 1015–1027.

Balcik, B., Beamon, B. M., Krejki, C. C., Muramatsu, K. M., & Ramirez, M. (2010). Coordination in humanitarian relief chains: Practice, challenges and opportunities. *International Journal of Production Economics, 16*, 22–34.

Barbarosoğlu, G., Özdamar, L., & Cevik, A. (2002). An interactive approach for hierarchical analysis of helicopter logistics in disaster relief operations. *European Journal of Operational Research, 140*(1), 118–133.

Bealt, J., Barrera, J. C. F., & Mansouri, S. A. (2016). Collaborative relationships between logistics service providers and humanitarian organizations during disaster relief operations. *Journal of Humanitarian Logistics and Supply Chain Management, 6*(2), 118–144.

Besiou, M., Pedraza-Martinez, A. J., & Van Wassenhove, L. (2014). Vehicle supply chains in humanitarian operations: Decentralization, operational mix, and earmarked funding. *Production and Operations Management, 23*(11), 1950–1965.

Bhattacharya, S., Hasija, S., & Van Wassenhove, L. N. (2014). Designing efficient infrastructural investment and asset transfer mechanisms in humanitarian supply chains. *Production and Operations Management, 23*(9), 1511–1521.

Blecken, A., Hellingrath, B., Dangelmaier, W., & Schulz, S. (2009). A humanitarian process reference model. *International Journal of Service Technology and Management, 12*(4), 391–413.

Chang, M. S., Tseng, Y. L., & Chen, J. W. (2007). A scenario planning approach for the flood emergency logistics preparation problem under uncertainty. *Transportation Research Part E: Logistics and Transportation Review, 43*(6), 737–754.

Coppola, D. P. (2015). *Introduction to international disaster management* (3rd. ed.). London, UK: Elsevier.

Directorate for Security and Preparedness. (2014). Nasjonalt risikobilde 2014. Katastrofer som kan ramme det norske samfunnet. DSB.

Duran, S., Gutierrez, M. A., & Keskinocak, P. (2011). Pre-positioning of emergency items for CARE international. *Interfaces, 41*(3), 223–237.

Elsharkawi, H. (2010). *Inside disaster.* Retrieved January 23, 2017, from https://www.youtube.com/watch?v=lYk-kUb1X-I

Fritz Institute. (2005). Lessons from the Tsunami: Top line findings. Retrieved January 11, 2007, from http://www.fritzinstitute.org

Gatignon, A., Van Wassenhove, L. N., & Charles, A. (2010). The Yogyakarta earthquake: Humanitarian relief through IFRC's decentralized supply chain. *International Journal of Production Economics, 126,* 102–110.

GHA. (2015). Report 2015. Retrieved October 3, 2017, from http://www.globalhumanitarianassistance.org/report/gha-report-2015

GPPI. (2010). Inter-agency real-time evaluation in Haiti: 3 months after the earthquake. Retrieved August 15, 2016, from http://www.unicef.org/evaluation/files/Haiti_IA_RTE_final_Eng.pdf

Haavisto, I., & Goentzel, J. (2015). Measuring humanitarian supply chain performance in a multi-goal context. *Journal of Humanitarian Logistics and Supply Chain Management, 5*(3), 300–324.

Harteveld, C., & Suarez, P. (2015). Guest editorial: Games for learning and dialogue on humanitarian work. *Journal of Humanitarian Logistics and Supply Chain Management, 5*(1), 61–72.

Heigh, I. (2006). *Case study terms of reference.* International Federation of the Red Cross and Red Crescent Societies Logistics Department (IFRC Logistics Supply Chain Award 2006, International Federation of the Red Cross and Red Crescent Societies Logistics Department). Geneva: IFRC Global Logistics Team.

Heigh, I., Jahre, M., Kovács, G., Listou, T., Spens, K., & Tatham, P. (2007). *Humanitarian logistics—The intermediating role of linking donors and beneficiaries.* WIP NOFOMA Conference, 2007.

Heigh, I., & Leonard, N. (2009). *Federation logistics of the future.* Geneva: IFRC. Unpublished report.

Holguín-Veras, J., Jaller, M., Van Wassenhove, L. N., Pérez, N., & Wachtendorf, T. (2012). On the unique features of post-disaster humanitarian logistics. *Journal of Operations Management, 30,* 494–506.

IFRC. (2008). Newsletter from the Logistics and Resource Mobilisation Department, Geneva.

IFRC. (2010). Logistics 2015—Strategic plan 2011–2015: Providing services to deliver Strategy 2020, January, International Federation Red Cross Red Crescent Society, Geneva, Switzerland.

IFRC. (2014). Case study: Unconditional cash transfers response to Typhoon Haiyan (Yolanda). Retrieved February 19, 2018, from https://www.preparecenter.org/sites/default/files/philippines_ctp_case_study_en.pdf

Jahre, M. (2008). *The organisational change of logistics in International Federation of the Red Cross Red Crescent Societies (IFRC)—A case study.* Unpublished, BI Norwegian School of Management.

Jahre, M. (2015). Impact on response from a changing service provision strategy: Case study of the IFRC Philippines Haiyan operation (MDRPH014) with focus on logistics. Unpublished, BI Norwegian Business School.

Jahre, M. (2017). Supply chain strategies in humanitarian logistics: A review of how actors mitigate supply chain risks. *Journal of Humanitarian Logistics and Supply Chain Management, 7*(2), 82–101.

Jahre, M., & Fabbe-Costes, N. (2015). How standards and modularity can improve humanitarian supply chain responsiveness: The case of emergency response units. *Journal of Humanitarian Logistics and Supply Chain Management, 5*(3), 348–386.

Jahre, M., & Grønland, S.-E. (2014). *Predicting the unpredictable—Deciding where to locate strategic stock using real data.* INFORMS annual meeting, San Francisco, November.

Jahre, M., & Heigh, I. (2008). Does the current constraints in funding promote failure in humanitarian supply chains? *Supply Chain Forum: An International Journal, 9*(2), 44–54.

Jahre, M., & Jensen, L.-M. (2010). Coordination in humanitarian logistics through clusters. *International Journal of Physical Distribution and Logistics Management, 40*(8/9), 657–674.

Jahre, M., Kembro, J., Rezvanian, T., Håpnes, S. J., Ergun, O., & Berling, P. (2016). Integrating supply chains for emergencies and ongoing operations in UNHCR. *Journal of Operations Management, 45*, 57–72.

Jahre, M., Navangul, K. A., Dieckhaus, D., Heigh, I., & Leonard, T-G. N. (2011). *Predicting the unpredictable—Demand forecasting in international humanitarian response.* NOFOMA-Proceedings 2011, Harstad University College, June, Norway.

Jahre, M., Pazirandeh, A., & Van Wassenhove, L. N. (2016). Defining logistics preparedenss: A framework and research agenda. *Journal of Humanitarian Logistics and Supply Chain Management, 6*(3), 372–398.

Kovács, G., & Spens, K. M. (2007). Humanitarian logistics in disaster relief operations. *International Journal of Physical Distribution and Logistics Management, 37*(2), 99–114.

Kunz, N., Reiner, G., & Gold, S. (2014). Investing in disaster management capabilities versus pre-positioning inventory: A new approach to disaster preparedness. *International Journal of Production Economics, 157*, 261–272.

Majewski, B., Navangul, K. A., & Heigh, I. (2010). A peek into the future of humanitarian logistics: Forewarned is forearmed. *Supply Chain Forum: An International Journal, 11*(3), 4–19.

McCoy, J. H., & Brandeau, M. L. (2011). Efficient stockpiling and shipping policies for humanitarian relief: UNHCR inventory challenge. *OR Spectrum, 33*(3), 673–698.

Meier, P. (2014). *Digital humanitarians: How big data is changing the face of humanitarian response.* Boca Raton, FL: CRC Press, Taylor & Francis Group.

Natarajan, K. N., & Swaminathan, J. M. (2014). Inventory management in humanitarian operations: Impact of amount, schedule, and uncertainty in funding. *Manufacturing & Service Operations Management, 16*(4), 595–603.

NOU. (2000). Et sårbart samfunn - Utfordringer for sikkerhets- og beredskapsarbeidet i samfunnet. Justis- og politidepartementet, 4.juli.

Pazirandeh, A., & Herlin, H. (2014). Unfruitful cooperative purchasing: A case of humanitarian purchasing power. *Journal of Humanitarian Logistics and Supply Chain Management, 4*(1), 24–42.

Rennemo, S. J., Fougner Rø, K., Hvattum, L. M., & Tirado, G. (2014). A three-stage stochastic facility routing model for disaster response planning. *Transportation Research Part E, 62*, 116–135.

Salmerón, J., & Apte, A. (2010). Stochastic optimization for natural disaster asset pre-positioning. *Production and Operations Management, 19*(5), 561–574.

Santarelli, G., Abidi, H., Klumpp, M., & Regatteri, A. (2015). Humanitarian supply chains and preformance measurement schemes in practice. *International Journal of Productivity and Performance Management, 64*(6), 784–810.

Schulz, S. (2008). *Disaster relief logistics. Benefits of and impediments to cooperation between humanitarian organizations.* Kuehne Foundation Book Series on Logistics 15, Germany.

Seuring, S., & Müller, M. (2008). From a literature review to a conceptual framework for sustainable supply chain management. *Journal of Cleaner Production, 16*(15), 1699–1710.

Sheppard, A., Tatham, P., Fisher, R., & Gapp, R. (2013). Humanitarian logistics: Enhancing the engagement of local populations. *Journal of Humanitarian Logistics and Supply Chain Management, 3*(1), 22–36.

Sphere Project. (2016). Retrieved October 3, 2017, from http://www.sphereproject.org/

Stalder-Olsen. (2011). Head GLS IFRC. Retrieved October 19, 2017, from http://www.hu-online.org/index.php/j-stuff/category-blog/265-ifrc-can-forecast-requirements-if-not-disasters

Stauffer, J. M., Pedraza-Martinez, A., & Van Wassenhove, L. N. (2015). Temporary hubs for the global vehicle supply chain in humanitarian operations. *Production and Operations Management, 25*(2), 192–209.

UNDP. (2015). *Act now-save later.* Retrieved May 2017, from http://www.dk.undp.org/content/undp/en/home/ourwork/get_involved/ActNow/

UNISDR. (2016). The United Nations Office for Disaster Risk Reduction. Retrieved October 3, 2017, from http://www.unisdr.org/we/inform/terminology

UNOCHA. (2016). Retrieved January 15, 2018, from http://www.unocha.org/what-we-do/coordination-tools/cluster-coordination

Van Wassenhove, L. N. (2006). Humanitarian aid logistics: Supply chain management in high gear. *Journal of the Operational Research Society, 57*(5), 475–489.

Van Wassenhove, L. N., & Pedraza-Martinez, A. (2012). Using OR to adapt supply chain management best practices to humanitarian logistics. *International Transactions in Operational Research, 19*, 307–322.

Wisner, B., Blaikie, P., Cannon, T., & Davis, I. (2003). *At risk: Natural hazards, people's vulnerability and disasters.* London, UK: Routledge.

2

Private Donations for Humanitarian Operations

Gloria Urrea and Alfonso J. Pedraza-Martinez

2.1 Introduction

Natural disasters have risen both in frequency and in impact over the years due to an increase of the global population, climate change and technological complexity (Starr & Van Wassenhove, 2014). Unfortunately, humanitarian funding is not growing as fast as humanitarian needs. In 2016, donations to international humanitarian assistance reached US$27.3 billion, up 6% from 2015. Although this is equivalent to collecting around US$3.6 from each person in the world, it still left a shortfall of 40% when compared to the appeals (Lattimer et al., 2017). This situation compels humanitarian organizations (HOs) to obtain new sources of donations and to manage current ones more efficiently.

G. Urrea (✉) • A. J. Pedraza-Martinez
Kelley School of Business, Indiana University, Bloomington, USA
e-mail: gloria.urrea@usi.ch; alpedraz@indiana.edu

Donations come from either institutional or private donors. Institutional donors are usually large government-based funding agencies, while private donors are individuals willing to give their money or time to humanitarian causes (Burkart, Besiou, & Wakolbinger, 2016). In this chapter, we use the terms "private" and "individual" donations interchangeably. Extant operations management literature has largely focused on institutional donors and how earmarked funds from these large donors shape humanitarian operations (Besiou, Pedraza-Martinez, & Van Wassenhove, 2012; Burkart et al., 2016). In contrast, the research into donations of cash, time or in-kind items from private donors has been rather limited, especially from an operations management perspective. In order to propose avenues for future research, we review the current studies linking private donations and humanitarian operations.

We first review the motivations that private donors have to donate. Next, we review the literature on private donations considering cash, time and in-kind donations from private donors, and categorize this research based on the four different phases of the disaster management cycle (DMC): preparedness, response, rehabilitation and mitigation (Tomasini & Van Wassenhove, 2009; Van Wassenhove & Pedraza-Martinez, 2012). For each category of donations (cash, time and in-kind), we identify open opportunities and suggest avenues for future studies on humanitarian operations management.

2.2 Donations for Humanitarian Operations

To carry out their programs, HOs interact with multiple stakeholders. Interactions with humanitarian supply chain actors such as donors, suppliers, governments and non-governmental organizations allow HOs to get the financial, material and informational resources to run their operations. Despite the diversity of actors in the humanitarian supply chain (Van Wassenhove & Pedraza-Martinez, 2012), the relationship with donors is the most critical one for the survival of HOs, because they depend on donations to fund their operations. Donations determine the scope, speed, effectiveness and efficiency of any humanitarian response (Burkart et al., 2016; Wakolbinger & Toyasaki, 2014). The nature of donations can be categorized as cash, time or in-kind. Cash donations refer to monetary resources that HOs can use to procure the items required for a response. In-kind donations refer to material resources such as relief items (e.g. food and medical kits) or anatomical donations (e.g. blood and organs), which allow HOs to avoid the procurement process. Time donations refer to volunteering activities, in which people donate their time and work to HOs (Burkart et al., 2016; Holguín-Veras, Jaller, Van Wassenhove, Pérez, & Wachtendorf, 2014).

Obtaining and managing donations is challenging for HOs. Obtaining donations is difficult due to the competition among HOs for donor attention and funding (Oloruntoba & Gray, 2006; Van Wassenhove, 2006). Competition for donations peaks during early phases of disaster response, when there is media attention and financial resources are readily available (Lindenberg, 2001; Stephenson & Schnitzer, 2006). Such competition can lead to negative operational outcomes, such as hampering coordination and reducing overall performance when it comes to aid distribution (Balcik, Beamon, Krejci, Muramatsu, & Ramirez, 2010; Stephenson, 2005). Managing donations is also challenging due to different pressures donors put on HOs. Institutional donors ask HOs to deliver aid in an accountable and cost-effective fashion (Eftekhar, Li, Van Wassenhove, & Webster, 2016; Leiras, de Brito, Queiroz Peres, Rejane Bertazzo, & Tsugunobu Yoshida Yoshizaki, 2014; Thomas & Kopczak, 2005; Van Wassenhove, 2006). This requirement usually means increasing the budget allocated to relief items while reducing the budget for training and other activities that can be considered overhead costs (Kovács & Spens, 2007). Another pressure point is the scope of the response, because some donors can use earmarking, or conditioning the use of funding provided (Besiou et al., 2012; Pedraza-Martinez, Stapleton, & Van Wassenhove, 2011). Earmarking usually focuses on short-term relief operations and aid distribution, instead of long-term investment in systems and processes (Oloruntoba & Gray, 2006; Besiou, Stapleton, & Van Wassenhove, 2011).

The challenges HOs face when obtaining and managing institutional donations are not likely to decrease. However, HOs might be able to relieve some of the pressure by relying more on private donors. Institutional and private donors have different motivations to donate. While institutional donors are strategic and decide where to allocate their resources based on efficiency considerations, private donors are motivated by factors such as altruism and prestige. By understanding the motivations of individuals to donate, HOs have the opportunity to learn how to access and manage donations from private donors.

2.3 Private Donors and Motivations to Donate

In the last decade, donations from private donors have become increasingly important for HOs (Kovács & Spens, 2007; Thomas & Kopczak, 2005). Individuals donate money to support humanitarian action, and their donations are significant. Private financial donations for humanitarian assistance added up to US$6.9 billion in 2016, 25% of the total donations (Lattimer et al., 2017). Therefore, HOs can maximize the opportunity to access private donations by understanding the motivations and incentives people have to donate.

Intrinsic motivations to donate have been a subject of previous research in different streams of literature. From a rational perspective, individuals are self-interested and do not have economic incentives to donate to a charitable cause out of pure altruism. Andreoni (1989, 1990) argues that a model of pure altruism cannot explain observed patterns of giving that a model of "impure" altruism can. An impure altruism model combines the assumption of altruism with the warm glow; that is the internal satisfaction people feel when giving to others. Other researchers consider that to understand the motives to donate, it is necessary to go beyond economic models and move toward other social and psychological incentives such as the desire to gain prestige, reputation, friendship, respect and social approval (Harbaugh, 1998; Holländer, 1990; Olson, 1965). Further experimental research shows evidence that people can actually have a prosocial tendency to cooperate, supporting the altruistic hypothesis (Eckel & Grossman, 1996; Fehr & Fischbacher, 2003; Fehr & Gächter, 2002; Henrich et al., 2006).

Beyond these intrinsic motivations, other research considers extrinsic incentives for people to donate or to exhibit other prosocial behavior. Extrinsic incentives for people to donate include interdependent preferences, seed capital, monetary rewards, identification and information, and fundraising activities.

- *Interdependent preferences*: Andreoni and Scholz (1998) find that private donations may depend on the level of charitable giving of a "reference group" determined by similar socio-demographic characteristics. Therefore, when a policy increases the donations of group A, it is expected that donations of other groups that take A as a reference will rise as well.
- *Seed capital*: According to public-good scholars, individuals tend to "crowd-out" from giving to a cause if the government or other donors have already contributed. Nevertheless, Andreoni (1998) finds that during the fundraising process of organizations, seed capital can serve as an incentive for other private donors to give as long as it is sufficiently high to achieve a critical mass, but "well below the amount required to build the good".
- *Monetary rewards*: Monetary rewards are one of the most controversial incentives for prosocial behavior. There is research that finds both negative and positive effects of rewarding people for carrying out activities (Bénabou & Tirole, 2003). In particular, when activities are altruistic, rewards may discourage potential donors because they do not want to appear greedy (Ariely, Bracha, & Meier, 2009; Bénabou & Tirole, 2006; Imas, 2014); instead, donors want to look prosocial (Lacetera & Macis, 2010). Exley (2017) finds that donors are less concerned with their social image when their reputation as "prosocial individuals" is established before they are offered the incentive. Therefore, when potential donors already have a reputation of being prosocial (due to past behavior), they are less discouraged to donate when there are monetary incentives.
- *Identification and information*: Andreoni and Petrie (2004) tested the social effects of donor identification in fundraising by conducting laboratory experiments with varying degrees of confidentiality. In line with the hypothesis of the importance of social image and reputation,

they find that when the identities of private donors and the amounts they donated is revealed, donations are 59% higher compared to when there is no such information. Moreover, when the option to remain anonymous is present, donations are higher than when it is compulsory to reveal information.
- *Fundraising activities*: Fundraising activities from charity organizations provide important incentives for private donors. Andreoni and Payne (2011) studied the negative effects of reducing expenditure for fundraising activities, finding that when organizations reduce fundraising spending by US$137, total contributions from private donors drop by US$772.

So far, we have recognized that private donors are important sources of donations for HOs and we have separated them from institutional donors by understanding the different motivations they have to donate. Next, we examine the existing literature linking private donations with humanitarian operations, so that we can identify research gaps and suggest future avenues for research.

2.4 Methodology

To classify the relevant literature, we used the keyword search methodology (Seuring & Gold, 2012). In particular, we used keywords related to individual donations and humanitarian operations. Due to the exploratory nature of this study, we opted for a purposive sample (Yin, 2014), which was not designed to achieve a significant representation of all the journals in areas related to operations management. Instead, we sampled leading journals in operations management and related disciplines such as operations research to identify impactful articles. First, we reviewed the literature in top operations management journals: Management Science, Manufacturing & Service Operations Management, Production and Operations Management, and Journal of Operations Management. Then, we expanded the search to other peer-reviewed journals such as Annals of Operations Research, European Journal of Operational Research, International Journal of Disaster Risk Reduction, Interfaces,

Journal of the Operational Research Society, and International Journal of Production Economics.

After an initial search, we assessed each paper to ensure those finally selected deal with the same topic we are analyzing in this chapter. The literature search resulted in a selection of 19 journal articles. Table 2.1 lists these papers with authors, topic, methods and journal, and categorizes them according to the nature of donation and the phases of the DMC.

2.5 Private Donations and the Disaster Management Cycle

HOs intend to alleviate human suffering caused by disasters and to improve the quality of life of the society through community sustainability (Beamon & Balcik, 2008; Besiou et al., 2011). HOs operate at different stages of the DMC (preparedness, response, rehabilitation and mitigation) through programs.

Preparedness: Programs implemented during preparedness aim to mitigate the impact of the hazard. An example of preparedness programs include the inventory prepositioning that the United States' Federal Emergency Management Agency (FEMA) carries out ahead of each hurricane season. As Table 2.1 shows, private donations for disaster preparedness have not received much scholarly attention. This lack of research can be explained by the general difficulty of raising funds for events that have not happened yet.[1] For instance, only 12% of the funds for disaster risk reduction from 1993 to 2013 were targeted to disasters before their occurrence (Kellett & Caravani, 2013). Only one paper (Ryzhov et al., 2016) investigates how HOs can convert one-time donors into recurrent donors for preparedness efforts. Therefore, we find ample scope for research into private donations for disaster preparedness.

Response: Programs implemented during the response phase aim to alleviate the most urgent needs of the population. A practical example of the work HOs perform during the response phase after a natural disaster is of Haiti after Hurricane Matthew struck the country on October 3, 2016, affecting over two million people. By October 10, an

Table 2.1 Research on the link between private donations and humanitarian operations

Authors	Topic	Methods	Nature of donation	Journal
Preparedness and response				
Ryzhov, Han and Bradić (2016)	Conversion of people into recurring donors for preparedness and response	Empirical	Cash	Management Science
Response				
Fritz and Mathewson (1957)	Personal, informational and material convergence during disaster response	Case study	Time In-kind	Report for Committee on Disaster Studies
Kendra and Wachtendorf (2001)	Volunteer convergence after the World Trade Center attack	Case study	Time	University of Delaware, Disaster Research Center
Holguín-Veras, Pérez, Ukkusuri, Wachtendorf and Brown. (2007)	Key logistical issues of the response to Hurricane Katrina	Case study	In-kind	Transportation Research Record: Journal of the Transportation Research Board
Destro and Holguín-Veras (2011)	Characteristics of donors contributing to material convergence	Empirical	In-kind	Transportation Research Board, 90th Annual Meeting
Holguín-Veras, Jaller, Van Wassenhove, Pérez and Wachtendorf (2012)	Post-disaster humanitarian logistics, including material convergence	Case study	In-kind	Journal of Operations Management

(continued)

Table 2.1 (continued)

Authors	Topic	Methods	Nature of donation	Journal
Toyasaki and Wakolbinger (2014)	Impacts of earmarked private donations for disaster relief	Analytical	Cash	Annals of Operations Research
Lassiter, Khademi and Taaffe (2015)	Task assignment and training of volunteers during disaster response	Optimization	Time	International Journal of Production Economics
Whittaker, McLennan and Handmer (2015)	Emerging and extending volunteerism in emergencies and disasters	Literature review	Time	International Journal of Disaster Risk Reduction
Lodree and Davis (2016)	Volunteer convergence after the 2011 tornado disaster in Tuscaloosa, Alabama	Empirical	Time	Natural Hazards
Response and rehabilitation				
Aflaki and Pedraza-Martinez (2016)	Trade-offs between earmarking and operational performance	Analytical	Cash	Production and Operations Management
Rehabilitation				
Wisner, Stringfellow, Youngdahl and Parker (2005)	Service design and operational factors relevant to volunteer satisfaction	Survey	Time	Journal of Operations Management

(continued)

Table 2.1 (continued)

Authors	Topic	Methods	Nature of donation	Journal
Sampson (2006)	Labor scheduling to reduce costs and maximize volunteer satisfaction	Optimization	Time	Journal of Operations Management
Falasca, Zobel and Ragsdale (2011)	Development of volunteer scheduling model for a development organization	Case study	Time	Interfaces
Falasca and Zobel (2012)	Multi-criteria model for volunteer assignment to tasks	Optimization	Time	Socio-Economic Planning Sciences
Lacetera, Macis and Slonim (2014)	Effects of economic incentives on volunteer activities	Field experiment	Time In-kind	Management Science
Kessler and Milkman (2016)	Impact of priming donor identity on individual donations	Field experiment	Cash	Management Science
Andreoni, Rao and Trachtman (2017)	Effects of verbally asking private donors to give funding	Field experiment	Cash	Journal of Political Economy
Mayorga, Lodree and Wolczynski (2017)	Management of spontaneous volunteers during recovery efforts	Analytical	Time	Journal of the Operational Research Society

appeal of US$119 million was launched and HOs started to respond to humanitarian needs with different projects in diverse sectors, such as emergency shelter (accommodating displaced population), food security (distributing food), and healthcare (preventing diseases such as cholera and malaria). A large proportion of extant research on private donors focuses on disaster response (Table 2.1). Most of these papers focus on time donations (i.e., volunteering) and in-kind donations. When individuals are moved by a tragic event, they are willing to help in any possible way. However, a great confluence of volunteers or materials can create managerial and logistical issues for the overall response. We find only two papers (Aflaki & Pedraza-Martinez, 2016; Toyasaki & Wakolbinger, 2014) that address cash donations during disasters, from the point of view of earmarking and operational performance. There is an opportunity for more research on cash donations for disaster response.

Rehabilitation: During rehabilitation, HOs' objective is to rebuild and improve the living conditions of the affected population. An example of rehabilitation is the long-term humanitarian action that followed the response to the Haiti earthquake in 2010. HOs such as the International Federation of Red Cross and Red Crescent Societies (IFRC) worked on improving the quality of life of victims of the earthquake years after the initial disaster response was over. As with disaster response, private donations for rehabilitation has received considerable attention from researchers (Table 2.1). This research focuses mainly on how HOs can motivate individual donors to continue giving after the response phase, both in cash and time. Moreover, scholars are interested in how to optimize the use of volunteers to maximize their satisfaction and the performance of HOs.

Mitigation: In the mitigation phase, HOs attempt to increase community resilience by looking for structural ways to reduce risk. Although it does not include direct involvement of HOs in the decision-making process, an example of mitigation is the relocation of housing in the New York City area following Hurricane Sandy, 2012. By moving neighborhoods away from high-risk areas, New York City reduced the long-term risk from disasters to these communities. Interestingly, as Table 2.1 shows, research on private donations for disaster mitigation has not received attention from scholars. One obvious research opportunity is the question of how HOs can increase individual donations for disaster mitigation.

2.6 Research Opportunities

After showing how the current research linking private donations with humanitarian operations has mainly focused on the response and rehabilitation phases of the DMC, we now move to reviewing in detail what we consider the avenues for future research, using the three forms of private donations: cash, time and in-kind. All three forms of donations can be used in every phase of the DMC. Table 2.2, at the end of this section, summarizes the research questions derived from our analysis.

2.6.1 Cash Donations

HOs attempt to align their organizational activities with the intrinsic and extrinsic motivations of private donors to raise funding mainly for their response and rehabilitation operations (Table 2.1). For instance, HOs appeal to donors' desire for the warm glow with advertisements and to social motivations by giving recognition to donors, such as small stickers or official acknowledgements on organizations' websites. HOs also use fundraising activities. Among these activities we can consider earmarking, which is one important topic in the literature on private cash donations for humanitarian operations (Aflaki & Pedraza-Martinez, 2016; Toyasaki & Wakolbinger, 2014).

HOs can decide how to ask for money from potential donors. They can have a general-purpose fund (non-earmarked) or a fund dedicated to responding to a specific crisis (earmarked). Earmarking reduces donors' uncertainty about how the funds will be used and, therefore, can increase donations. However, earmarking may negatively affect HOs' operational efficiency, resulting in higher costs and distribution delays. Toyasaki and Wakolbinger (2014) model earmarking from the perspective of donors, HOs and policy-makers, considering the earmarking decision as an optimization problem. They find that the decision to implement earmarking or not is not trivial. For both donors and HOs, there are different variables that influence their preference such as fundraising goals and fundraising costs. Aflaki and Pedraza-Martinez (2016) link the earmarking decision, both in relief and development situations, with the operational performance of HOs. They find the following trade-offs. On the one hand, earmarking increases donations but imposes constraints that decrease the operational performance of HOs. On the other hand, non-earmarking leads to a reduced amount of funds but increases operational performance. The authors propose alternatives to total earmarked funding.

In addition to the incentives and fundraising activities, HOs use different messages and channels to reach potential donors. To increase donations, HOs use communication strategies such as emphasizing their commitment to preparedness and training programs or giving cards to identify the donor as an organization's supporter (Ryzhov et al., 2016). Moreover, HOs can spur the generosity of private donors by priming their identity with certain messages. Priming messages include being previous supporters of the organization or members of a community (Kessler & Milkman, 2016). Regarding channels, HOs can have volunteers go on the streets to raise funds by talking directly to people and taking advantage of the empathy such face-to-face interactions create (Andreoni et al., 2017). They can also use direct-mail marketing to foster repeated contributions from previous donors.

A new channel to reach potential money donors is through the use of social media. In particular, we consider the high potential of online crowdfunding platforms to raise money for humanitarian causes. Crowdfunding is a mechanism through which individuals and organizations raise money from a large number of people (i.e. the "crowd"), whose individual contributions are usually small (Belleflamme, Lambert, & Schwienbacher, 2014). Crowdfunding not only allows HOs to reach out to private donors more directly, but also to provide more targeted information about the operations performed using a specific given donation. Considering that people tend to directly reward organizations that are transparent with their operations (Buell, Kim, &

Tsay, 2017; Buell & Norton, 2011), we believe that HOs will benefit from actions that disclose their operations to individual donors in a more accessible way.

There is currently an opportunity to advance the research at the intersection of the humanitarian operations literature, operational transparency and crowdfunding. First, building on previous findings, future research can investigate how HOs can make the best use of new online channels such as crowdfunding to raise cash donations from individual donors. Second, future studies can look into the effect of operational transparency on private donations in general, and on online crowdfunding donations in particular. Finally, a third possible research topic is how HOs can potentiate these online communications to raise funding for their preparedness and mitigation operations. Possible research questions include: *How can HOs leverage current technologies such as crowdfunding to make their operations more transparent? How does this transparency affect the outcome of crowdfunding campaigns? How can HOs communicate more efficiently their operational transparency?*

2.6.2 Time Donations

In addition to financial support, individual donors give their time to HOs, which is also known as volunteering. In fact, around 45% of US residents reported to have volunteered for charities at least once a month during 2015 (Independent-Sector, 2016). However, volunteer management can be challenging for HOs, given the particularities of this kind of donations. First, given the lack of formal contracts between HOs and volunteers, there is always uncertainty regarding volunteer arrivals and the length of their stay in the organization (Sampson, 2006; Wisner et al., 2005). Second, volunteer skills and experience are highly variable, which creates a challenge for HOs, forcing them to plan their activities without having a stable skill set (Lassiter et al., 2015).

Most of the recent research about volunteer management focuses on the rehabilitation phase of the DMC (Table 2.1). Extant research studies how to keep volunteers motivated and satisfied with their tasks. The abundance of this research is justified by the finding that when volunteers are satisfied, they stay for longer periods of time, and are more likely to also donate financially to the organization and to recommend the volunteer experience to family and friends (Wisner et al., 2005). Researchers have studied enhancers of volunteer satisfaction such as schedule flexibility, training, empowerment, recognition, social interaction and economic rewards (Lacetera et al., 2014; Wisner et al., 2005). They have also considered how to use labor assignment to match volunteers' skill levels and preferences with the requirements of the HO and beneficiaries (Falasca & Zobel, 2012; Falasca et al., 2011; Lassiter et al., 2015; Sampson, 2006). In addition to match volunteer preferences, this last work on labor assignment has also included how to improve the performance of HOs by using scheduling and training in an attempt to minimize possible future organizational costs, reduce volunteer labor shortage and minimize unmet task demand (Falasca & Zobel, 2012; Falasca et al., 2011; Lassiter et al., 2015; Sampson, 2006).

However, a focus on volunteer satisfaction framed only within the rehabilitation phase prevents a complete understanding of the various decisions and operational consequences involved in managing volunteers in all stages of the DMC. Furthermore, as limited previous research has considered that volunteers may not have the required skill set to complete a task (Lassiter et al., 2015), there is currently a gap in the literature on how HOs can best manage the different skills and experience levels of volunteers.

There is an opportunity to advance the research in volunteer management by filling these gaps. Future research should move beyond volunteer satisfaction to consider the consequences of volunteer management on HOs' operational performance measures such as order fulfillment rate, delivery delays and efficiency. Moreover, research on volunteers should incorporate the uncertainty of volunteers' skills and experience to perform the assigned task, including the training and learning processes. Additionally, future studies should explore other stages of the DMC. For instance, volunteer management during the preparedness stage may include research topics such as volunteer training and learning in teams, building on the positive effects of collaboration and information sharing previously found in the literature (Siemsen, Balasubramanian, & Roth,

2007; Urrea, Villa, & Gonçalves, 2016). Volunteer management in the response phase could study the best ways to team together volunteers of different skill levels to obtain the optimum performance measures for the HO. Possible research avenues in this stream are: *How does volunteer uncertainty affect order fulfillment, delivery time and efficiency in humanitarian operations at the different stages of the DMC? How does volunteer experience affect order fulfillment, delivery time and efficiency during disaster response operations? How do volunteer learning processes and volunteer pairing decisions affect order fulfillment, delivery time and efficiency during both preparedness and response operations?*

2.6.3 In-Kind Donations

Convergence during disasters refers to large amounts of information, people and material arriving at a particular area after a disaster occurs, creating congestion in the system and even hindering the response (Fritz & Mathewson, 1957; Mayorga et al., 2017; Whittaker et al., 2015). Research on this topic has been rather scarce and has mainly taken a descriptive approach on how both material and people convergence can be challenging to manage for HOs.

Fritz and Mathewson (1957) define convergence of people and materials, and identify an initial categorization of the different types of people that arrive after a disaster occurs: returnees, anxious, helpers, curious and exploiters. Moreover, the authors describe the negative consequences of convergence for disaster response efforts, given that HOs would need to manage high volumes (above those of the actual needs) of people and materials, which would deviate attention and effort from more vital tasks.

Subsequent research focused on the convergence of people and material includes a study of on people or volunteer convergence increases after the 2001 World Trade Center attack, which saw a high number of people coming to the affected area out of a desire to help, as well as out of curiosity to know what happened (Kendra & Wachtendorf, 2001). More recent research tries to describe the advantages and disadvantages of people convergence, such as the advantage of receiving volunteers when you most need them and the disadvantage of creating congestion in the response (Whittaker et al., 2015). Some have attempted to quantify the problem of convergence by studying the arrivals of volunteers and modeling them as a queuing system (Lodree & Davis, 2016).

Research on material convergence is more recent. As the World Trade Center attack served as a trigger for studying people convergence after a disaster, the crisis caused by Hurricane Katrina served as the trigger for research on material convergence (Destro & Holguín-Veras, 2011; Holguín-Veras et al., 2007). Destro and Holguín-Veras (2011) were among the first to study this topic by collecting evidence on the problems created by unsolicited in-kind donations in the wake of Hurricane Katrina. The authors used econometric models to identify the demographic characteristics of potential donors of unsolicited donations, and found that unsolicited in-kind donations increase with geographical proximity to the disaster area (Destro & Holguín-Veras, 2011). Subsequent research categorizes types of unsolicited donations, separating them in high priority, low priority and non-priority, emphasizing that most of the problems are caused by non-priority items (Holguín-Veras et al., 2012).

By definition convergence occurs after a disaster; i.e. during the response and rehabilitation phases of the DMC (Table 2.1). Therefore, there are not many opportunities to study this phenomenon outside these phases. However, past research on convergence of both people and materials has mainly taken a descriptive approach, discussing the challenges and difficulties of managing convergence. Little has been said about the potential relocation of unsolicited donations. In-kind items that are not needed in a particular operation may be useful elsewhere. Hence, one research avenue is to go beyond the challenges of managing convergence, and take a more holistic and quantitative approach to studying how convergence affects the operational performance measures of HOs and even of the response as a whole. Possible research questions are: *How does congestion created by convergence of people and materials affect order fulfillment, delivery time and efficiency during disaster response operations? What are the best policies to manage convergence of people and in-kind items? How do these policies affect order fulfillment, delivery time and efficiency? How do these policies affect private donors' motivations and future willingness to donate?*

Table 2.2 Summary table of research questions

Type of donation	Preparedness	Response	Rehabilitation	Mitigation
Cash donations	How can HOs leverage current technologies such as crowdfunding to make their operations more transparent? How does this transparency affect the outcome of crowdfunding campaigns? How can HOs communicate their operational transparency more efficiently?			
Time	How do volunteer learning processes and volunteer pairing decisions affect order fulfillment, delivery time and efficiency during both preparedness and response operations?	How does volunteer experience affect order fulfillment, delivery time and efficiency during disaster response operations?		
	How does volunteer uncertainty affect order fulfillment, delivery time and efficiency in humanitarian operations at the different stages of the DMC?			
In-kind donations		How does congestion created by convergence of people and materials affect order fulfillment, delivery time and efficiency during disaster response operations?		
	What are the best policies to manage convergence of people and in-kind items? How do these policies affect order fulfillment, delivery time and efficiency? How do these policies affect private donors' motivations and future willingness to donate?			

2.7 Conclusion

This chapter highlights the importance of private donations for humanitarian operations and the need to conduct research in this realm. Previous studies have only started to open a way to understand the behavior of private donors when giving money and time. We believe that there is still much to uncover about how to access and manage private donations. Therefore, we indicate possible avenues to carry out future research.

We propose three avenues for future research on private donations for humanitarian operations. First, crowdfunding is a new channel HOs have to obtain private cash donations. An interesting problem related to crowdfunding has to do with operational transparency as a strategy to increase donations. Second, volunteering is an almost unexplored area of research in humanitarian operations management. Some interesting problems regarding volunteering include the exploration of the uncertainty generated by the variability in volunteers' skills and experience, and how HOs can manage that uncertainty in different phases of the DMC to reduce possible negative impacts operational performance. Finally, in-kind items are a common yet operationally challenging source of donations for HOs. The material convergence of in-kind items, including unsolicited donations, requires a careful examination of logistics network flows. While unsolicited in-kind donations may not match the current needs of an ongoing operation, such contributions may be very helpful to HOs either later in the DMC or in a different operation elsewhere.

The major limitation of this book chapter, as with any literature review, is the high dependence we have on the search process and hence on the final selection of articles we have used to analyze and draw our conclusions. We hope that our efforts to summarize the existing literature and propose future research avenues inspire researchers and practitioners in their next projects.

Note

1. As fundraising for future disasters is difficult, there are only few cases in which preparedness efforts exist. Moreover, these efforts are mostly funded by institutional donors such as governmental agencies and not private donors, which is the focus of the chapter. In sum, given the lack of cases to study, there is lack of research as well.

References

Aflaki, A., & Pedraza-Martinez, A. J. (2016). Humanitarian funding in a multi-donor market with donation uncertainty. *Production and Operations Management, 25*(7), 1274–1291.

Andreoni, J. (1989). Giving with impure altruism: Applications to charity and ricardian equivalence. *Journal of Political Economy, 97*(6), 1447–1458.

Andreoni, J. (1990). Impure altruism and donations to public goods: A theory of warm-glow giving. *The Economic Journal, 100*(401), 464–477.

Andreoni, J. (1998). Toward a theory of charitable fund-raising. *Journal of Political Economy, 106*(6), 1186–1213.

Andreoni, J., & Payne, A. A. (2011). Is crowding out due entirely to fundraising? Evidence from a panel of charities. *Journal of Public Economics, 95*(5–6), 334–343.

Andreoni, J., & Petrie, R. (2004). Public goods experiments without confidentiality: A glimpse into fund-raising. *Journal of Public Economics, 88*(7–8), 1605–1623.

Andreoni, J., Rao, J. M., & Trachtman, H. (2017). Avoiding the ask: A field experiment on altruism, empathy, and charitable giving. *Journal of Political Economy, 125*(3), 625–653.

Andreoni, J., & Scholz, J. K. (1998). An econometric analysis of charitable giving with interdependent preferences. *Economic Inquiry, 36*, 410–428.

Ariely, D., Bracha, A., & Meier, S. (2009). Doing good or doing well? Image motivation and monetary incentives in behaving prosocially. *American Economic Review, 99*(1), 544–555.

Balcik, B., Beamon, B. M., Krejci, C. C., Muramatsu, K. M., & Ramirez, M. (2010). Coordination in humanitarian relief chains: Practices, challenges and opportunities. *International Journal of Production Economics, 126*(1), 22–34.

Beamon, B. M., & Balcik, B. (2008). Performance measurement in humanitarian relief chains. *International Journal of Public Sector Management, 21*(1), 4–25.

Belleflamme, P., Lambert, T., & Schwienbacher, A. (2014). Crowdfunding: Tapping the right crowd. *Journal of Business Venturing, 29*(5), 585–609.

Bénabou, R., & Tirole, J. (2003). Intrinsic and extrinsic motivation. *Review of Economic Studies, 70*(3), 489–520.

Bénabou, R., & Tirole, J. (2006). Incentives and prosocial behavior. *American Economic Review, 96*(5), 1652–1678.

Besiou, M., Pedraza-Martinez, A. J., & Van Wassenhove, L. N. (2012). The effect of earmarked funding on fleet management for relief and development. *INSEAD Working Paper No. 2012/10/TOM/INSEAD*, Social Innovation Centre.

Besiou, M., Stapleton, O., & Van Wassenhove, L. N. (2011). System dynamics for humanitarian operations. *Journal of Humanitarian Logistics and Supply Chain Management, 1*(1), 78–103.

Buell, R. W., Kim, T., & Tsay, C.-J. (2017). Creating reciprocal value through operational transparency. *Management Science, 63*(6), 1673–1695.

Buell, R. W., & Norton, M. I. (2011). The labor illusion: How operational transparency increases perceived value. *Management Science, 57*(9), 1564–1579.

Burkart, C., Besiou, M., & Wakolbinger, T. (2016). The funding-humanitarian supply chain interface. *Surveys in Operations Research and Management Science, 21*(2), 31–45.

Destro, L., & Holguín-Veras, J. (2011). Material convergence and its determinants: The case of Hurricane Katrina. *Transportation Research Record: Journal of the Transportation Research Board, 2234*(1), 14–21. https://doi.org/10.3141/2234-02

Eckel, C. C., & Grossman, P. J. (1996). Altruism in anonymous dictator games. *Games and Economic Behavior, 16*(2), 181–191.

Eftekhar, M., Li, H., Van Wassenhove, L. N., & Webster, S. (2016). The role of media exposure on coordination in the humanitarian setting. *Production and Operations Management, 0*(0), 1–15.

Exley, C. (2017). Incentives for prosocial behavior: The role of reputations. *Management Science, 64*(5), 1–12.

Falasca, M., & Zobel, C. (2012). An optimization model for volunteer assignments in humanitarian organizations. *Socio-Economic Planning Sciences, 46*(4), 250–260.

Falasca, M., Zobel, C., & Ragsdale, C. (2011). Helping a small development organization manage volunteers more efficiently. *Interfaces, 41*(3), 254–262.

Fehr, E., & Fischbacher, U. (2003). The nature of human altruism. *Nature, 425*(6960), 785–791.

Fehr, E., & Gächter, S. (2002). Altruistic punishment in humans. *Nature, 415*(6868), 137–140.

Fritz, C. E., & Mathewson, J. (1957). *Convergence behavior in disasters: A problem in social control. A special report prepared for the Committee on Disaster Studies.* Washington, DC: National Academy of Sciences—National Research Council.

Harbaugh, W. T. (1998). What do donations buy? A model of philanthropy based on prestige and warm glow. *Journal of Public Economics, 67*, 269–284.

Henrich, J., McElreath, R., Barr, A., Ensminger, J., Barrett, C., Bolyanatz, A., … Ziker, J. (2006). Costly punishment across human societies. *Science, 312*(5781), 1767–1770. Retrieved from http://www.ncbi.nlm.nih.gov/pubmed/16794075

Holguín-Veras, J., Jaller, M., Van Wassenhove, L. N., Pérez, N., & Wachtendorf, T. (2012). On the unique features of post-disaster humanitarian logistics. *Journal of Operations Management, 30*(7–8), 494–506.

Holguín-Veras, J., Jaller, M., Van Wassenhove, L. N., Pérez, N., & Wachtendorf, T. (2014). Material convergence: Important and understudied disaster phenomenon. *Natural Hazards Review, 15*(1), 1–12.

Holguín-Veras, J., Pérez, N., Ukkusuri, S., Wachtendorf, T., & Brown, B. (2007). Emergency logistics issues affecting the response to Katrina: A synthesis and preliminary suggestions for improvement. *Transportation Research Record: Journal of the Transportation Research Board, 2022*(1), 76–82. https://doi.org/10.3141/2022-09

Holländer, H. (1990). A social exchange approach to voluntary cooperation. *American Economic Review, 80*(5), 1157–1167.

Imas, A. (2014). Working for the "warm glow": On the benefits and limits of prosocial incentives. *Journal of Public Economics, 114*, 14–18.

Independent-Sector. (2016). *United for Charity: How Americans trust and value the charitable sector*. Washington, DC.

Kellett, J., & Caravani, A. (2013). *Financing disaster risk reduction: A 20 year story of international aid*. Retrieved March 22, 2018, from https://www.odi.org/sites/odi.org.uk/files/odi-assets/publications-opinion-files/8574.pdf

Kendra, J. M., & Wachtendorf, T. (2001). Rebel food… renegade supplies: Convergence after the world trade center attack. *University of Delaware, Disaster Research Center, 316*, 1–25.

Kessler, J. B., & Milkman, K. L. (2016). Identity in charitable giving. *Management Science, 64*(2), 1–17.

Kovács, G., & Spens, K. M. (2007). Humanitarian logistics in disaster relief operations. *International Journal of Physical Distribution & Logistics Management, 37*(2), 99–114.

Lacetera, N., & Macis, M. (2010). Social image concerns and prosocial behavior: Field evidence from a nonlinear incentive scheme. *Journal of Economic Behavior & Organization, 76*(2), 225–237.

Lacetera, N., Macis, M., & Slonim, R. (2014). Rewarding volunteers: A field experiment. *Management Science, 60*(5), 1107–1129.

Lassiter, K., Khademi, A., & Taaffe, K. M. (2015). A robust optimization approach to volunteer management in humanitarian crises. *International Journal of Production Economics, 163*, 97–111.

Lattimer, C., Swithern, S., Sparks, D., Tuchel, L., Evans, H., Johnson, M., ... Wasiuk, D. (2017). *Global humanitarian assistance report 2017*. Retrieved March 22, 2018, from http://reliefweb.int/report/world/global-humanitarian-assistance-report-2017.

Leiras, A., de Brito, I., Jr., Queiroz Peres, E., Rejane Bertazzo, T., & Tsugunobu Yoshida Yoshizaki, H. (2014). Literature review of humanitarian logistics research: Trends and challenges. *Journal of Humanitarian Logistics and Supply Chain Management, 4*(1), 95–130.

Lindenberg, M. (2001). Are we at the cutting edge or the blunt edge? Improving NGO organizational performance with private and public sector strategic management frameworks. *Nonprofit Management and Leadership, 11*(3), 247–270.

Lodree, E. J., & Davis, L. B. (2016). Empirical analysis of volunteer convergence following the 2011 tornado disaster in Tuscaloosa, Alabama. *Natural Hazards, 84*(2), 1109–1135.

Mayorga, M. E., Lodree, E. J., & Wolczynski, J. (2017). The optimal assignment of spontaneous volunteers. *Journal of the Operational Research Society, 68*(9), 1106–1116.

Oloruntoba, R., & Gray, R. (2006). Humanitarian aid: An agile supply chain? *Supply Chain Management: An International Journal, 11*(2), 115–120.

Olson, M. (1965). *The logic of collective action*. Cambridge: Harvard University Press.

Pedraza-Martinez, A. J., Stapleton, O., & Van Wassenhove, L. N. (2011). Field vehicle fleet management in humanitarian operations: A case-based approach. *Journal of Operations Management, 29*(5), 404–421.

Ryzhov, I. O., Han, B., & Bradić, J. (2016). Cultivating disaster donors using data analytics. *Management Science, 62*(3), 849–866.

Sampson, S. E. (2006). Optimization of volunteer labor assignments. *Journal of Operations Management, 24*(4), 363–377.

Seuring, S., & Gold, S. (2012). Conducting content-analysis based literature reviews in supply chain management. *Supply Chain Management: An International Journal, 17*(5), 544–555.

Siemsen, E., Balasubramanian, S., & Roth, A. V. (2007). Incentives that induce task-related effort, helping, and knowledge sharing in workgroups. *Management Science, 53*(10), 1533–1550.

Starr, M. K., & Van Wassenhove, L. N. (2014). Introduction to the special issue on humanitarian operations and crisis management. *Production and Operations Management, 23*(6), 925–937.

Stephenson, M. (2005). Making humanitarian relief networks more effective: Operational coordination, trust and sense making. *Disasters, 29*(4), 337–350.

Stephenson, M., & Schnitzer, M. H. (2006). Interorganizational trust, boundary spanning, and humanitarian relief coordination. *Nonprofit Management & Leadership, 17*(2), 211–233.

Thomas, A. S., & Kopczak, L. R. (2005). *From logistics to supply chain management: The path forward in the humanitarian sector*. San Francisco. Retrieved March 22, 2018, from http://www.fritzinstitute.org/PDFs/WhitePaper/FromLogisticsto.pdf

Tomasini, R., & Van Wassenhove, L. N. (2009). *Humanitarian logistics*. Basingstoke: Palgrave Macmillan.

Toyasaki, F., & Wakolbinger, T. (2014). Impacts of earmarked private donations for disaster fundraising. *Annals of Operations Research, 221*(1), 427–447.

Urrea, G., Villa, S., & Gonçalves, P. (2016). Exploratory analyses of relief and development operations using social networks. *Socio-Economic Planning Sciences, 56*, 27–39.

Van Wassenhove, L. N. (2006). Humanitarian aid logistics: Supply chain management in high gear. *Journal of the Operational Research Society, 57*(5), 475–489.

Van Wassenhove, L. N., & Pedraza-Martinez, A. J. (2012). Using OR to adapt supply chain management best practices to humanitarian logistics. *International Transactions in Operational Research, 19*, 307–322.

Wakolbinger, T., & Toyasaki, F. (2014). *Impacts on funding systems on humanitarian operations* (P. Tatham & M. Christopher, Eds., 2nd ed.). Kogan Page.

Whittaker, J., McLennan, B., & Handmer, J. (2015). A review of informal volunteerism in emergencies and disasters: Definition, opportunities and challenges. *International Journal of Disaster Risk Reduction, 13*, 358–368.

Wisner, P. S., Stringfellow, A., Youngdahl, W. E., & Parker, L. (2005). The service volunteer–loyalty chain: An exploratory study of charitable not-for-profit service organizations. *Journal of Operations Management, 23*(2), 143–161.

Yin, R. K. (2014). *Case study research: Design and methods* (5th ed.). London, UK: Sage Publications.

3

Strategy and Knowledge Management in Humanitarian Organizations

Margarita Cruz and Achim Schmitt

3.1 Introduction

> *An almost universal weakness of NGOs is found within their often limited capacity to learn, adapt and continuously improve the quality of what they do. This is a serious concern because the future usefulness of NGOs for the world's poor will depend on their ability to overcome their learning disabilities. Crudely put, if NGOs do not learn from their experience, they are destined for insignificance and will atrophy as agents of social change.* (Fowler, 1997)

According to the knowledge-based view of the firm, sustainable competitive advantage is based on exploiting, exploring, and retaining an organization's knowledge (e.g., Grant, 1996).[1] Consequently, a firm's ability to acquire, exploit and explore existing and new knowledge is a crucial element in strategic decision-making as well as organizational performance

---

M. Cruz (✉) • A. Schmitt
Ecole hôtelière de Lausanne, HES-SO // University of Applied Sciences Western Switzerland, Lausanne, Switzerland
e-mail: margarita.cruz@ehl.ch; Achim.schmitt@ehl.ch

and survival (Berdrow & Lane, 2003; Bosua & Venkitachalam, 2013). In the past, scholars have explored various antecedents (i.e. environmental conditions, firm structure) and moderators (i.e. leadership team, organizational resources) of knowledge exploitation (Stettner & Lavie, 2014), knowledge exploration (Raisch, Birkinshaw, Probst, & Tushman, 2009), as well as knowledge retention (Schmitt, Borzillo, & Probst, 2012). While most of these studies have focused on the firm level of analysis, more recent studies have started to uncover these elements at the group or business level of analysis (Jansen, Simsek, & Cao, 2012; Josserand, Schmitt, & Borzillo, 2017; Simsek, Heavey, Veiga, & Souder, 2009). How teams, project groups, and departments are able to utilize and develop existing as well as new knowledge throughout the firm uncovers not only efficiency gains but also sources of competitive advantage. For instance, Kotabe, Jiang, and Murray (2011) show how multinational firms are able to leverage local ties to access new knowledge and exploit this knowledge throughout the organization. Similarly, Josserand et al. (2017) emphasize how individuals' external network connections can help to foster knowledge creation and dissemination. Unfortunately, there are not many studies analyzing the role of individual internal networks for knowledge exploitation and exploration (see Giuffre, 2013 for a rare example). This is surprising as many international organizations, such as humanitarian ones, face the challenge of identifying and utilizing the knowledge gained in operations in various parts of the world. By providing a social capital approach to knowledge sharing and creation, this chapter addresses this shortcoming and outlines how humanitarian organizations can overcome current knowledge barriers in their international operations, creating a competitive advantage.

We offer a theoretical framework on social capital and knowledge management followed by the case of the World Health Organization (WHO). In this section, we identify knowledge challenges facing the WHO and its initiatives to overcome them. We then discuss implications for humanitarian organizations derived from the WHO example and conclude by suggesting future research avenues.

3.2 A Social Capital Approach for Knowledge Sharing and Creation

Organizations can be considered as social groups that combine and transform individual and social expertise into economically valuable outputs (Kogut & Zander, 1992). In this respect, employees' social relationships become a valuable resource for organizational activity (Nahapiet & Ghoshal, 1998) and strategic actions (Carpenter & Westphal, 2001; Cross, Borgatti, & Parker, 2002). The knowledge stocks embedded in and dispersed through organizational actors' external and internal relationships, defined as social capital (Adler & Kwon, 2002), are a potential source for knowledge exploitation, exploration, and retention.[2] For instance, scholars have argued that external social capital helps firms to pursue exploration or exploitation (e.g., Lin, Yang, & Demirkan, 2007) by offering access to novel ideas (Inkpen & Tsang, 2005) and complementary knowledge outside a firm's boundaries (Taylor & Helfat, 2009).

The relationship between employees can be analyzed in terms of their structural, relational, and cognitive dimension (Adler & Kwon, 2002; Granovetter, 1992). The structural dimension describes the overall connection between actors in a social network (Maurer & Ebers, 2006).[3] Conversely, social capital's relational dimension describes the nature of personal ties built through a history of interaction. It encompasses all elements (i.e. shared norms, trust, understanding) that shape and determine the relationship (Nahapiet & Ghoshal, 1998). Finally, the cognitive dimension concerns the shared systems of meaning, representation and understanding among individuals (Kang & Snell, 2009). Additionally, research has distinguished between social capital's internal and external social network dimensions (Payne, Moore, Griffis, & Autry, 2011).

Prior research has emphasized the facilitating role of internal relational embeddedness in exploitation and exploration (Jansen, Van Den Bosch, & Volberda, 2006; Mom, Van Den Bosch, & Volberda, 2009; Taylor & Helfat, 2009). An organization's social capital enables it to increase internal connectedness, which helps explore new technologies while exploiting existing capabilities (Taylor & Helfat, 2009;

Urrea, Villa, & Gonçalves, 2016). Conversely, other scholars (e.g., Harryson, Dudkowski, & Stern, 2008; Lechner, Frankenberger, & Floyd, 2010; Reagans & Zuckerman, 2001) argue that the firm's social relationships have more task-contingent effects. These studies consider weak internal network ties as beneficial for exploration by providing access to non-redundant knowledge and strong network ties as a condition for knowledge sharing and exploitation (e.g., Hansen, 1999). Consequently, Simsek (2009) has called for more research on the role of social networks in knowledge exploitation, exploration, and retention. According to Payne et al. (2011), seeking for more insights into the impact that individuals and groups have on organizational strategic action is a promising approach to better understanding the role that social capital plays for organizations. Jansen and colleagues' study (2006)—one of the few to address this question—highlights that high internal network ties enable firms to balance and resolve the conflicting tasks of knowledge exploitation and knowledge exploration within a business unit.

Motivated by these results, we explore how humanitarian organizations can use (a) the individual employee's social capital for knowledge exploitation, exploration and retention, and (b) the appropriate mechanisms and conditions that allow humanitarian organizations to leverage these relationships for strategic action. We focus on the relational dimension of social capital. Prior internal social capital research has emphasized this dimension as critical for achieving knowledge exploitation and exploration (Kang & Snell, 2009). The dimension can be characterized in terms of the strength of the ties resulting from a combination of time, emotional intensity, and intimacy (Granovetter, 1973). It is thus an indication of how well individuals know their exchange partners (McFadyen & Cannella, 2004). Their interactions build the foundation that allows individuals to access and leverage resources and knowledge embedded in these relationships. In line with Payne and colleagues' (2011) suggestions, we discuss the effects of employees' social capital (lower level of analysis) on the organizational level for strategic action (higher level construct).

3.3 Knowledge Barriers and Problems in Humanitarian Organizations: The Case of the WHO

To illustrate how humanitarian organizations use individual employees' social capital for knowledge management and how this form of social capital can be used for strategic action within the context of humanitarian organizations, we explore the case of the WHO. Building on secondary data, we use an exploratory approach to identify the challenges facing the WHO with regard to knowledge management and their initiatives to support knowledge exploitation, exploration and retention. We rely on publicly available reports such as WHO's country cooperation strategy guidelines (World Health Organization, 2016a), multiple issues of WHO's framework for action (e.g. World Health Organization, 2007), WHO's mid-term programmatic and financial reports, as well as several reports by WHO's Secretariat, including the transformation agenda for 2015–2020 (World Health Organization, 2015), progress on the eHealth programs, and HR initiatives. In addition to this, our secondary sources include reports on the World Alliance for Patient Safety (World Health Organization, 2008), the Geographical Mobility Policy reports, as well as WHO's bulletins (e.g. Kwankam, 2004).

The WHO was established in 1948 as the United Nations' specialized agency for health with the purpose of building "a better, healthier future for all people all over the world" (World Health Organization, 2017). Health, as defined in the WHO constitution, is a "state of complete physical, mental and social well-being, and not merely the absence of disease or infirmity" (World Health Organization, 1946). With headquarters (HQ) in Geneva (Switzerland), the WHO has 194 member states and is present in over 150 countries in six regions. To manage its operations, the WHO employs more than 7000 fixed-term and short-term employees, of whom over 50% are based in country offices in the six regions, while approximately 2500–3000 employees work at the Geneva HQ (World Health Organization, 2017).

Three main bodies govern the WHO: the World Health Assembly (WHA), the Executive Board (EB) and the Secretariat. The WHA is the supreme governing body of the WHO, with delegates from all member states who meet annually in Geneva. The main function of the WHA is to determine the organization's biennial budget and policies. In addition, the WHA is responsible for appointing the HQ's Director-General (DG) every 5 years. The EB consists of 34 members, all technically qualified in the field of health. The main function of the Board is to promote the decisions and policies determined by the WHA, while also submitting the general work program for the WHA's consideration and approval. The Secretariat is the WHO's managerial body, thus overseeing the over 7000 employees in the HQ and country offices (World Health Organization, 2017).

3.3.1 The Problem of Knowledge Management at WHO

In recent years, the challenges facing the WHO have increased in complexity. In 2016 alone, it responded to 47 emergencies worldwide—of which five required the highest level of response of the organization in the Eastern Mediterranean Region (i.e. the development of a strategy and action plan for refugee and migrant health in the WHO European Region) and two related to the largest ever virus disease outbreaks: Zika and Ebola[4]). In addition to this, the WHO has to deal with more than 100 outbreaks of infectious diseases annually and provides health aid to over 200,000 people affected by natural and man-made disasters (World Health Organization, 2016b).

The increased diversity and complexity of the emergencies facing the WHO also makes strategy formulation challenging. New disease outbreaks, refugee crises, and numerous terrorist attacks in traditionally safe regions have required the WHO to be prepared for the unexpected and to have programs in place that allow it to respond swiftly. One way to do this is by managing the knowledge that flows throughout the organization (Grant, 1996). Being able to create, share, use, and manage the knowledge within an organization has proven beneficial for organizations, particularly when undertaking strategic decisions and transforming their strategic intent into achievable actions (Berdrow & Lane, 2003; Bosua & Venkitachalam, 2013). However, as an international and highly centralized organization, the WHO has traditionally concentrated functions such as strategic decision-making, design, and planning in the hands of the HQ with limited input from the country offices. Particularly, because of a general lack of trust toward the countries and the regions, the WHO's HQ kept resources and decisions centralized. With presence in six regions and over 150 countries, the WHO's centralization strategies created small organizational islands with no connecting communication channels that would allow the exchange of information and thereby support strategic action pertaining the WHO regions and countries. As a result, the WHO's limited absorption from and exchange of knowledge with country offices has led to bureaucratic strategic decision-making processes, operational inefficiency, limited communication channels, and deteriorating relationships between the HQ and the country offices (Probst & Schmitt, 2005).

3.3.2 WHO's Initiatives for Knowledge Exploitation, Exploration, and Retention

Aware of the barriers to knowledge management and the consequent barriers to strategy-making, the WHO has adopted a number of initiatives in recent years to enhance knowledge exploitation, exploration, and retention throughout the organization (World Health Organization, 2005). Particular attention has been given to virtual and face-to-face initiatives enhancing staff's social capital and providing them with opportunities for sharing and exchanging knowledge with members of different duty stations at the HQ, regional offices, and country offices. Three prominent recent initiatives stand out: employee mobility, eHealth collaborations, and eLearning networks. These initiatives offer face-to-face or virtual arenas (or both) for interactions and knowledge transfer.

3.3.2.1 Staff Mobility Program

The staff mobility program and job rotation plan offer the opportunity to move to a different duty station in one of the six regional offices or country offices for periods of two to six years. The main purpose of the program is to harvest the knowledge gained at local and regional offices while eliminating cultural barriers that interfere in the decision-making process within the organization. All WHO employees are expected to take the mobility initiative and rotate across the HQ, regional offices, and country offices to enhance their understanding of and improve the quality of their contributions to the WHO (World Health Organization, 2016c).

By reassigning employees to new duty stations for two to six years, the program gives employees the opportunity to interact face-to-face and develop strong ties with staff at the host office. Being physically present at the new duty station also provides WHO employees with further opportunities to discuss technical and operational topics in detail while having constant professional exchanges with local WHO employees. As a result, the program enhances the exchange of non-redundant information (Ruef, 2002) between local and relocated employees, creates diversity in the working groups within regional and country offices, and fosters knowledge exploration and innovation in the long run (Carnabuci & Operti, 2013; Leahey, Beckman, & Stanko, 2017).

By encouraging all employees to rotate across all levels of the organization, the WHO is preparing to make more informed strategic planning and improve efficiency in the strategy-making in the long run. The adoption rate of the program provides an overview of the staff members who are acquiring knowledge about different duty stations. For instance, in 2012 alone, 10.9% out of 184 staff moves were to the HQ, 28.8% to the African region, 6.5% to the Americas, 10.3% to South-East Asia, 9.8% to the Eastern Mediterranean region, 20.7% to Europe, and 13% to the Western Pacific. Africa ranked number one in sending employees to different duty stations (28% of all rotations), while Europe accounted for the second largest region in putting in place the mobility program (21% of all staff mobility reassignments). As far as the top receiving offices, Africa, Europe, and the Western Pacific accounted together for 62.5% of all relocations. Africa received the largest inflow of reassigned staff, however the vast majority came from different duty stations within the African territory itself. The European region received 12.5% employees from the WHO South-East Asia region and 10.7% from the HQ. In the Western Pacific, 28.6% of all relocated employees camefrom the HQ in Geneva. In total, 22% of all 184 reassignments were to another WHO region or to HQ (World Health Organization, 2013a).

3.3.2.2 eHealth Collaborations

Within the framework of the eHealth initiatives,[5] cross-country collaborations with both WHO staff and other humanitarian organizations have emerged. The eHealth collaborations are present all around the world and encourage long-term collaborations as well as virtual and face-to-face networking opportunities among countries and regions to share knowledge and experience (World Health Organization, 2017). These collaborations also provide scientific exchange and learning forums for knowledge exploration activities within the WHO. By recognizing that the field of eHealth is changing the delivery of health initiatives around the world, the WHO and eHealth collaborations are playing an important role in shaping and transforming the future of health particularly for developing countries (World Health Organization, 2013b).

For instance, the eHealth collaboration between the WHO and the Norwegian Centre of Telemedicine (NST) at the University Hospital of North Norway,[6] has provided an arena for interaction and provision of expert advice in the field of telemedicine. The collaboration has led to the development of "mhealth" applications -health applications for mobile devices- oriented to aging and chronic-care patients. By developing, evaluating, and providing guidelines on mobile phone-based applications for aged care, the eHealth collaborations between the NST and the WHO have successfully led to knowledge creation and exploration within the organization (World Health Organization, 2017).

The collaboration with the International Telecommunication Union (ITU) provides a similar experience for knowledge exploration within the WHO. With the purpose of monitoring, reviewing, and providing actions that improve the life of women and children, the collaboration has allowed for innovative ways of supporting mothers and their children's lives. For instance, by having access to mobile devices and applications, mothers and pregnant women receive information on healthy pregnancy, safe delivery, and child protection. While 62% of 64 countries report that eHealth is supporting major women's and children's health initiatives, 48% have adopted an eHealth initiative (i.e. mHealth) for the monitoring and surveillance of maternal, neonatal, and pediatric patients. Under the collaboration, 69% of the countries report to have at least partially implemented eHealth systems (World Health Organization, 2014).

3.3.2.3 eLearning Networks

Finally, virtual learning communities by region or area of expertise are an additional initiative particularly for knowledge exploitation and retention within the WHO (World Health Organization, 2013a).

For example, the Asia eHealth Information Network (AeHIN) is an eLearning Network dedicated to WHO staff based in the Western Pacific and South-East Asia regions. The AeHIN uses a peer-to-peer assistance and knowledge-sharing approach to support better quality and more timely health information for greater country-level impacts across the Western Pacific and South-East Asia (World Health Organization, 2013b). Network membership is open not only to WHO staff but also to other healthcare practitioners and organizations. Membership is free of charge and after filling out a form, users are ready to join the eLearning community. The AeHIN offers a community-driven platform that brings together tools, guidelines, and personal experience in an accessible and user-friendly atmosphere. The platform facilitates productive exchange of information between members. In addition to the information made available through the platform, members can also engage in spontaneous conversations about topics of interest pertaining to technical or regional health problems. Between January and March 2014, Cambodia, Philippines, and India were the top three countries in terms of number of interactions and posts between members of the AeHIN. Cambodia alone accounted for the 33% of all exchanges, the Philippines for 28%, and India for 13% (Asia eHealth Information Network, 2017).

By engaging with these communities, WHO staff members exchange knowledge on a sporadic basis with colleagues or experts from different health organizations in other countries. Participating actively and contributing regularly to these communities enhance the WHO's social capital, particularly with regards to socially weak network ties. These exchanges allow the organization to exploit, integrate, share, and replicate current regional and technical knowledge (Landry, Amara, Pablos-Mendes, Shademani, & Gold, 2006).

Sporadic interactions between members of the eLearning Networks have also supported the process of knowledge exploration and creation within the WHO, particularly around the field of eHealth. For example, a number of eHealth mobile initiatives have been pitched and designed via eLearning Networks. Hence, by providing a context to exchange information with members all around the world, the eLearning Networks are encouraging collaborations between experts and are thereby fostering the entry of new actors and innovations into the field of eHealth. These weak and spontaneous collaborations are reinforced by annual meetings, workshops, and conferences where members can interact face-to-face and showcase their projects (Asia eHealth Information Network, 2012).

Table 3.1 summarizes the initiatives for knowledge exploration, exploitation, and retention implemented by the WHO.

Table 3.1 WHO initiatives for knowledge exploration, exploitation, and retention

Initiative	Mechanism	Outcome	Tie strength
Staff mobility program	Regular and face-to-face interactions among WHO employees from different duty stations.	Knowledge exploitation and exploration in the long run. Can lead to knowledge retention too.	Strong
eHealth collaborations	Virtual as well as face-to-face networking opportunities among countries and regions (including partners outside the WHO).	Knowledge exploitation and exploration. Can lead to knowledge retention too.	Strong
eLearning networks	Sporadic interactions between WHO's staff. Face-to-face exchanges possible through conferences and yearly meetings.	Mainly knowledge exploitation, but knowledge exploration also possible.	Weak

The combination of initiatives relying on weak and strong ties lead to WHO's knowledge retention

3.4 Implications for Humanitarian Organizations

As the WHO case shows, social capital developed at the individual level contributes to knowledge exploration, exploitation, and retention at the organizational level (see Table 3.1). While sporadic weak ties play a fundamental role to access, identify, and exploit existing knowledge within a virtual e-learning network, the WHO also fosters strong network ties through long-lasting collaborations and mobility programs. Such strong network ties pave the way not only to emphasize knowledge exploitation but also to new explorative avenues and health initiatives. The combination of weak and strong ties enables the organization to ensure knowledge retention and organizational learning.

From a theoretical standpoint, these insights from the humanitarian field can shed light on the role of social capital for knowledge management. First, in alignment with prior research (Lechner et al., 2010), our study suggests that a more fine-grained distinction of the task-contingent social capital effect of knowledge exploration and exploitation is required. For instance, prior research such as Hansen (1999), emphasizes weak ties as a source of knowledge exploration as it provides individuals with access to non-redundant knowledge sources. Conversely, strong ties create mutual understandings and are thus an efficient tool for knowledge exploitation and retention (Hansen, 1999; Reagans & Zuckerman, 2001). Given its complexity and mission, the WHO example follows a different approach. Strong ties not only enable knowledge exploitation but also provide the basis for knowledge exploration (i.e. mobility program). In the context of humanitarian organizations, the capacity to create new knowledge is essentially dependent on strong local and international relationships that create trust, constant exchange, and a profound understanding of each other's mission. In this respect, weak ties play a very important support role in exploiting established standards, new regulations, and best practices. This does not necessarily contradict prior findings that have indicated a positive relationship between weak ties and exploration (Hansen, 1999), but shows that such prior findings may rather be context-dependent and do not hold in cases where knowledge exploration and exploitation relates to international standards and common practices for humanitarian activities. Knowledge retention instead happens through the continuous offer of initiatives relying on both weak and strong ties, and an active employee participation in these initiatives. We believe that such insights can contribute to a better understanding of the combination of weak and strong network ties for knowledge exploration, exploitation and retention (Im & Rai, 2008; Lin et al., 2007).

Second, the WHO example also enhances our understanding of the antecedents of knowledge exploitation, exploration, and retention (Raisch & Birkinshaw, 2008). Prior research has argued that knowledge sharing and development are built on "enabling bureaucracies" (Adler, Goldoftas, & Levine, 1999) that adapt, align, and combine individual networks and knowledge effectively (Kauppila, 2010). The WHO example reveals that the use of technology enabled the organization to create an environment characterized as highly "user-friendly", "voluntary", and "valuable". Humanitarian employees may connect to a digital platform for multiple reasons: they need advice, they are searching for an answer, or they would like to learn more about a global health initiative. In this way, the organization provides an autonomous context in which individuals can nurture their weak as well as strong network ties when needed. Prior research has often emphasized the role of autonomy in creating and maintaining individual social networks (Güttel & Konlechner, 2009) but called for more insights into how organizations are able to create a context that enables individual participation in knowledge exploitation, exploration, and retention (Gibson & Birkinshaw, 2004; Simsek, 2009). By providing structures and programs to support the individual needs of international employees, the organization is able to participate, adapt, align, and source organizational knowledge for strategic action.

Third, by exploring the case of knowledge management at the WHO and their different initiatives to explore, exploit, and retain knowledge, this chapter highlights knowledge as a resource upon which humanitarian organizations can rely on to build competitive advantage (Barney, 1991). From this point of view, knowledge can be considered a unique resource with which humanitarian organizations can create and maintain competitive advantages in dynamic environments. As illustrated by the WHO example, one of the main knowledge-related challenges facing humanitarian organizations pertains to their international scope and the

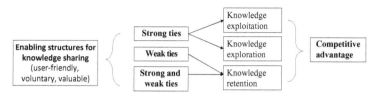

Fig. 3.1 Antecedents of knowledge exploration, exploitation, and retention at the WHO

disconnect between headquarters and regional offices. Being able to breach these knowledge challenges is paramount for humanitarian organizations to increase cost efficiency, improve coordination, and increase visibility in the eyes of different stakeholders. These are factors that can help humanitarian organizations stand out and to achieve cost leadership through cost efficiency (Porter, 1985). By providing arenas for interaction similar to the eHealth and mobility programs, humanitarian organizations can build their source of competitive advantage. Figure 3.1 provides an overview of the main ideas underlying this chapter.

3.5 Future Research and Limitations

While the WHO case provides insights and contributions, it is not without its limitations, and researchers should be cautious about generalizing our findings. While our findings provide a starting point, future research should confirm them in different contexts—other humanitarian, international, non-governmental, governmental, and private sector organizations—to advance our knowledge of contingent effects for knowledge exploitation, exploration and retention. For instance, future researchers should consider both empirical and experimental studies to test the role of networks and tie strength on the use of existing knowledge (exploitation), creation of new knowledge (exploration), and the transfer of knowledge to other humanitarian tasks and regional offices (retention). Our arguments push for an association between social capital and knowledge management, and the insights derived from the WHO example provide initial evidence about this relationship. However, future research should test whether strong ties lead not only to higher knowledge exploitation but also to exploration and effective knowledge transfer in humanitarian organizations. Being able to use empirical as well as experimental methods would not only help to validate our insights but they might also be particularly useful to avoid relying solely on the self-reporting character of the WHO case study.

Furthermore, our focus is on investigating the relationship between individual social networks and the organizational level, without considering the role of middle-managers and regional departments. While this approach responds to calls to bridge multi-level perspectives for social capital research (Payne et al., 2011), we encourage future research that explores the role of social capital stemming from intra-firm regional networks and groups for knowledge exploration, exploitation, and retention. Finally, past studies (Casanueva & Gallego, 2010) have frequently emphasized that the individual network's performance depends on whether it contains useful resources for the individual and/or the organization. While our study focused on relational embeddedness, we encourage future research analyzing the content, quality, and integration potential of resources available through an individual's external network.

Notes

1. Knowledge exploitation refers to an organization's repeated use of its existing knowledge, leading to the further development of its competencies. Knowledge exploration instead refers to the acquisition of new knowledge that can result in new competencies (March, 1991). While knowledge exploitation results in moderate but certain returns, knowledge exploration is uncertain and its returns are unpredictable (Liu, 2006). Knowledge retention deals with the firm's storage of and capability to use the knowledge it creates (Argote, McEvily, & Reagans, 2003).
2. We follow Nahapiet and Ghoshal's view on social capital (1998), which defines it as "the sum of the actual and potential resources embedded within, available through, and derived from the network of relationships possessed by an individual or social unit. Social capital thus comprises

both the network and the assets that may be mobilized through the network" (p. 243).
3. Also known as embeddedness (Granovetter, 1985).
4. While Zika affected 76 countries in the Americas, South-East Asia, and the Western Pacific Regions, the impact of Ebola was limited to the WHO African Regions, where it took approximately 11,310 lives.
5. According to the WHO, eHealth refers to the use of information and communication technologies for health (World Health Organization, 2017). In 2005, the WHA acknowledged the potential of eHealth to strengthen health systems and recommended that the WHO's member states incorporate eHealth into their health systems and services.
6. Collaboration established in 2002 and still ongoing by mid-2018.

References

Adler, P., Goldoftas, B., & Levine, D. (1999). Flexibility versus efficiency? A case study of model changeovers in the toyota production system. *Organization Science, 10*, 43–68.

Adler, P., & Kwon, S. W. (2002). Social capital: Prospects for a new concept. *Academy of Management Review, 27*, 17–40.

Argote, L., McEvily, B., & Reagans, R. (2003). Managing knowledge in organizations: An integrative framework and review of emerging themes. *Management Science, 49*(4), 571–582.

Asia eHealth Information Network. (2012). *Workshop proceedings, United Nations Conference Centre*, Bangkok, Thailand, August 2012.

Asia eHealth Information Network. (2017). Retrieved July 2017, from http://Www.Aehin.Org/

Barney, J. (1991). Firm resources and sustained competitive advantage. *Journal of Management, 17*(1), 99–120.

Berdrow, I., & Lane, H. W. (2003). International joint ventures: Creating value through successful knowledge management. *Journal of World Business, 38*(1), 15–30.

Bosua, R., & Venkitachalam, K. (2013). Aligning strategies and processes in knowledge management: A framework. *Journal of Knowledge Management, 17*(3), 331–346.

Carnabuci, G., & Operti, E. (2013). Where do firms' recombinant capabilities come from? Intraorganizational networks, knowledge, and firms' ability to innovate through technological recombination. *Strategic Management Journal, 34*(13), 1591–1613.

Carpenter, M. A., & Westphal, J. D. (2001). The strategic context of external network ties: Examining the impact of director appointments on board involvement in strategic decision making. *Academy of Management Journal, 44*(4), 639–660.

Casanueva, C., & Gallego, Á. (2010). Social capital and individual innovativeness in university research networks. *Innovation: Management, Policy & Practice, 12*, 105–117.

Cross, R., Borgatti, S. P., & Parker, A. (2002). Making invisible work visible: Using social network analysis to support strategic collaboration. *California Management Review, 44*(2), 25–46.

Fowler, A. (Ed.). (1997). *Striking a balance: A guide to enhancing the effectiveness of non-governmental organisations in international development*. Earthscan, London.

Gibson, C., & Birkinshaw, J. (2004). The antecedents, consequences and mediating role of organizational ambidexterity. *Academy of Management Journal, 47*, 209–226.

Giuffre, K. (2013). *Communities and networks: Using social network analysis to rethink urban and community studies*. John Wiley & Sons.

Granovetter, M. (1973). The strength of weak ties. *American Journal of Sociology, 78*, 1360–1380.

Granovetter, M. (1985). Economic action and social structure: The problem of embeddedness. *American Journal of Sociology, 91*(3), 481–510.

Granovetter, M. (1992). Problems of explanation in economic sociology. In N. Nohria & R. Eccles (Eds.), *Networks and organizations: Structure, form and action*. Boston, MA: Harvard Business School Press.

Grant, R. M. (1996). Toward a knowledge-based theory of the firm. *Strategic Management Journal, 17*, 109–122.

Güttel, W. H., & Konlechner, S. W. (2009). Continuously hanging by a thread: Managing contextually ambidextrous organizations. *Schmalenbach Business Review, 61*, 149–171.

Hansen, M. T. (1999). The search transfer problem: The role of weak ties in sharing knowledge across organizational sub-units. *Administrative Science Quarterly, 44*, 82–111.

Harryson, S. J., Dudkowski, R., & Stern, A. (2008). Transformation networks in innovation alliances—The development of volvo c70. *Journal of Management Studies, 45*, 745–773.

Im, G., & Rai, A. (2008). Knowledge sharing ambidexterity in long-term interorganizational relationships. *Management Science, 54*, 1281–1296.

Inkpen, A., & Tsang, E. W. K. (2005). Social capital, networks, and knowledge transfer. *Academy of Management Review, 30*, 146–165.

Jansen, J. J. P., Simsek, Z., & Cao, Q. (2012). Ambidexterity and performance in multiunit contexts: Cross-level moderating effects of structural and resource attributes. *Strategic Management Journal, 33*, 1286–1303.

Jansen, J. J. P., Van Den Bosch, F. A. J., & Volberda, H. (2006). Exploratory innovation, exploitative innovation, and performance: Effects of organizational antecedents and environmental moderators. *Management Science, 52*, 1661–1674.

Josserand, E., Schmitt, A., & Borzillo, S. (2017) Balancing present needs and future options: How employees leverage social networks with clients. *Journal of Business Strategy, 38*, 14–21.

Kang, S.-C., & Snell, S. A. (2009). Intellectual capital architectures and ambidextrous learning: A framework for human resource management. *Journal of Management Studies, 46*, 65–92.

Kauppila, O.-P. (2010). Creating ambidexterity by integrating and balancing structurally separate interorganizational partnerships. *Strategic Organization, 8*, 283–312.

Kogut, B., & Zander, U. (1992). Knowledge of the firm, combinative capabilities and the replication of technology. *Organization Science, 3*, 383–397.

Kotabe, M., Jiang, C. X., & Murray, J. Y. (2011). Managerial ties, knowledge acquisition, realized absorptive capacity and new product market performance of emerging multinational companies: A case of China. *Journal of World Business, 46*(2), 166–176.

Kwankam, S. Y. (2004). What e-Health can offer. *Bulletin of the World Health Organization, 82*(10), 800–802.

Landry, R., Amara, N., Pablos-Mendes, A., Shademani, R., & Gold, I. (2006). The knowledge-value chain: A conceptual framework for knowledge translation in health. *Bulletin of The World Health Organization, 84*(8), 597–602.

Leahey, E., Beckman, C. M., & Stanko, T. L. (2017). Prominent but less productive: The impact of interdisciplinarity on scientists' research. *Administrative Science Quarterly, 62*(1), 105–139.

Lechner, C., Frankenberger, K., & Floyd, S. W. (2010). Task contingencies in the curvilinear relationships between intergroup networks and initiative performance. *Academy of Management Journal, 53*, 865–889.

Lin, Z., Yang, H., & Demirkan, I. (2007). The performance consequences of ambidexterity in strategic alliance formations: Empirical investigation and computational theorizing. *Management Science, 53*, 1645–1658.

Liu, W. (2006). Knowledge exploitation, knowledge exploration, and competency trap. *Knowledge and Process Management, 13*(3), 144–161.

March, J. G. (1991). Exploration and exploitation in organizational learning. *Organization Science, 2*(1), 71–87.

Maurer, I., & Ebers, M. (2006). Dynamics of social capital and their performance implications: Lessons from biotechnology start-ups. *Administrative Science Quarterly, 51*, 262–292.

Mcfadyen, M. A., & Cannella, A. A. (2004). Social capital and knowledge creation: Diminishing returns of the number and strength of exchange relationships. *Academy of Management Journal, 47*, 735–746.

Mom, T. J. M., Van Den Bosch, F. A. J., & Volberda, H. (2009). Understanding variation in managers' ambidexterity: Investigating direct and interaction effects of formal structural and personal coordination mechanisms. *Organization Science, 20*, 812–828.

Nahapiet, J., & Ghoshal, S. (1998). Social capital, intellectual capital and the organizational advantage. *Academy of Management Review, 23*, 242–266.

Payne, T. G., Moore, C. B., Griffis, S. E., & Autry, C. W. (2011). Multilevel challenges and opportunities in social capital research. *Journal of Management, 37*, 491–520.

Porter, M. E. (1985). *The competitive advantage: Creating and sustaining superior performance* (p. 167). New York, NY: Free Press.

Probst, G., & Schmitt, A. (2005). *The World Health Organization: Change in an international organization*. The Case Centre: Reference No. 405-047-1, Geneva.

Raisch, S., & Birkinshaw, J. (2008). Organizational ambidexterity: Antecedents, outcomes, and moderators. *Journal of Management, 34*, 375–409.

Raisch, S., Birkinshaw, J., Probst, G., & Tushman, M. L. (2009). Organizational ambidexterity: Balancing exploitation and exploration for sustained performance. *Organization Science, 20*, 685–695.

Reagans, R., & Zuckerman, E. W. (2001). Network, diversity and performance: The social capital of r&d teams. *Organization Science, 12*, 502–518.

Ruef, M. (2002). Strong ties, weak ties and islands: Structural and cultural predictors of organizational innovation. *Industrial And Corporate Change, 11*(3), 427–449.

Schmitt, A., Borzillo, S., & Probst, G. (2012). Don't let knowledge walk away: Knowledge retention during employee downsizing. *Management Learning, 43*, 53–74.

Simsek, Z. (2009). Organizational ambidexterity: Towards a multilevel understanding. *Journal of Management Studies, 46*, 597–624.

Simsek, Z., Heavey, C., Veiga, J. F., & Souder, D. (2009). A typology for aligning organizational ambidexterity's conceptualizations, antecedents, and outcomes. *Journal of Management Studies, 46*, 864–894.

Stettner, U., & Lavie, D. (2014). Ambidexterity under scrutiny: Exploration and exploitation via internal organization, alliances, and acquisitions. *Strategic Management Journal, 35*, 1903–1929.

Taylor, A., & Helfat, C. E. (2009). Organizational linkages for surviving technological change: Complementary assets, middle management, and ambidexterity. *Organization Science, 20*, 718–739.

Urrea, G., Villa, S., & Gonçalves, P. (2016). Exploratory analyses of relief and development operations using social networks. *Socio-Economic Planning Sciences, 56*, 27–39.

World Health Organization. (1946). Constitution of the World Health Organization. Retrieved July 2017, from http://www.who.int/governance/eb/who_constitution_en.pdf

World Health Organization. (2005). Bridging the "Know-Do" gap. *Meeting on knowledge translation in Global Health*, Geneva, 2005. Retrieved July 2017, from https://www.measureevaluation.org/resources/training/capacity-building-resources/high-impact-research-training-curricula/bridging-the-know-do-gap.pdf

World Health Organization. (2007). *Everybody business: Strengthening health systems to improve health outcomes: WHO's framework for action.* Retrieved July 2017, from http://www.who.int/healthsystems/strategy/everybodys_business.pdf

World Health Organization. (2008). *World Alliance for patient safety. Progress report 2006–2007.* Retrieved July 2017, from http://apps.who.int/iris/handle/10665/75169

World Health Organization. (2013a). Human resources: Annual report. *Sixty-sixth World Health Assembly*, May 2013. Retrieved July 2017, from http://apps.who.int/gb/e/e_wha66.html

World Health Organization. (2013b). eHealth and health Internet domain names. *Sixty-sixth World Health Assembly*, May 2013. Retrieved July 2017, from http://apps.who.int/gb/e/e_wha66.html

World Health Organization. (2014). eHealth and innovation in women's and children's health: A baseline review: Based on the findings of the 2013 survey of CoIA countries by the WHO Global Observatory for eHealth, March 2014. Retrieved July 2017, from http://apps.who.int/iris/bitstream/10665/111922/1/9789241564724_eng.pdf

World Health Organization. (2015). The transformation agenda of the World Health Organization Secretariat in the African region 2015–2020. Retrieved July 2017, from http://www.afro.who.int/sites/default/files/pdf/generic/Transformation_agenda_english.pdf

World Health Organization. (2016a). *WHO country cooperation strategy. Guide 2016*. Retrieved July 2017, from http://apps.who.int/iris/handle/10665/251734

World Health Organization. (2016b). *Mid-term programmatic and financial report for 2016–2017*. Retrieved July 2017, from http://apps.who.int/gb/ebwha/pdf_files/WHA70/A70_40-en.pdf?ua=1

World Health Organization. (2016c). *Geographical mobility policy*. Retrieved July 2017, from http://www.who.int/employment/WHO-mobility-policy.pdf

World Health Organization. (2017). Retrieved July, 2017, from http://www.who.int/en/

4

Innovating Short-Term Preparedness Actions Using Climate Information

Gloria Urrea and Meghan Bailey

4.1 Introduction

The human cost of weather-related disasters, especially for the world's poorest people is sizeable and growing. During the last two decades, over 90% (6457) of natural disasters were caused by weather-related events—most notably, floods, droughts, storms, landslides, and hurricanes—claiming a total of over 600,000 lives and leaving over 4 billion people injured, homeless or in need of assistance from governments and humanitarian organizations (CRED & UNISDR, 2015). The vast majority of people affected during these weather-related disasters were located in lower-income countries where the capacity of national governments to

---

G. Urrea (✉)
Kelley School of Business, Indiana University, Bloomington, USA
e-mail: gloria.urrea@usi.ch

M. Bailey
Red Cross Red Crescent Climate Centre, The Hague, Netherlands
e-mail: bailey@climatecentre.org

prepare for and respond to disaster risk is lower. As such, humanitarian actors play a strong role in efforts to both reduce the risks of weather-related disasters and respond to affected populations during and following disaster events.

Moreover, the frequency of weather-related disasters is on the rise. The Emergency Events Database (EM-DAT) recorded an average of 335 weather-related disasters per year between 2005 and 2014, which is an increase of 14% as compared to the period of 1995–2004. Further, the most recent averages are nearly double the level recorded between 1985 and 1994. The number of floods and storms each year is rising steadily. Nearly half (47%) of all weather-related disasters between 1995 and 2015 were floods, affecting a total of 2.3 billion people. Storms are less frequent than floods, but have the highest death toll, killing more than 242,000 people in the same period of time, which corresponds to 40% of the global total for all weather-related disasters (CRED & UNISDR, 2015). A range of climate change models indicate this upward trend in weather-related disasters will continue or increase in most carbon-emission scenarios (IPCC, 2015).

Humanitarian institutions, which work to reduce the impacts of these weather-related disasters, are grappling with the increasing demand disasters place on the humanitarian system. Many humanitarian institutions are adapting their practices to adjust to these demands, including by taking advantage of emerging technology to better inform them of where, when and how to take action in light of growing demand and finite financial resources. This chapter will provide an introduction to climate change and the demands that weather disasters in a changing climate place on the humanitarian system. It will then review how climate information can be used to inform both policy makers and humanitarian actors. We focus on an innovative approach—forecast-based actions—where scientific forecasting has been used to reduce disaster impacts. This approach is innovative because it uses a recombination of knowledge in climate information and short-term preparedness actions, which has not been considered before in the humanitarian setting. The chapter finishes by giving practical examples that highlight the use of climate information services to design and inform on-the-ground actions before a disaster occurs.

4.2 Climate Change

Climate change is the increase of the earth's temperature due to human-induced changes in atmospheric composition, mainly caused by the emission of greenhouse gases. The change in the earth's global mean temperature leads to changes in weather extremes, producing high levels of variability in both temperature and precipitation, as well as decreases in snow and ice extent, and increases in the sea level (Karl & Trenberth, 2003). The consequences of these changes vary around the globe, but they are frequently experienced as changes in natural biological systems and negative effects over the population.

The interest and study of climate change has gone through two main "eras". The first one took place between 1980 and 2000, when climate change was considered solely an environmental issue under the responsibility of climate scientists and politicians, with little or no concern for the impact on the population (Birkmann & von Teichman, 2010). For instance, Parmesan and Yohe (2003) conduct a meta-analysis of the early research on climate change in order to define an adequate "climate fingerprint". They were interested in quantitative estimates of the global biological impacts of climate change and found that the range limits of species have moved on average 6.1 km per decade northward or meters per decade upward, which is the direction predicted by climate change. Moreover, they find an average change toward earlier spring timing of 2.3 days per decade (Parmesan & Yohe, 2003).

The second era started in 2000, when the negative effects of climate change on the population became evident. In this stage, more actors such as social scientists and humanitarian organizations took a more active role to protect exposed people (Birkmann & von Teichman, 2010). Therefore, social scientists and organizations are currently including in their analysis of climate change the vulnerability and exposure levels of the population, in addition to the magnitude of the weather-related hazard. In particular, governments and humanitarian organizations are focusing on communities who are the most vulnerable as a result of population trends, unmanaged urban development and reduced economic development.

During this second era, recent studies of climate change have documented not only observed changes and their causes; future climate change, risks and impacts; but also future pathways for adaptation, mitigation and sustainable development (IPCC, 2015). There are currently some confirmed facts about climate change:

- There is no credible doubt that humans are having an influence on the climate system due to the emission of greenhouse gases. The changes in the climate system have broad consequences for both natural ecosystems and population.
- If emissions of greenhouse gases are not reduced, global warming will continue and the changes in the climate system will be irreversible, increasing the likelihood of having negative impacts for people and ecosystems.
- Possible actions to limit the risks caused by climate change include sustained reductions of greenhouse emissions and the implementation of adaptation and mitigation policies and actions to increase the resilience of communities to deal with changes in their climate.
- There is no one mitigation or adaptation strategy that will reduce the impact of climate change in its entirety. A collaborative approach is required, bringing together different stakeholders at all levels and integrating climate change adaptation and mitigation actions with other societal objectives.

Research on climate change and its impacts on global mean temperatures and climatic variability gives an indication of the kinds of weather-related disasters we are likely to see more of in future. However, understanding whether a specific weather-related disaster can be attributed to climate change, or whether it would have happened without human-induced changes in the climate is a complicated task. This is because weather-related disasters have always occurred and as such, understanding whether a specific weather-related disaster was caused by climate change involves assigning probabilities of occurrence. Weather-related disasters are typically categorized based on return periods, such as a 1-in-2 year flood, which is the level of flooding one would expect to happen once in a two-year period.

By way of example, in a country like Bangladesh, a 1-in-2 year flood in the rainy season is low-level flooding that Bangladeshi farmers are typically well prepared to deal with, and indeed rely on for their production of rice. Likewise, a 1-in-5 year flood is of a higher magnitude, being expected to happen once in a five year period of time, likely requiring those same farmers to either use bricks to raise their furniture and continue living in inundated houses, or evacuate for a period of time. In an extreme 1-in-30 year event those same farmers would likely be part of a large scale movement of people to evacuate, perhaps for a long period of time and returning to find all their belongings gone. In this context the 1-in-30 year flood would certainly be classified as a disaster requiring humanitarian assistance, while the 1-in-2 year flood would not. The 1-in-5 year flood could also require humanitarian assistance for specific subsets of the population, such as households located in highly exposed areas or disadvantaged groups such as refugees. All three of these example floods could occur without the influence of climate change, but may be occurring more frequently in a changing climate.

Understanding whether a flood with a specific return period was caused by climate change requires statistical analysis comparing two scenarios using computer models—the world as it is now with climate change and a world without these human-induced changes based on what is known about the climate in the past. While the humanitarian imperative to support populations in need is unaffected by whether a specific weather-related disaster can be attributed to climate change, understanding these trends and the disasters we can expect to see more of in future is important for service delivery and the coping capacity of populations. In the example of the Bangladeshi farmers, a farmer might have experienced the extreme 1-in-30 year flood which robs her of all assets one to three times in a lifetime, allowing time in between for families to rebuild their lives and asset-bases. If these events increase in frequency as a result of climate change, that periodic depletion of assets also becomes more frequent, effectively trapping the farmer in poverty.

As the serious consequences of climate change become unavoidable, global willingness to take action to mitigate the impact of climate change has increased. Evidence of this willingness is the Paris Agreement, which aims "to undertake ambitious efforts to combat climate change and adapt to its effects"; these efforts include limiting temperature increases and enhancing the ability of countries to deal with the impacts of climate change (UNFCCC, 2017).[1] Beyond the global agreements, governments and humanitarian organizations are also participating in these initiatives by using climate information services to design long-term policies and implement short-term actions. In the next few sections, we describe how scientific information can help reduce the impact of weather-related disasters, and the long-term and short-term actions that can be taken to reduce the negative consequences of weather-related phenomena that are exacerbated by climate change.

4.3 Climate Information to Prevent Disasters

Advances in technology have increased the prevalence and quality of the types of hydro-meteorological and climate information available to scientists, governments and organizations. According to the Global Framework for Climate Services (GFCS), "[climate] services involve high-quality data from national and international databases on temperature, rainfall, wind, soil moisture and ocean conditions, as well as maps, risk and vulnerability analyses, assessments, and long-term projections and scenarios" (GFCS, 2017). Ideally, these types of data could be combined with other socio-economic variables such as population distributions, agricultural activities, or location of roads and other infrastructure to evaluate the possible impacts of a weather event and help decision-makers improve long- and short-term policies and actions to enhance community resilience (Fig. 4.1).

However, despite the current predictability of many weather-related events, the use of this scientific information remains limited. Several authors have asserted that the limited applicability of climate information in the design and implementation of policies to reduce the risk of communities is due to a failure in communication between climate scientists and practitioners. For instance, the transfer of information between these parties has focused mainly on averages in regions (e.g. rainfall average in Africa), giving useful information on the general trend of climate change but ignoring extreme events, variability and uncertainty ranges

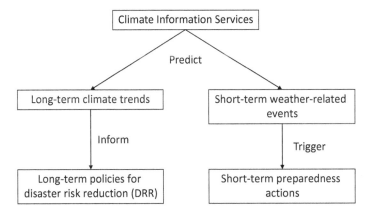

Fig. 4.1 Ideal use of climate information services

that have a direct impact on the population (Coughlan de Perez, Monasso, van Aalst, & Suarez, 2014). In fact, it has been shown that in some regions of Africa the number of extreme rainfall events in a season serve as a better predictor for the probability of seasonal flooding than the total seasonal rainfall does (Coughlan de Perez et al., 2017).

In order to increase the usability of climate science to help prevent the impact of disasters, several steps need to be taken regarding both the presentation of climate information and the methods of increasing collaboration between scientific and humanitarian organizations. To address the first point and improve the presentation of the information, climate scientists should go beyond averages and include additional information in their forecasts. According to Coughlan de Perez et al. (2014), first, climate scientists could include information about the frequency of extreme events, which is directly connected to disasters, because humanitarian organizations actually find these critical thresholds useful to spur actions when real conditions approach those critical values. Second, as using averages usually gives the wrong perception that phenomena is linearly progressing, climate scientists could also present information about variability and uncertainty ranges of a phenomenon. It is important to understand the range of possible outcomes of the weather event to adequately design policies and prepare communities to be resilient to all the possibilities (not only to the average). And third, communication between climate scientists and practitioners should be clear, graphical, concise and should avoid the use of jargon (Coughlan de Perez et al., 2014).

To increase collaboration between climate scientists and humanitarian organizations, we need to consider practices that go beyond the presentation of climate information. Building on the partnership between the Red Cross Red Crescent Climate Centre (RCCC) and the Research Institute for Climate and Society, Coughlan de Perez and Mason (2014) suggest that climate scientists should prioritize the needs of humanitarian practitioners, provide only information that is relevant to them and give support when required. Climate scientists tend to give aggregate information with technical details, while practitioners are usually interested in information on specific weather events occurring in the next days that may serve as proxy for risks that can inform decision-making and trigger early action (Coughlan de Perez & Mason, 2014).

The expectation is that building the bridge to connect climate scientists with policy makers and humanitarian practitioners will allow a better use of climate information. Having a better idea of the kind of weather events that will affect a population can help design long-term policies and trigger short-term actions to reduce vulnerability and, therefore, the risk associated with the weather event. In the next section, we address the types of policies and actions that could be implemented with the right scientific information.

4.4 Taking Action with Climate Information

The temporal nature of climate information means that different types of data are appropriate to inform different types of decisions and are therefore useful for different types of decision-makers. Long-range climate forecasts that indicate, for example, whether a region will experience greater or lesser dryness on average in subsequent decades, may be useful for government or large private sector actors engaged in long-term planning and investing, but are typically of little use to small-scale farmers or herders, who have limited means to make meaningful decisions on those time-scales. In contrast, the timing and severity of near-term disaster events for specific areas is often of keen interest to farmers and herders, as well as the government and humanitarian institutions that aim to support them. In this chapter, we make the distinction between long-term and short-term actions that are taken by government and humanitarian actors to support vulnerable populations, and at least in part, are based on climate information. First we will we review the long-term actions, using examples that fall under the auspices of disaster-risk reduction and climate change adaptation. Then we will turn to an emerging set of innovative short-term actions based on a forecast of an imminent weather event.

4.4.1 Long-term Actions: Disaster-Risk Reduction and Climate Change Adaptation

Disaster-risk reduction (DRR) and climate change adaptation (CCA) have been two different perspectives taken by practitioners and climate scientists respectively to address the concern of reducing vulnerability with long-term actions. DRR is defined as "the development and application of policies, strategies and practices to reduce vulnerabilities and disaster risks throughout society" (Twigg, 2015). DRR actions are usually implemented over a long time period and involve investment in infrastructure such as flood embankments to reduce the threat of the hazard and the vulnerability of the population (Thomalla, Downing, Spanger-Siegfried, Han, & Rockström, 2006). CCA has the main objective of reducing the vulnerability of the population to the specific impacts of climate change, using a long-term approach. For instance, CCA actions can be geared toward the diversification of agricultural activities including crops resistant to natural hazards, early warning systems and training and awareness campaigns (Mercer, 2010).

The main differences between DRR and CCA correspond to their scope and spatial scales. DRR tools and interventions are implemented considering the protection of the population and infrastructure against all types of hazards, while CCA focuses on climate-related hazards (Mercer, 2010). Moreover, CCA is usually analyzed and monitored at a global level, while DRR actions are considered at the community local level (Birkmann & von Teichman, 2010). Despite these differences, there is an opportunity to integrate both approaches building on their complementarity. CCA could be integrated into the DRR approach to design and implement programmatic interventions based on an understanding of future climate and expected weather extremes (Twigg, 2015). Such an integration could reduce the mortality rate and material losses (calculated as a share of the exposed population and gross domestic product respectively) and close the vulnerability gap between high- and low-income countries (Jongman et al., 2015).

Therefore, government and humanitarian actors should consider projections that give an indication of the kinds of conditions one might expect in the future, for example, average precipitation, temperature and seasonal timings, as well as climatic variability and expected extremes. Government and humanitarian actors can then use this information to make better-informed decisions on the kinds of negative impacts that local populations can expect, and in turn design long-term programs that aim to alleviate those specific climate-sensitive vulnerabilities. For instance, the choice of which alternative crop to promote to increase nutrient intake would best be made with some level of understanding of how that crop would perform in both the present and future expected climatic conditions, in addition to a host of socio-economic factors.

In summary, there are a number of long-term actions that can be taken to reduce risk without knowing exactly when and where a weather-related disaster will occur. Climate information that is both long-term, looking at decades, and medium-term, looking at the upcoming season, can help identify the variety of disaster events to prioritize in preparedness and DRR efforts. For instance, the Red Cross Red Crescent societies in Pacific Island countries will typically devote more resources to helping communities develop and rehearse cyclone contingency plans during years of El Niño (identified by climate information), during which cyclones can be expected to be more frequent and unpredictable.

4.4.2 Short-term Actions: Forecast-Based Actions

Weather-related disasters tend to be categorized as either slow onset, such as droughts and extreme winter conditions, or fast onset, including floods, cyclones, storms, heat waves and cold waves (Chantarat, Barrett, Mude, & Turvey, 2007). Both types of weather-related disasters can be anticipated, with varying levels of certainty and time-scales, using climate and weather information. Short-term projections can provide a valuable early warning if the warning information is used in a meaningful way to take action. While there are limitations of reliability such that one can never know for sure that a disaster will occur, and important differences between regions and disaster type that affect how well forecasts can accurately predict a disaster event in time and space, forecasts can provide valuable lead time for short-term actions before a disaster occurs.

However, the humanitarian system, especially the systems which release and move humanitarian funds to where they are needed, have traditionally not been well set-up to operate on the time-scale of a forecast (Stephens, Coughlan de Perez, Kruczkiewicz, Boyd, & Suarez, 2015). Actors within the Red Cross Red Crescent movement and other humanitarian institutions have traditionally focused on efforts to support populations once they have already experienced a disaster—most notably in emergency response, reconstruction and rehabilitation. Remarkably, only 12% of funding was allocated to reducing the risk of disaster before it occurred, in the time period between 1993 and 2013 (Coughlan De Perez et al., 2015)—the remainder of which was spent post-disaster. While there is substantial experience within the humanitarian system operating rapidly to response post-disaster, there is little experience of initiating similar rapid efforts in the lead up to an anticipated disaster. Further, pre-disaster efforts to reduce risk have focused on the long-term preparedness and DRR-type actions outlined in the previous section.

4.4.2.1 The Innovation Behind Forecast-Based Actions

Both the time-scale of working pre-disaster based on a forecast, and the uncertainty inherent in spending humanitarian funds based on a forecast, are considerable operational challenges. These operational challenges, combined with the increasing demand that weather-related disasters place on the humanitarian system, plus steady improvements in climate and hydro-meteorological science and big data, have created a space for innovation. This section will highlight one stream of innovation in this space, which has been called forecast-based financing (FbF). The FbF concept is a new approach developed by the Red Cross Red Crescent movement and supporting partners (RCCC, 2018) and is innovative because it uses a recombination of knowledge in climate information and short-term preparedness actions (Kaplan & Vakili, 2015), which has not been used before in the humanitarian setting.

Forecast-based financing was born out of considerable institutional learning about implementing early actions based on early warnings. A significant bottleneck to doing early action based on a credible warning is the need for a financial mechanism specifically designed for operating on the timescale of a forecast (Slatyer, 2016). It is for this reason that the finance aspect of this concept is highlighted in the concept name—FbF—however there are multiple applications of FbF systems to date that go beyond enabling the timely release of funds. The concept has been piloted by a handful of humanitarian, development and UN agencies, and its potential benefits are starting to be recognized by governments and academia (Slatyer, 2016; Stephens et al., 2015; WFP, 2016). For instance, the Australian government proposes FbF as a way to more efficiently use the scarce global funding for humanitarian action and is currently supporting the implementation of pilot projects in the Pacific (Slatyer, 2016). The World Food Program (WFP) is also building on the FbF concept in their FoodSECuRE initiative. FoodSECuRE uses climate forecasts to trigger actions aiming to prepare the community and reduce the impact of climate-related disasters. Moreover, WFP has established that "early action using a climate-triggered forecast mechanism would reduce the cost of emergency response by approximately 50%" (WFP, 2016).

The following are the key innovative elements of an FbF system: selecting a trigger, matching forecast probabilities with appropriate actions, and designing post-trigger plans to carry out those actions. We explain these elements below and illustrate the implementation of FbF systems with practical examples in the next section. These examples were implemented by actors within the Red Cross Red Crescent movement, as many of these programs have been the first to trigger forecast-based humanitarian operations and because the operations have been trialed on a diversity of weather-disaster types and geographic locations. Further, the authors of this chapter have contributed to the design and development of these programs as advisers. Additional information on FbF programming, including guidance on design, implementation, and evaluation can be found in FbF manuals available publicly online: http://fbf.drk.de/.

4.4.2.2 Elements of FbF Systems

Selecting a trigger: In order to act early based on a forecast, the government or humanitarian institution must choose a pre-existing forecast, or where one is not available or suitable, they must design a new model with the help of climate scientists. The aim is to use a weather forecast or seasonal climate forecast that is as reliable as possible for the country or region of interest, and for the specific weather hazard one is trying to pre-empt, such as a flood, drought or cyclone. All forecasts have some level of uncertainty, as it is not possible given current forecasting capacity to know with absolutely certainty the timing and extremity of future weather conditions. However, some forecasts are correct more often than others, due a number of factors, including how much historical data exists for the area, how difficult the specific weather phenomenon is to model and how many resources have been devoted to modeling specific areas, through which a scientist might be able to find agreement between multiple models, thus giving the user more confidence in what the forecast is projecting. It is important for humanitarian actors to know how reliable a forecast is so an informed decision can be made on whether to use it to make decisions that involve spending humanitarian funds, and if so, how much to spend. This involves thinking through in a systematized way, how often the user might expect a forecast to be wrong, and therefore how often the humanitarian institution could spend funds in anticipation of a weather-related disaster that does not happen or does not happen to the extremity that was expected.

Matching forecast probabilities with appropriate actions: The government or humanitarian institution must also specify the extremity of the expected weather-related disaster that the system should anticipate. For example, a local population might rightly be assumed to be able to cope using their own means with a 1-in-2 year flood and as such, no action is initiated if the forecast indicates this is the level of flooding to expect. However, in anticipation of a 1-in-5 year flood, a humanitarian actor might deem lower-level supports appropriate, such as the distribution of water purification supplies to address the increased risk of waterborne disease. In anticipation of an extreme 1-in-30 year flood, a humanitarian actor might deem higher-level action support necessary, such as the distribution of supplies to build evacuation centers in anticipation of farmers needing to leave their homes for a prolonged period.

Designing post-trigger plans: Designing post-trigger plans to carry out those actions involves selecting actions that meet a number of criteria. Most notably, the forecast-based actions selected must address a specific risk associated with the weather-related disaster which is reasonably expected to produce a positive change that ultimately improves upon the lived experience of the intended beneficiary population. This may involve developing a theory of change for specific actions, to work through specifically how actions taken following a forecast are expected to lead to improved outcomes. Further, the action must be right-sized, meaning it is implemented at the right dosage to have the desired effect. For example, if the intention is to supply water purification supplies to reduce waterborne disease, those supplies must be sufficient for the household water needs of all family members for the duration of the higher risk period.

Consideration of how much time an action takes to implement is essential. For example, while is not possible to build a cyclone shelter in the days or hours before an expected cyclone hits, it may be possible to engage in minor repairs and cleaning of existing cyclone shelters, or fill them with helpful supplies. In contrast, for slower onset weather-related disasters like a drought, it may be possible to take actions following a forecast for drought that are implemented over weeks or even months, such as the repair of water infrastructure to reduce water waste or the distribution of cash or food to address an expected spike in food prices.

The selection of forecast-based actions also includes determining the desirable actions to perform from the perspective of both the affected population and the implementing organization, regardless of whether the expected weather-related disaster occurs. This may involve community and household level consultations as well as costing exercises. Each of these processes of selecting a trigger, matching forecast probabilities with appropriate actions, and designing post-trigger plans to carry out those actions were trialed in the case studies presented in the next section.

4.5 Practical Approach: Case Studies of Forecast-Based Actions

The case studies described in this section are built on primary information collected during our collaboration as advisers with the Red Cross Red Crescent movement. These cases have the spirit of giving an intuition of the process, potential benefits and challenges the FbF approach entails for different weather-related disasters. We highlight first a case where the FbF concept has been put to test to reduce impacts of flooding in Bangladesh and second, an example of a new effort currently being established to reduce the impacts of extreme winter conditions on Mongolian herders. After the description of the two case studies, Table 4.1 summarizes the most relevant aspects.

Table 4.1 Summary of the case studies

	Bangladesh	Mongolia
Weather-related disaster	Floods	*Dzud* (extreme winter conditions)
Main problem for the population that FbF is trying to address	Negative coping strategies to have financial resources during evacuation	Livestock death causing emotional burden, loss of livelihood and possible forced migration
FbF input—Trigger (climate information)	1-in-10 year forecast	Evaluated according to Dzud Risk Map
FbF output—Action (problem reduction)	Unconditional cash distribution	Emergency distribution of animal feed or cash distribution
FbF—Lead Time to Act	7–10 days	3 months
FbF—Current status	Positive outcomes after pilots in 4 villages. Currently at initial design stages for scale-up	Early stages of design and evaluation following the first pre-dzud implementation of action

4.5.1 Floods in Bangladesh

In Bangladesh a community-level assessment was completed by the authors, which identified a number of negative coping strategies that subsistence-oriented, often landless, farmers engage in during flooding events that are beyond their coping capacity. During the process of evacuating, vulnerable people take-out high interest informal loans and sell assets at destitution prices in order to pay for the costs associated with evacuating and living in evacuation, including food and temporary shelter supplies. This is especially pronounced for households who gain subsistence from working on other people's land, and for whom food is purchased daily from day-labor, which gives little financial cushion. Many households are also forced to evacuate inefficiently, reducing the amount of goods they can carry to evacuation points, as they are unable to pay for boat or road transport and must instead wade through waist deep water with their belongings, at considerable personal risk.

Given these pressures, the dearth of cash at the time period before evacuation was identified as an entry point for support that could be initiated by a reliable flood forecast. As such, an unconditional cash transfer was selected as the primary forecast-based action to reduce the extent to which households would need to engage in negative coping strategies in the process of evacuating and in the early days and weeks of evacuation before traditional post-disaster humanitarian assistance (if needed) arrives. It was agreed that the system would trigger for floods with an approximate return period of 1-in-10 years, which is when it is believed that the flooding level outstrips the coping capacity of the local population. As Bangladesh and its catchment areas have experienced a particularly wet couple of years, the FbF system has triggered in the last two years—once in 2016 and once in 2017—initiating a cash distribution to pre-identified households. This program was implemented by the German Red Cross and the Bangladesh Red Crescent Society. While this program was small, targeting only four flood-prone villages, the pilot has produced promising results, leading to a program scale-up which was in the initial design stages at the time of writing. The new scaled-up forecast-based program will operate at a national level with the ability to trigger forecast-based action where the forecast indicates the greatest impacts are to be expected.

4.5.2 Dzud in Mongolia

In Mongolia, extreme winter conditions causing widespread livestock death, which is locally referred to as *dzud* in the Mongolian language, were identified as a weather-related disaster that could benefit from forecast-based programming. The extreme conditions which lead to winter deaths of livestock are a combination of many sub-hazards, including cold and snowy conditions during the peak winter months, as well as dry conditions in the preceding summer months. The dry conditions limit summer grazing and therefore reduce the plumping of herd animals, which they need to be in an appropriate body condition to survive the winter months (Shinoda, 2017). Large scale losses of herds is emotionally traumatic for herders, destroys herder livelihoods, and in the extremist form, can lead herders to make destitution migrations to cities and towns where they often live in poverty with no way to recover their livelihoods.

There are multiple categories of *dzud*, highlighting the different winter conditions under which animals die en masse: unique combinations of ice and snow that prevent the animals from grazing for long periods, and very cold temperatures reaching as low as −48 Celsius degrees, under which the animals use all their energy to keep warm. In all scenarios, the animals waste and die from starvation, dehydration or cold-exposure. *Dzud* has occurred six times in the last two decades, often happening in consecutive years, although the severity of animal death has varied between years and geographic regions of Mongolia.

Supporting herder populations experiencing *dzud* is challenging. Many herders live in remote areas which are difficult to access after the onset of the winter season. Typically, once *dzud* is confirmed based on observed winter weather conditions and reports of large scale animal deaths, it is often too late to take action to save the animals. Providing emergency feeding and veterinary care in the capacity of a humanitarian response may make little demonstrable difference, as once the animals enter a highly weakened state from starvation, they are no longer able to digest emergency fodder or hay. As such, if supports are to be provided to help herders save their animals, and therefore their livelihoods, it would be far more impactful to provide that support in the lead up to *dzud*, rather than in response to it.

Predicting winter conditions in Mongolia is challenging and relies on seasonal climate forecasting. While advancements in seasonal forecasting are being made, the forecasts for Mongolia remain low-skill, and as such a user must accept a lower likelihood that the forecast will be correct. This poses a challenge to humanitarian actors wishing to use the seasonal forecast to make decisions, especially since any action taken to support herders would need to be a substantial investment in finances as well as in operational capacity to reach remote areas.

Fortunately, a new methodology for forecasting impact on animals has recently been co-developed by Nagoya University and the government of Mongolia, called the Dzud Risk Map (Shinoda, 2017). Given that livestock deaths are highly related to the body condition of animals going into the winter season, the Dzud Risk Map captures the indicators important to animal survival into the winter season, including the conditions of summer pasture, and adds the expected winter conditions based on a seasonal climate forecast. In doing so, the projection is not solely based on a seasonal forecast, giving the user of the forecast greater confidence in the maps results. The Dzud Risk Map will be released each year in November before the winter season sets in and will indicate specific localities that are at heightened risk of *dzud*.

In the new forecast-based financing program implemented by the Mongolian Red Cross Society with support from the British Red Cross, the disaster management officers of the Mongolian Red Cross Society will use the Dzud Risk Map to identify vulnerable herder households at high risk of losing large portions of their herds. These will receive either a pre-winter emergency distribution of animal feed or an unconditional cash transfer where animal feed and other necessary veterinary supplies are available in the local market. This program is in its early stages, preparing for the upcoming winter season. It will be the subject of a rigorous evaluation to ascertain that the benefits expected from acting early, as compared to responding post-disaster, are achieved. The initiative represents a new way of working in Mongolia: using a forecast of *dzud* impacts to pre-empt the loss and hardship that jeopardize the traditional way of life for many herders.

4.6 Conclusion

Both long-term planning and short term-preparedness actions can be better informed by climate and weather information if the appropriate systems are in place to address their inherent uncertainty and often very short operational timescales. Forecast-based financing (FbF) is one of such innovative systems. The innovation behind FbF consists of integrating climate information systems into humanitarian efforts in three steps: selecting a trigger, matching forecast probabilities with appropriate actions, and designing post-trigger plans to carry out those actions. The two case studies of short-term preparedness actions using the FbF concept exemplify the potential benefits this approach has in terms of reducing the impact of weather-related disasters on vulnerable populations.

We acknowledge that these practical examples have limitations when it comes to showing the real extent of the benefits that can be reached with the FbF approach. The current evidence is based on a small number of case studies. However, we see this limited evidence as an opportunity for future research to test the concept. The use of field experiments is an optimal means of doing so, however attention needs to be given to ethical issues arising from selecting who, how and why some beneficiaries can receive help while others cannot. In the longer term, the FbF community of practice could also complete longitudinal or ethnographic studies on populations where forecast-based actions have been implemented and their evolution documented over time.

The FbF approach has multiple implications for practitioners. We emphasize that governments and humanitarian actors can build on the FbF concept to consider climate information in new or existing programs and thereby improve preparedness actions and the lives of the most vulnerable. However, in order for these efforts to succeed realistically, there are a number of operational and strategic issues that should be addressed.

First, governments and humanitarian actors should have the adequate human resources, with the right knowledge and skills, to make appropriate use of climate information and forecasts. Second, depending on the region and specific country, there might be technological constraints that would limit the availability and accuracy of forecasts. Last, but not least, one of the main challenges of the practical application of the FbF concept is that of access to funding. Donors are usually reluctant to give funding to actions based on forecasts because given their probabilistic nature, there is a chance to "act in vain" (i.e. implement the action when no disaster occurs). Practitioners should address the above concerns before implementing forecast-based actions.

In summary, we consider that the FbF concept and other innovations within the humanitarian setting are important advancements which allow the sector to perform better, and ultimately help keep up with the demand that climate change has begun to place and will continue to place on the humanitarian system.

Note

1. At the time of writing this chapter, all countries in the world have signed the agreement. Only the US has notified its intention to withdraw from it.

References

Birkmann, J., & von Teichman, K. (2010). Integrating disaster risk reduction and climate change adaptation: Key challenges-scales, knowledge, and norms. *Sustainability Science, 5*(2), 171–184.

Chantarat, S., Barrett, C. B., Mude, A. G., & Turvey, C. G. (2007). Using weather index insurance to improve drought response for famine prevention. *American Journal of Agricultural Economics, 89*(5), 1262–1268.

Coughlan de Perez, E., & Mason, S. J. (2014). Climate information for humanitarian agencies: Some basic principles. *Earth Perspectives, 1*(1), 1–11.

Coughlan de Perez, E., Monasso, F., van Aalst, M., & Suarez, P. (2014). Science to prevent disasters. *Nature Geoscience, 7*(2), 78–79.

Coughlan de Perez, E., Stephens, E., Bischiniotis, K., van Aalst, M., van den Hurk, B., Mason, S., ... Pappenberger, F. (2017). Should seasonal rainfall forecasts be used for flood preparedness? *Hydrology and Earth System Sciences, 21*(9), 4517–4524.

Coughlan De Perez, E., Van Den Hurk, B., Van Aalst, M. K., Jongman, B., Klose, T., & Suarez, P. (2015). Forecast-based financing: An approach for catalyzing humanitarian action based on extreme weather and climate forecasts. *Natural Hazards and Earth System Sciences, 15*(4), 895–904.

CRED, & UNISDR. (2015). *The human cost of weather-related disasters 1995–2015*. Brussels. Retrieved March 2018, from. http://cred.be/HCWRD

GFCS. (2017). What are weather/climate services? Retrieved March 2018, from http://www.wmo.int/gfcs/what_are_climate_weather_services

IPCC. (2015). *Climate change 2014: Synthesis report*. Geneva. Retrieved March 2018, from http://www.ipcc.ch/report/ar5/syr/

Jongman, B., Winsemius, H. C., Aerts, J. C. J. H., Coughlan de Perez, E., van Aalst, M. K., Kron, W., & Ward, P. J. (2015). Declining vulnerability to river floods and the global benefits of adaptation. *Proceedings of the National Academy of Sciences of the United States of America, 112*(18), E2271–E2280.

Kaplan, S., & Vakili, K. (2015). The double-edged sword of recombination in breakthrough innovation. *Strategic Management Journal, 36*(10), 1435–1457.

Karl, T. R., & Trenberth, K. E. (2003). Modern global climate change. *Science, 302*, 1719–1723.

Mercer, J. (2010). Disaster risk reduction or climate change adaptation: Are we reinventing the wheel? *Journal of International Development, 22*(2), 247–264.

Parmesan, C., & Yohe, G. (2003). A globally coherent fingerprint of climate change impacts across natural systems. *Nature, 421*, 37–42.

RCCC. (2018). Forecast-based financing. Retrieved March 2018, from http://www.climatecentre.org/programmes-engagement/forecast-based-financing

Shinoda, M. (2017). Evolving a multi-hazard focused approach for arid eurasia. In T. Sternberg (Ed.), *Climate hazard crises in Asian societies and environments*. New York, NY: Routledge.

Slatyer, J. (2016). Disaster preparation means forecast-based financing not band-aids. Retrieved March 2018, from http://www.internationalaffairs.org.au/australianoutlook/disaster-preparation-means-forecast-based-financing-not-band-aids/

Stephens, E., Coughlan de Perez, E., Kruczkiewicz, A., Boyd, E., & Suarez, P. (2015). *Forecast-based action*. Reading, UK. Retrieved March 2018, from http://www.climatecentre.org/downloads/files/Stephens%20et%20al.%20Forecastbased%20Action%20SHEAR%20Final%20Report.pdf

Thomalla, F., Downing, T., Spanger-Siegfried, E., Han, G., & Rockström, J. (2006). Reducing hazard vulnerability: Towards a common approach between disaster risk reduction and climate adaptation. *Disasters, 30*(1), 39–48.

Twigg, J. (2015). *Disaster risk reduction. Good practice review*. London, UK: Humanitarian Policy Group.

UNFCCC. (2017). The Paris Agreement. Retrieved March 2018, from http://unfccc.int/paris_agreement/items/9485.php

WFP. (2016). *FoodSECuRE—Food Security Climate Resilience Facility Supporting community resilience-building before and after climatic shocks*. Retrieved March 2018, from http://documents.wfp.org/stellent/groups/public/documents/communications/wfp279583.pdf?_ga=2.176477091.743910230.1518825155-912470856.1518825155

5

Refugees and Social Inclusion: The Role of Humanitarian Information Technologies

Sonia Camacho, Andrea Herrera, and Andrés Barrios

5.1 Introduction

At the time of this writing, refugees' emergencies are increasing in frequency and complexity. In accordance with the United Nations High Commissioner for Refugees (UNHCR), tens of millions of people have been violently displaced worldwide by war or other forms of armed hostilities. For example, the number of Syrians registered as refugees rose to 5 million in 2017 (Aljazeera, 2017). Among refugees, more than 50 percent are under the age of 18. Many of these children were unaccompanied or separated from their families (UNHCR, 2015a). This situation has devastating consequences, including horrific human suffering:

S. Camacho (✉) • A. Barrios
School of Management, Universidad de los Andes, Bogotá, Colombia
e-mail: so-camac@uniandes.edu.co; andr-bar@uniandes.edu.co

A. Herrera
Department of Systems and Computing Engineering, School of Engineering, Universidad de los Andes, Bogotá, Colombia
e-mail: a-herrer@uniandes.edu.co

refugees are forcibly separated from a context and introduced in a new one in a vulnerable way. The phenomenon also affects the regions the refugees leave and where they pass through and/or permanently settle. In the former, the region loses human capital, which limits its development (e.g., Syria, Colombia, Bosnia and Herzegovina, and Cambodia). In the latter, the regions face unexpected demands on communities, socio-economic systems and ecosystems (e.g. Germany, Italy, U.S., and Canada).

The massive challenges of these refugee crises call for interdisciplinary approaches. One of the perspectives to help address this phenomenon is that of information technology (IT). IT has become an active part of individuals' lives. For example, there were almost 4 billion internet users around the world in 2017, accounting for about 50% of the world population (Internet World Stats, 2017). In addition, the combined global sales of electronic devices (i.e., PCs, mobile phones, and tablets) were estimated to be 2.3 billion units in 2018 (Gartner, 2018). The widespread availability of IT makes it a useful support tool to reap benefits at the individual, organizational, and social levels (Laudon & Laudon, 2014; Majchrzak, Markus, & Wareham, 2016). IT can help to develop services and technologies that facilitate (i) social inclusion, (ii) mitigation of risks associated with natural disasters, and (iii) improved access to low-cost healthcare and education (The Earth Institute at Columbia University & Ericsson, 2016; United Nations, 2016). In the refugee context, IT can be utilized to assuage refugees' suffering or perhaps even to contribute to address refugee crises via transformative solutions and practices. Therefore, this chapter aims to revise the IT solutions that have been developed to address the refugees' phenomenon and that have been covered by literature and practitioners. This chapter contributes to the literature by (i) summarizing the IT solutions intended to be used by both refugees and the organizations assisting them in different regions of the world, and (ii) classifying those solutions according to a framework that addresses refugees' vulnerabilities along their journey (i.e., the refugee pathway model).

The chapter has been organized as follows: Section 5.2 presents a description of the refugee pathways model, which will function as an organizing framework to account for the IT solutions aimed at addressing refugees' needs. Section 5.3 introduces IT in a formal way, as well as its benefits for organizations and individuals. In addition, this section presents how IT have been utilized in the humanitarian sector. Then, Sect. 5.4 will summarize the IT solutions intended to address the refugee phenomenon in each step of the refugee pathways. Section 5.5 presents the limitations of this chapter and the implications for research and practice in this domain. Finally, Sect. 5.6 will conclude the chapter.

5.2 Refugee Pathways

The United Nations (UN) General Assembly (1967) established a definition of refugee as "any person who owing to well-founded fear of being persecuted for reasons of race, religion, nationality, membership of a particular social group or political opinion, is outside the country of his nationality and is unable or, owing to such fear, is unwilling to avail himself of the protection of that country; or who, not having a nationality and being outside the country of his former habitual residence as a result of such events, is unable or, owing to such fear, is unwilling to return to it" (p. 152). Implicit in this definition is the forced nature of departure of refugees and that the fear of persecution makes them move beyond their countries' borders. This differentiates refugees from regular immigrants, who cross borders looking for a better future. According to the definition of refugee, such situation terminates once the person does not experience a life threat, and decides to return to her country of origin or become a resident of another country.

This chapter uses the refugees' pathway as framework to provide specific and detailed guidance about IT's positive role in the refugees' humanitarian crisis. Research indicates this pathway involves refugees' unique experiences in their quest for safety, with important meanings for the rest of their lives (BenEzer, 2002). Different academic and non-academic studies have aimed to describe the refugees' pathway by aggregating the shared identifiable characteristic in their journey. For example, Gonsalves (1992) puts forth a three-step pathway model (preflight, flight, and resettlement) identifying different psychological risks at every stage. According to Gonsalves (1992), the intensity and duration of the life threat during each stage create different psychological traumas that further limit refugees' opportunities to resettle in a new country. Outside of the academic literature, World Vision (2010) suggests a four-step journey (leaving home, on the road, seeking refuge in another country, returning home or resettlement), describing what occurs in each step. These and other approaches have been subject of criticism for focusing only on refugees' actions and milestones, while ignoring the particular needs experienced in the process (BenEzer & Zetter, 2014).

Fundamental to the development of any beneficial approach for refugees is an understanding of the vulnerabilities associated with their situation. For Baker and Mason (2012, p. 544), a vulnerability analysis serves as a "theoretical lens through which to view at-risk groups, social injustices or hazardous situations". For this reason, this chapter uses as a framework a 4-stage refugee pathway described by Schultz et al. (2017). In this pathway, each stage comes with a description of the specific manifestations of victims' vulnerabilities. This is useful to capture how humanitarian IT can be used to assuage those vulnerabilities regardless of whether the pathway lasts for just a few days or a lifetime. Figure 5.1 illustrates the refugee pathway, and each step is further described below:

1. *Displacement*: The pathway is precipitated by a triggering event (e.g. war). At this time, victims' lives are under threat, and as such, they need to rapidly plan an exit. This plan includes establishing a safe destination that may work as temporary or permanent settlement for them and their relatives.

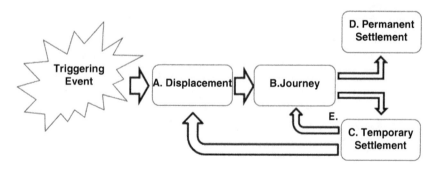

Fig. 5.1 Refugee pathway (Source: Schultz et al., 2017)

2. *Journey*: Once the destination is set, the displacement starts with a journey from home to a safer place. Usually, there is a collapse of the transportation infrastructure at this time. This makes victims vulnerable due to the limited access to essential economic, social, and psychological resources. For instance, they experience difficulties in obtaining access to basic food and shelter, as well as to affordable, reliable, and safe modes of transportation (BenEzer & Zetter, 2014).
3. *Temporal settlement*: Along the journey, victims usually arrive at temporary places, like refugee camps, where they stay until they can continue to their final destination. At this time, victims face vulnerabilities that are common in their transient status: disconnection from existing social networks, depressed socio-economic status, and lack of the protections afforded to citizens (Derose, Escarce & Nicole, 2007; Wang & Tian, 2014).
4. *Permanent settlement*: This step occurs when victims reach their envisioned destination and obtain a residence. At this time, victims face vulnerabilities regarding acculturation, accessing social services, and stigmatization/marginalization. Despite their permanent status, victims could experience discrimination resulting from their refugee status.

It is worth noting that refugees can enter sometimes into *protracted* situations (see arrow E in Fig. 5.1). Depending on different local policies, victims may either remain in temporary settlements for long periods (without access to durable solutions), or enter into cyclical process with temporary settlements and repeated displacements. In this situation, they face the vulnerabilities related to the displacement and temporary settlement, but not necessarily face a direct risk or threat to life (UNHCR, 2010).

In the following section, a description is provided on how IT is becoming central to humanitarian aid. Then the focus moves to describing the different IT applications that can help refugees and organizations providing services to them, in each step of the pathway.

5.3 IT and the Humanitarian Sector

IT can be defined as technologies that allow storage, processing, retrieval and communication of information (Gartner, 2013; Ralston, Reilly, & Hemmendinger, 2003). IT has provided different benefits to organizations, such as task automation (Laudon & Laudon, 2014), reduction in coordination costs to locate new suppliers (e.g., Hitt & Brynjolfsson, 1996; Malone, 1987), promotion of information sharing and collaboration inside and across organizations (e.g., Barua, Lee, & Whinston, 1995; Lind & Zmud, 1995), and fostering innovations (e.g., Dewett & Jones, 2001). Non-profit organizations have also used IT to provide information to their stakeholders (e.g., Lovejoy & Saxton, 2012), find donors and volunteers (e.g., Lee, Cheng, & Zhang, 2001; Lee-Won, Abo, Na, & White, 2016), as well as improve their learning and knowledge management practices (e.g., Burt & Taylor, 2000; Hackler & Saxton, 2007).

Considering the benefits IT has given to different types of organizations, as well as individuals (e.g., increasing convenience and saving time in daily transactions, providing access to health information and education, reducing social inequality; Atkinson & Castro, 2008; Ganju, Pavlou, & Banker, 2016), it is important to analyze IT's role in the humanitarian sector. IT can play an important role in this context, considering the need for timely, relevant, and reliable information (Van de Walle, Van Den Eede, & Muhren, 2009). The benefits provided by IT (e.g., better communication and data collection practices) can have a further positive impact on risk assessment, targeted prevention and the effectiveness of humanitarian operations (Altay & Labonte, 2014; Van de Walle et al., 2009). In order to analyze the role of IT in the humanitarian sector, we will henceforth use the term humanitarian IT. Humanitarian IT is understood in this chapter as the technologies used to collect, process, and analyze information that may contribute to improve the livelihoods of people affected by a devastating event.

In the literature, three main streams of these humanitarian IT can be found. First, IT has become an important tool for effective information management in relief operations (Pettit & Beresford, 2009). For example, in tasks related to humanitarian logistics, IT can provide field staff with timely and accurate information regarding inventory management (e.g., procurement activities), distribution of supplies (to better monitor and evaluate activities), and funds (to better plan budgets), while reducing duplication of data stored across organizations (Howden, 2009; Lee & Zbinden, 2003). Second, IT can also be designed to support decision making, a category known as Decision Support Systems (DSS). In the humanitarian context, the UN has developed a DSS to improve coordination among different agencies and organizations, facilitate information exchange, and build capacity (Kovács & Spens, 2007). Those systems can also contribute to develop local and regional plans (e.g., evacuation plans). Third, organizations can leverage the large audiences that form around online communities in what is known as "digital humanitarianism". This concept refers to large numbers of virtual volunteers that rapidly assemble situational awareness at the onset of an emergency event through crowdsourcing, data analysis, and crisis mapping to aid in the emergency response. A very well-known example of this stream is the destructive earthquake in Haiti in 2010, which taught us an unexpected lesson: the power of IT and public participation to coordinate, inform, and guide relief efforts. The Ushahidi Haiti Crisis Map was created hours after the earthquake using a popular and open source platform from Kenia. This crisis map gathered thousands of crowd-sourced SMS and social media posts reporting damages and emergencies. As a result, humanitarian forces were able to carry out more targeted and efficient emergency relief efforts (Lambert & Carlson, 2011). Even though this particular example is not directly related to refugees, it is recognized as one of the first digital humanitarianism initiatives and it has served as an example for others such as "Refugees Welcome".[1] This housing initiative matches refugees with locals that are willing to share their accommodations. The concept behind this type of IT platform is to help not only address the big challenge of finding adequate housing for newcomers, but also develop social integration processes.

The examples in the three identified streams show that humanitarian IT has been used across the world in managing emergency incidents and humanitarian crises. Moreover, three-quarters of refugees have a smartphone, making those devices not only useful in terms of remote communication but also in terms of transferring geospatial information that can be helpful when coordinating preparedness, response, and recovery actions (Benton & Glennie, 2016). In the next section, details are provided on how humanitarian IT can be used in each step of the refugee pathway.

5.4 Uses of IT Along the Refugee Pathway

In accordance with the UNHCR, "humanitarian" is understood as to "save lives and alleviate suffering in a manner that respects and restores personal dignity" (UNHCR, 2017). Humanitarian IT has emerged to provide governments and non-governmental organizations (NGOs) as well as individuals with tools to respond to the vulnerabilities (e.g., limited access to social services) experienced by the refugee population. The utilization of IT to assuage refugees' suffering or even to contribute to address refugee crises is relatively recent and not extensively documented. Given the early stage of exploration of this phenomenon, our main objective is to revise the IT solutions that have been developed to address the refugees' needs along their pathway, providing an initial classification based on how these IT solutions are supporting those needs (Gregor, 2006). In this section, different IT innovations are presented and an overview of these is shown in Table 5.1.

In order to collect information about IT innovations, both academic and practitioner sources were employed. Two criteria were applied in the search and inclusion of cases. First, it was ensured that IT innovations intended for both organizations and individuals as main users were covered. The reason behind selecting those two groups as main users was to include IT innovations utilized not only by refugees (individual users), but also by the organizations that may act as intermediaries in delivering IT's intended outcomes (Majchrzak et al., 2016). Second, IT innovations were included if their main purpose or the main need they address was explicitly documented. It is worth noting that some of these innovations have been developed specifically for refugee support. However, others that may have had related events (e.g. natural disaster relief) as goals, are also suitable for application to the refugee context.

Table 5.1 Overview of examples of IT usage along the refugee pathway

Pathway stage	Main user	Specific need	IT example
Displacement	Organizations and individuals	Information collection	ReliefWeb is a specialized digital service of the UN Office for the Coordination of Humanitarian Affairs. Its aim is to be the main information source on global crises and disasters.
Journey	Individuals	Route planning	Google maps can be used to help migrants to cross borders and avoid trouble.
	Individuals	Family reunification	Trace the Face is a service maintained by the International Committee of the Red Cross that allows people to check if their families are looking for them or publish their photos to facilitate contact with their family members.
Temporary settlement	Organizations	Health	TWINE is a standardized health information system across different countries to monitor the health programs of refugee camps.
	Organizations and individuals	Navigating services	REACH is an addressing system that provides maps that facilitate access to services and help in increasing refugees' familiarity with the camp. It also helps humanitarian organizations orientate within the camp.
Permanent settlement	Individuals	Language learning	Online Linguistic Support allows refugees to improve their knowledge of a particular language.
	Individuals	Finding work	LinkedIn for Good is a talent initiative in order to provide refugee services that focus on career development and job accessibility.
	Organizations and individuals	Registration and safety	TRIS is a tracking refugee information system to have updated information of the refugees arriving at or living in Malaysia.

5.4.1 Displacement

As mentioned in Sect. 5.2 above, the displacement begins with a triggering event (e.g., a threat of a terrorist attack). In this first step, two stages are recognized: a pre event stage and after the triggering event occurs. In the former, "when people are under threat, perceived or actual, they go into intensified information seeking period" (Winerman, 2009, p. 376) and IT sites are viewed as "places for harvesting information… to determine what is happening on the ground" (Vieweg, Hughes, Starbird, & Palen, 2010, p. 1079). For example, with the Refugee Crisis in Europe, there are multiple sites where people can look for updated information. One of these sites is the ReliefWeb,[2] a website that provides 24-hour coverage of disasters, conflicts, and crises (OCHA, n.d.). It collects information from over a thousand sources (e.g., NGOs, UN, and the media) and provides a centralized repository for emergency response information (Van de Walle et al., 2009). In addition to official sites, individuals can seek information directly via social media. In the particular case of Europe, there is a Facebook group called "Refugee crisis in Europe",[3] which provides news about the situation. These two types of humanitarian IT help both organizations and individuals to gain some perspective of changing conditions and perhaps to prompt survival actions.

In the latter stage (i.e., after the event occurs), the management and exchange of information is critical for a successful response (Altay & Labonte, 2014; Long & Wood, 1995). Collecting reliable information to characterize the emergency situations (e.g., location of those in need) facilitates the coordination of different organizations involved (e.g., relief organizations, governments) to provide humanitarian assistance (OCHA, n.d.). The UN Office for the Coordination of Humanitarian Affairs (OCHA) is in charge of collecting and analyzing information to have an overview of emergencies. In this task, OCHA counts with several humanitarian IT (e.g., websites, bulletins). Three examples of these are Financial Tracking Service (FTS), Humanitarian Response and ReliefWeb. FTS provides a tool to track international humanitarian funding flows via a website or an application program interface (API), with the aim of facilitating the mobility of resources (e.g., efficient allocation and use of donated funds) (FTS, n.d.). Humanitarian Response is also a website where humanitarian organizations can find and collaborate on information related to protracted or sudden-onset emergencies, in order to inform operations and decision making (Humanitarian Response, n.d.).

During the Displacement step, other technologies can be used to generate useful information, as it has been shown during the occurrence of natural disasters. There are public participation initiatives such as the crisis map of the 2010 earthquake in Haiti described above (Lambert & Carlson, 2011) and Tweak the Tweet (TtT), a syntax also deployed at the aftermath of the Haiti earthquake, created with the aim of distributing prescriptive tweets about the emergency situation at predefined time intervals in English and French (Starbird & Palen, 2011). Social media provide communities the opportunity to get involved in the generation and exchange of information in the aftermath of an emergency event, generating an awareness of the situation and allowing for the development of citizen advocacy (e.g., pet-family matching) (Vieweg et al., 2010; White, Palen, & Anderson, 2014).

The main idea behind IT supporting this first stage of the pathway is for such technologies to be used by both individuals and organizations in their quests to improve situational awareness and therefore, to better support them when making crucial decisions.

5.4.2 Journey

The recent European refugee crisis has created an explosion of examples of technological innovations. In this particular step, refugees depend on real-time geospatial information about routes, border guard movements, places to stay, and transport, all while staying in contact with their families. Therefore, some grass-roots initiatives such as smartphone apps have sprung up, giving information about the closest services on a map to refugees, volunteers, and aid workers. A specific example of humanitarian IT covering refugees' needs in this step is *Trace the Face*, a service maintained by the International Committee of the Red Cross (ICRC) that allows people to check if their families are looking for them or publish their photos to facilitate contact with their family members[4] (Benton & Glennie, 2016).

Fig. 5.2 A refugee's journey walking from Syria to Serbia (Source: Huber, 2016)

Another example is the use of very well-known tools like Google Maps, which help refugees cross borders and avoid trouble. Figure 5.2 shows the walking directions for a family fleeing Aleppo, Syria and trying to get to Horgos, Serbia. This map could also help other refugees that are willing to make that uncertain and dangerous journey arrive safe at their destination.

In this stage, the range of needs that refugees have is wider (safety, travel, family reunification, among others) and information that could help them to reach successfully a safer place is crucial. Thus, the role of IT in this stage is mainly targeted to individuals and such innovations may even become a lifeline for them.

5.4.3 Temporary Settlement

In this step, refugees may arrive at temporary camps. In these camps, having access to accurate and timely information regarding housing, sanitation, food, and healthcare is critical. In relation to the last aspect, health information is also crucial for humanitarian organizations to identify emerging health issues and the current needs of the refugees, as well as to prioritize their interventions (Spiegel, Sheik, Woodruff, & Burnham, 2001). Starting in 2005, UNHCR led the implementation of a standardized health information system (HIS) across different countries to monitor the health programs of refugee camps (Haskew, Spiegel, Tomczyk,

Cornier, & Hering, 2010). Data is collected using an online tool called TWINE, which creates report cards with indicators related to water, sanitation, and hygiene (Harvey, 2015). With the goal of improving refugees' health, this HIS not only addresses the unique needs of refugees in terms of health (e.g., higher risk of cross-border exposure to diseases), but also provides the countries hosting the refugee camps with information that complies with their national reporting requirements. In addition to facilitating the coordination between NGOs implementing services in refugee camps and local governments, HIS has reduced the time allocated to prepare reports and to analyze data. The increased efficiency of health data management at the refugee camps has led to improved program decision making and resource allocations (Haskew et al., 2010).

Another IT that has proved useful in the management of refugee camps is Geographic Information Systems. Those systems are becoming an essential part of the planning, response, and monitoring actions of organizations addressing humanitarian emergencies to the point that those organizations have specialized units (e.g., UNHCR has a geographic information and mapping unit) (Kaiser, Spiegel, Henderson, & Gerber, 2003). Specific to refugee camps, the UN Operational Satellite Applications Program established an initiative called REACH, along with the organizations ACTED and IMPACT Initiatives (ACTED, 2014). Inside REACH, an addressing system was established in a Jordan refugee camp, providing maps that facilitate access to services, increase refugees' familiarity with the camp and help humanitarian organizations orientate within the camp. To build REACH maps, the information is collected with GPS-enabled smartphones and satellite images. The maps retain the original Arabic names of places, to facilitate refugees' recognition of them. Data collected by the maps are continuously updated and they help to inform decision making and planning (e.g., location of new hospitals) (ACTED, 2014).

One of the alternatives refugees have during this step is to return to their home areas. For example, the UNHCR established along with the Iraqi Ministry of Migration and Displacement and the International Organization for Migration a Voluntary Repatriation Program in 2008 (Iaria, 2011). The program was established to facilitate the return of nationals that wanted to go back to their places of origin. However, refugees may not trust official institutions due to previous experiences with them or to the experiences of others returning home (Iaria, 2011). In such situations, refugees may rely on informal information systems to gather information about the political and economic situations of their home area and to inform their return decisions. From the systems found by Iaria (2011), the one supported by IT is the use of mobile phones. Through daily or weekly phone calls, Iraqi refugees learn of the security and well-being of their relatives in Iraq. They are also able to maintain their virtual presence and connection with their families by sharing audio, text, and visual messages (Iaria, 2011).

In this stage, the range of needs of both refugees and humanitarian organizations continues to grow and thus, the role of IT is preponderant in order to find more effective and efficient ways of meeting these needs in innovative ways.

5.4.4 Permanent Settlement

When refugees arrive at their final destination, they may experience social exclusion. This exclusion may lead to limited access to job markets and education, as well as to negative personal outcomes such as feelings of loneliness, stress, and social isolation (George & Chaze, 2009; Lloyd, Kennan, Thompson, & Qayyum, 2013; Vinson, 2009).

Different IT-based initiatives have been designed and implemented to help refugees participate in their new local communities. In terms of education, refugees located in Europe can access the Online Linguistic Support (OLS) offered by the Erasmus Plus initiative. With OLS, refugees can improve their knowledge of a particular language (there are 18 languages available) for free through the courses offered in the platform (Erasmus+, 2014). In Germany, Integreat was developed as an Information Platform for Refugees across different municipalities. The aim of this platform is to provide refugees with an app where they can access relevant information (e.g., procedures related to asylum processes) in languages they are familiar with, as well as to enable authorities, volunteers, and social services workers to share information and offerings with those refugees (Informatik 17, n.d.). In terms of job seeking, LinkedIn runs a talent initiative in order to provide refugee services that focus on career development and job accessibility (LinkedIn for Good). This humanitarian IT program also seeks to match refugees looking for jobs with employers willing to hire them (Benton & Glennie, 2016).

Although the development of those apps and programs aims at keeping refugees informed of their new local surroundings, caution may be exercised. Providing information in large quantities may have the purpose of socially including refugees. However, this may prove counterproductive: refugees may experience information overload and may have to make decisions before they are able to process the information they received (Lloyd et al., 2013).

Government agencies and NGOs can also utilize IT to manage refugees arriving at their countries. For example, the Malaysian government has implemented a Tracking Refugee Information System (TRIS) to have up to date information of the refugees arriving at or living in the country. Refugees can input their biometric information into the system, which will allow the government to close loopholes that could lead to illegal activities (e.g., terrorism, human trafficking) (Nasa, 2017).

In the Middle East, IT is being used to help humanitarian efforts led by UN agencies, national governments, and NGOs to aid Syrian refugees.[5] IT is used there in several fronts such as digital registration, delivery of aid, and telemedicine (Favell, 2015). Syrian refugees arriving at host countries are registered in the database of the UNHCR, which entitles them to protection and makes them eligible for aid. This registration process includes scanning barcodes of Syrian ID cards, as well as identity verification of refugees based on biometric information (i.e., fingerprints, iris data, and facial images) (Accenture, 2015). This database is complemented by the Refugee Assistance Information System (RAIS), which is also owned and operated by UNHCR (UNHCR, 2015b). This system was originally deployed to collect refugees' demographic and health data (Mateen et al., 2012). The system piloted in Jordan with Iraqi refugees and has been extended to include all assistance and assessment (e.g., access to sanitation) data linked to refugees and their families (UNHCR, 2014).

In addition to registering refugees and keeping track of their information, IT has also been used to deliver aid to refugees in the Middle East.

In-kind aid is being replaced by electronic vouchers and smart cards that refugees can use to buy the goods they need. In terms of health, SMSs are used to notify refugees of upcoming medical checkups and vaccines; tablets are used to report cases of diseases and to prescribe medications; and services of telemedicine and telesurgery are provided (e.g., a physician in North America may oversee a surgery and communicate remotely with the patient and the local staff) (Favell, 2015).

Finally, the Department of State counts with the Worldwide Refugee Admission Processing System (WRAPS) to process refugee resettlement in the U.S (Bureau of Population, Refugees and Immigration, 2016). WRAPS was created by the Refugee Processing Center (RPC; operated by the Department of State). It works as a centralized and standardized tool to process refugee cases and it allows RPC to (i) track refugee case status information; (ii) process statistics of resettlement to be shared with other partners (e.g., at the federal or state levels); and (III) enhance coordination and integration with other agencies, so processing issues can be addressed in an effective manner (RPC, 2016). In addition, the U.S. Centers for Disease Control and Prevention have an Electronic Disease Notification System. This system collects health information of refugees arriving at the country (for example, those that require treatment or follow-up of medical conditions) and distributes it to health departments of all states across the country (Lee, 2013).

For individuals and organizations facing the reality of these humanitarian emergencies, IT continues to be vital in this last stage of the refugee pathway. Yet, there are still a number of barriers to overcome (e.g., language, literacy) in order to ensure that these IT innovations are available, accessible and impactful.

5.5 Limitations and Implications for Research and Practice

The main limitation of this chapter is that it focused solely on providing a description of this phenomenon, as it has not been extensively documented. This chapter is based on a review of secondary sources and as such, the extent of usage of the IT described and the consequences of that usage for refugees and the organizations assisting them were not explored. The findings and limitations of the chapter open up new avenues for future research in the field of humanitarian IT. First, future studies could investigate factors that determine how humanitarian IT transforms potential benefits into concrete improvements along the refugees' pathway. Second, the potential negative effects of humanitarian IT (e.g., privacy risks) can be examined. This is particularly important in the initial stages of the refugees' pathway, as their quest for safety is crucial; information regarding where refugees have been relocated and where their families are could prove harmful if it falls in the wrong hands.

Third, future research can analyze the impact of IT on specific steps of refugee pathways. For example, studies can explore the extent to which IT is utilized by refugees to inform their decision to return home or to resettle in a different country (i.e., permanent settlement step). Future research can also analyze how IT can help in improving the provision of services at refugee camps (i.e., temporary settlement). In addition, future studies can analyze if and how IT can be utilized by NGOs and government agencies in order to reduce protracted refugee situations. Finally, researchers may focus on particular uses refugees give to an IT (e.g., a computer, a smartphone) and the benefits obtained from such use. An example of such research was conducted by Diaz Andrade & Doolin (2016), who analyzed a New Zealand initiative that trains refugees in the use of computers (e.g., using email) and provides them with a refurbished computer. These authors analyzed the different uses refugees gave to computers (e.g., communicating with government agencies and with members of their community of origin) in their search for social inclusion in this country.

Practitioners can also benefit from the revision provided in this chapter. The IT solutions designed to address the refugee phenomenon fall mainly in two of the three streams of humanitarian IT identified in Sect. 5.3 above. IT supporting refugees during the displacement step fall mainly in the category of information management in relief operations. In addition, IT solutions supporting refugees in the journey and temporary settlement steps fall mostly in the decision making support category. This opens up opportunities for NGOs and government agencies to leverage alternatives of digital humanitarianism such as Refugees Welcome (e.g., to assemble online volunteers to provide in-kind aid to refugees during the step of temporary settlement, to establish an online market to provide products or services to refugees during the permanent settlement step).

In addition, a new category of humanitarian IT that is specific to the refugees' phenomenon can be identified: social integration or inclusion of refugees. The IT solutions identified during the permanent settlement step aim at achieving this goal by providing refugees with information and access to different services (e.g., health, education, legal advice). Organizations in the private sector can work in tandem with government agencies and NGOs in the development of initiatives supported by IT, which can facilitate the social integration of refugees (e.g., finding schools or day-care centers for children, facilitating refugees' participation in community projects).

5.6 Conclusion

Sadly, approximately 28 countries are currently involved in violent conflicts—wars and other forms of protracted fighting (Council on Foreign Relations, 2017). Consequently, refugee crises have increased in frequency and complexity. The challenges posed by those crises call for interdisciplinary approaches to address the refugee needs. This chapter summarized how humanitarian IT can help refugees or the organizations assisting them at each step of the refugee pathway. In the first step, *displacement*, the life of individuals is threatened after a triggering event and the need for a safer location arises. At this point, humanitarian IT can be useful for individuals to collect information about the current situation (e.g., ReliefWeb), for communities to mobilize and help individuals in need (e.g., social media) and for humanitarian organizations to provide better assistance (e.g., Humanitarian Response). In the second step, *journey*, refugees start moving from their home to a safer place. During the journey, humanitarian IT can provide refugees with geospatial information about services and routes (e.g., Google Maps), as well as with means to keep connected to family members (e.g., *Trace the Face*).

In the third step, *temporary settlement*, refugees arrive at temporary locations (e.g., refugee camps). At those locations, humanitarian IT may be useful to obtain accurate information related to the health status of refugees (e.g., HIS), to create maps and plan the provision of services (e.g., addressing system of REACH) and to inform the decision of whether or not refugees can return to their home country (e.g., mobile phones). In the fourth and final step, *permanent settlement*, refugees arrive at their desired destination. In this step, humanitarian IT can help refugees navigate their new environment with activities supporting learning new languages (e.g., OLS) or job seeking (e.g., LinkedIn for Good). In addition, those IT can also help government agencies and NGO manage the arrival of refugees by facilitating their registration (e.g., TRIS) and aid delivery (e.g., smart cards).

The examples provided in this chapter show how humanitarian IT can help organizations and governments coordinate efforts in providing services to refugees, while diminishing the refugees' uncertainties associated with the stressful events they have to endure. We hope these examples serve to enrich the discussion about the different approaches to providing humanitarian assistance.

Notes

1. http://www.refugees-welcome.net/.
2. https://reliefweb.int/report/greece/unicef-refugee-and-migrant-crisis-europe-regional-humanitarian-situation-report-26-15.
3. https://www.facebook.com/refugeecrisiseu/.
4. https://familylinks.icrc.org/europe/en/Pages/Home.aspx.
5. Most Syrian refugees arrive at the following neighboring countries: Egypt, Iraq, Jordan, Lebanon, and Turkey (Favell, 2015).

References

Accenture. (2015). *UNHCR: Innovative identity management system uses biometrics to better serve refugees*. Retrieved January 2018, from https://www.accenture.com/us-en/success-unhcr-innovative-identity-management-system

ACTED. (2014). *How do geographic information systems inform humanitarian action?* Retrieved January 2018, from http://www.acted.org/en/how-do-geographic-information-systems-inform-humanitarian-action

Aljazeera. (2017). *UN: Number of Syrian refugees passes five million.* Retrieved January 2018, from http://www.aljazeera.com/news/2017/03/number-syrian-refugees-passes-million-170330132040023.html

Altay, N., & Labonte, M. (2014). Challenges in humanitarian information management and exchange: Evidence from Haiti. *Disasters, 38*(s1), s50–s72.

Atkinson, R. D., & Castro, D. (2008). *Digital quality of life: Understanding the personal and social benefits of the information technology revolution.* Retrieved from SSRN: https://ssrn.com/abstract=1278185 or https://doi.org/10.2139/ssrn.1278185

Baker, S., & Mason, M. (2012). Towards a process theory of consumer vulnerability and resilience: Illuminating its transformative potential. In D. Mick, S. Pettigrew, C. Pechmann, & J. Ozanne (Eds.), *Transformative consumer research for personal and collective well-being.* New York, NY: Routledge.

Barua, A., Lee, C. H. S., & Whinston, A. B. (1995). Incentives and computing systems for team-based organizations. *Organization Science, 6*(4), 487–504.

BenEzer, G. (2002). *The Ethiopian Jewish Exodus: Narratives of the migration journey to Israel 1977–1985.* London, UK: Routledge.

BenEzer, G., & Zetter, R. (2014). Searching for directions: Conceptual and methodological challenges in researching refugee journeys. *Journal of Refugee Studies, 28*(3), 297–318.

Benton, M., & Glennie, A. (2016). *Digital humanitarianism: How tech entrepreneurs are supporting refugee integration.* Washington, DC: Report for Migration Policy Institute.

Bureau of Population, Refugees, and Immigration. (2016). *The refugee processing and screening system (text version of infographic).* U.S. Department of State. Retrieved January 2018, from https://2009-2017.state.gov/j/prm/releases/factsheets/2016/264501.htm

Burt, E., & Taylor, J. A. (2000). Information and communication technologies: Reshaping voluntary organizations? *Nonprofit Management and Leadership, 11*(2), 131–143.

Council of Foreign Relations. (2017). *Global Conflict Tracker.* Retrieved January 2018, from https://www.cfr.org/interactives/global-conflict-tracker

Derose, K. P., Escarce, J. J., & Lurie, N. (2007). Immigrants and health care: Sources of vulnerability. *Health Affairs, 26*(5), 1258–1268.

Dewett, T., & Jones, G. R. (2001). The role of information technology in the organization: A review, model, and assessment. *Journal of Management, 27*(3), 313–346.

Diaz Andrade, A., & Doolin, B. (2016). Information and communication technology and the social inclusion of refugees. *MIS Quarterly, 40*(2), 405–416.

Erasmus+. (2014). *OLS for refugees*. Retrieved January 2018, from https://erasmusplusols.eu/ols4refugees/

Favell, A. (2015). *How technology is helping deliver aid to Syrian refugees in the Middle East*. Retrieved January 2018, from http://www.computerweekly.com/feature/How-technology-is-helping-deliver-aid-to-Syrian-refugees-in-the-Middle-East

FTS. (n.d.). *About FTS*. Retrieved January 2018, from https://fts.unocha.org/content/about-fts-1

Ganju, K. K., Pavlou, P. A., & Banker, R. D. (2016). Does information and communication technology lead to the well-being of nations? A country-level empirical investigation. *MIS Quarterly, 40*(2), 417–430.

Gartner. (2013). *IT (Information Technology)*. Retrieved January 2018, from http://www.gartner.com/it-glossary/it-information-technology/

Gartner. (2018, January 29). *Gartner says worldwide device shipments will increase 2.1 percent in 2018*. Retrieved January 2018, from http://www.gartner.com/newsroom/id/3187134

George, U., & Chaze, F. (2009). "Tell me what i need to know": South Asian women, social capital and settlement. *Journal of International Migration and Integration/Revue de l'integration et de la migration internationale, 10*(3), 265–282.

Gonsalves, C. J. (1992). Psychological stages of the refugee process: A model for therapeutic interventions. *Professional Psychology: Research and Practice, 23*(5), 382–389.

Gregor, S. (2006). The nature of theory in information systems. *MIS Quarterly, 30*(3), 611–642.

Hackler, D., & Saxton, G. D. (2007). The strategic use of information technology by nonprofit organizations: Increasing capacity and untapped potential. *Public Administration Review, 67*(3), 474–487.

Harvey, B. (2015). *UNHCR WASH manual*. Retrieved January 2018, from http://www.ben-harvey.org/UNHCR/WASH-Manual/Wiki/index.php/Monitoring_the_effectiveness_of_WASH_interventions

Haskew, C., Spiegel, P., Tomczyk, B., Cornier, N., & Hering, H. (2010). A standardized health information system for refugee settings: Rationale, challenges and the way forward. *Bulletin of the World Health Organization, 88*(10), 792–794.

Hitt, L. M., & Brynjolfsson, E. (1996). Productivity, business profitability, and consumer surplus: Three different measures of information technology value. *MIS Quarterly, 20*(2), 121–142.

Howden, M. (2009). How humanitarian logistics information systems can improve humanitarian supply chains: A view from the Field. In *Proceedings of the 6th International ISCRAM Conference* (pp. 1–10), Gothenburg.

Huber, C. (2016). *Google map perspective: A refugee's journey walking from Syria to Serbia*. Retrieved January 2018, from https://www.worldvision.org/refugees-news-stories/syrian-refugee-google-map-perspective

Humanitarian Response. (n.d.). *About us*. Retrieved January 2018, from https://www.humanitarianresponse.info/en/about

Iaria, V. (2011). Iraqi refugees' informal information systems in Syria and Jordan. *Bulletin for the Council for British Research in the Levant, 6*(1), 43–49.

Informatik 17. (n.d.). *Integreat—Information platform for refugees*. Retrieved January 2018, from https://www.i17.in.tum.de/index.php?id=345

Internet World Stats. (2017, December 31). *World internet usage and population statistics*. Retrieved January 2018, from http://www.internetworldstats.com/

Kaiser, R., Spiegel, P. B., Henderson, A. K., & Gerber, M. L. (2003). The application of geographic information systems and global positioning systems in humanitarian emergencies: Lessons learned, programme implications and future research. *Disasters, 27*(2), 127–140.

Kovács, G., & Spens, K. M. (2007). Humanitarian logistics in disaster relief operations. *International Journal of Physical Distribution & Logistics Management, 37*(2), 99–114.

Lambert, N., & Carlson, S. (2011). The virtual field: Remote crisis mapping of the Haitian earthquake. *PRAXIS: The Fletcher Journal of Human Security, 15*, 87–92.

Laudon, K. C., & Laudon, J. P. (2014). *Management information systems*. Upper Saddle River, NJ: Pearson.

Lee, D. (2013). *Disease surveillance among newly arriving refugees and immigrants—Electronic disease notification system, United States, 2009*. Retrieved January 2018, from https://www.cdc.gov/mmwr/preview/mmwrhtml/ss6207a1.htm

Lee, H. W., & Zbinden, M. (2003). Marrying logistics and technology for effective relief. *Forced Migration Review, 18*(3), 34–35.

Lee, T. E., Chen, J. Q., & Zhang, R. (2001). Utilizing the internet as a competitive tool for non-profit organizations. *Journal of Computer Information Systems, 41*(3), 26–31.

Lee-Won, R. J., Abo, M. M., Na, K., & White, T. N. (2016). More than numbers: Effects of social media virality metrics on intention to help unknown others in the context of bone marrow donation. *Cyberpsychology, Behavior, and Social Networking, 19*(6), 404–411.

Lind, M. R., & Zmud, R. W. (1995). Improving interorganizational effectiveness through voice mail facilitation of peer-to-peer relationships. *Organization Science, 6*(4), 445–461.

Lloyd, A., Anne Kennan, M., Thompson, K. M., & Qayyum, A. (2013). Connecting with new information landscapes: Information literacy practices of refugees. *Journal of Documentation, 69*(1), 121–144.

Long, D. C., & Wood, D. F. (1995). The logistics of famine relief. *Journal of Business Logistics, 16*(1), 213.

Lovejoy, K., & Saxton, G. D. (2012). Information, community, and action: How nonprofit organizations use social media. *Journal of Computer-Mediated Communication, 17*(3), 337–353.

Malone, T. W. (1987). Modeling coordination in organizations and markets. *Management Science, 33*(10), 1317–1332.

Majchrzak, A., Markus, M. L., & Wareham, J. (2016). Designing for digital transformation: Lessons for information systems research from the study of ICT and societal challenges. *MIS Quarterly, 40*(2), 267–277.

Mateen, F. J., Carone, M., Al-Saedy, H., Nyce, S., Ghosn, J., Mutuerandu, T., & Black, R. E. (2012). Medical conditions among iraqi refugees in Jordan: Data from the United Nations refugee assistance information system. *Bulletin of the World Health Organization, 90*(6), 444–451.

Nasa, A. (2017). *Gov't introduces Tracking Refugee Information System to update, gather data on refugees.* Retrieved December 2017, from https://www.nst.com.my/news/nation/2017/08/263348/govt-introduces-tracking-refugee-information-system-update-gather-data

OCHA. (n.d.). *Information management.* Retrieved from https://www.unocha.org/our-work/information-management

Pettit, S., & Beresford, A. (2009). Critical success factors in the context of humanitarian aid supply chains. *International Journal of Physical Distribution & Logistics Management, 39*(6), 450–468.

Ralston, A., Reilly, E., & Hemmendinger, D. (2003). *Encyclopedia of computer science.* Chichester: John Wiley and Sons Ltd.

RPC. (2016). *About us.* Retrieved from http://www.wrapsnet.org/about-us/about/

Schultz, C., Barrios, A., Krasinoff, A., Bennett, A., Becker, I., Sierra, J., & Santos, M. (2017). Humanitarian business for the refugee pathway. Manuscript submitted for publication.

Spiegel, P. B., Sheik, M., Woodruff, B. A., & Burnham, G. (2001). The accuracy of mortality reporting in displaced persons camps during the post-emergency phase. *Disasters, 25*(2), 172–180.

Starbird, K., & Palen, L. (2011, May). Voluntweeters: Self-organizing by digital volunteers in times of crisis. In *Proceedings of the SIGCHI conference on human factors in computing systems* (pp. 1071–1080). ACM.

The Earth Institute at Columbia University & Ericsson. (2016). *ICT & SDGs: How information and communication technology can accelerate action on the Sustainable Development Goals*. Retrieved January 2018, from https://www.ericsson.com/assets/local/news/2016/05/ict-sdg.pdf

United Nations. (2016). *Information and communications technologies integrally tied to sustainable development, speakers say at second committee debate*. Retrieved January 2018, from https://www.un.org/press/en/2016/gaef3454.doc.htm

UN General Assembly. (1967). *Protocol relating to the status of refugees*. Retrieved January 2018, from http://www.refworld.org/docid/3ae6b3ae4.html

UNHCR. (2010). *Protracted refugee situations*. Retrieved January 2018, from http://www.unhcr.org/research/eval/4a1d43986/protracted-refugee-situations.html

UNHCR. (2014) *Inter-sectoral meeting*. Retrieved January 2018, from data.unhcr.org/syrianrefugees/download.php?id=4369

UNHCR. (2015a). *Figures at a glance*. Retrieved January 2018, from http://www.unhcr.org/en-us/figures-at-a-glance.html

UNHCR. (2015b). *Inter agency meeting*. Retrieved January 2018, from data.unhcr.org/syrianrefugees/admin/download.php?id=9586

UNHCR. (2017). *Humanitarian principles*. Retrieved January 2018, from https://emergency.unhcr.org/entry/44766/humanitarian-principles

Van de Walle, B., Van Den Eede, G., & Muhren, W. (2009). Humanitarian information management and systems. In J. Löffler & M. Klann (Eds.), *Mobile response, LNCS 5424* (pp. 12–21). Berlin: Springer.

Vieweg, S., Hughes, A. L., Starbird, K., & Palen, L. (2010). Microblogging during two natural hazards events: What Twitter may contribute to situational awareness. *CHI 2010* (pp. 1–10). Atlanta: ACM.

Vinson, T. (2009). Social inclusion: The origins, meaning, definitions and economic implications of the concept of inclusion/exclusion. Australian Department of Education, Employment and Workplace Relations.

Wang, J. J., & Tian, Q. (2014). Consumer vulnerability and marketplace exclusion: A case of rural migrants and financial services in China. *Journal of Macromarketing, 34*(1), 45–56.

White, J. I., Palen, L., & Anderson, K. M. (2014). Digital mobilization in disaster response: The work & self-organization of on-line pet advocates in response to hurricane sandy. In *Proceedings of the 17th ACM conference on computer supported cooperative work & social computing* (pp. 866–876). ACM.

Winerman, L. (2009). Social networking: Crisis communication. *Nature News, 457*, 376–378.

World Vision. (2010). The journey. *Get Connected*. Retrieved January 2018, from https://www.worldvision.com.au/docs/default-source/school-resources/get-connected-full-issues/getconnected-08-migration.pdf?sfvrsn=8

Part II

Behavior

6

Behavioral Experiments in Single-Agent Operational Problems

Jaime Andrés Castañeda

6.1 Introduction

Behavioral operations (BeOps) is a branch of operations management that considers the effects of human behavior on operational performance. Since people are involved in almost all operational settings, BeOps can inform the design and management of operational processes (Gino & Pisano, 2008; Loch & Wu, 2007; Sankaranarayanan, Castañeda, & Villa, 2018). Research in BeOps has studied a broad range of issues, ranging from how cognitive biases affect inventory control to how social preferences and cultural traits affect supply chain performance. Although BeOps is not limited to the use of behavioral experiments (BeExs), the branch has brought BeExs into the mainstream of research methodologies in operations management (Siemsen, 2011).

People in humanitarian operations (HuOps) are also likely to affect HuOps performance; however, BeOps studies in HuOps are scant

---

J. A. Castañeda (✉)
School of Management, Universidad del Rosario, Bogotá, Colombia
e-mail: jaime.castaneda@urosario.edu.co

(Sankaranarayanan et al., 2018). The example of planning for hurricane seasons illustrates how human behavior affects operations. Several firms ran out of stock in 2004 because they were not prepared to meet the demand created by the multiple hurricanes that struck the southeastern United States. In 2005, these firms again experienced stock outs because of the extreme demand surge caused by Hurricane Katrina. These experiences motivated firms to be more aggressive in their approach to stocking supplies the following year. However, because of an inactive hurricane season in 2006, several firms were left with excess inventory (Lodree & Taskin, 2009; Taskin & Lodree, 2010). Biased stocking and forecasting behaviors could have played a role in the supply–demand mismatches documented in this example.

This chapter explores the application of BeExs in HuOps. It first describes the BeExs methodology and then reviews several BeExs in single-agent problems, focusing on newsvendor and forecasting studies. Based on the reviewed studies, the chapter discusses BeOps issues that could be studied in HuOps. The chapter concludes with a summary of the work.

6.2 Behavioral Experiments

A BeEx is a controlled test of decision making. It is composed of three main elements: an environment, an institution and the observed behavior (Smith, 1976, 1982). The environment corresponds to the circumstances that define the setting under which the experiment's participants make decisions (e.g., environmental parameters, available information, etc.). The institution refers to the rules that govern how participants should behave in the experiment. It is usually defined by the experimental instructions given to participants. The observed behavior refers to participants' decisions, which are interpreted as a function of the environment and the institution (Smith, 1994).

The relative advantage of BeExs over other research methodologies is the control that researchers can exert over the environment and the institution (Katok, 2010; Siemsen, 2011). When running BeExs, researchers manipulate one or several components of the environment and/or the institution to test decision making under different environmental and/or institutional configurations. These configurations are usually called treatments. At the same time, researchers are not interested in the effect of observable and unobservable variables that might confound the effect of the treatments (Katok, 2010; Morton & Williams, 2010). Control allows researchers to state that confounding variables either do or do not differ in a specified way between several treatments, which makes it possible for researchers to establish causal inferences. BeExs achieve such control by using two mechanisms: randomization and induced valuation.[1]

6.2.1 Randomization

Treatment variables are systematically manipulated in a BeEx; however, confounding variables must be held constant across treatments so that any treatment effects cannot be attributed to the confounding variables and/or to interaction effects between the treatment and confounding variables (Katok, 2010). Randomization refers to the random assignment of treatments to avoid any systematic composition of participants in the treatments (Katok, 2010). That is, confounding variables are randomized such that they do not correlate with the treatments, avoiding or sidestepping the problem of confounding (Morton & Williams, 2010; Siemsen, 2011).

6.2.2 Induced Valuation

This mechanism refers to the use of a reward structure to induce experimental motivations in the participants in order to reduce the effect of their unobservable variables on their behavior during the experiment (Morton & Williams, 2010; Smith, 1976). Induced valuation postulates that four conditions should be considered when attempting to induce experimental motivations by a reward structure: monotonicity, saliency, dominance and privacy (Smith, 1976, 1982). A reward structure is:

- *Monotonic* if participants prefer more of the reward medium to less.
- *Salient* if the amount of the reward medium that participants receive is a by-product of their behavior during the experiment.
- *Dominant* if participants' behavior during the experiment is based on the reward medium.
- *Private* if participants' interpersonal utility considerations are minimized. Privacy is closely related to dominance since a reward structure's dominance may be lost if participants hold interpersonal utility considerations. A private reward structure implies that participants are given information only on their reward medium such that they cannot estimate the amount of the reward medium that the other participants receive.

Overall, the intuition behind randomization and induced valuation is that the researcher can choose any relationship between participants' actions and the reward structure if he can explain this relationship to the participants (saliency), and they are motivated by the reward medium (monotonicity) and not by other influences (dominance, privacy and randomization) (Fatás & Roig, 2004; Sankaranarayanan et al., 2018). However, these conditions are not intended to be necessary conditions. A valid BeEx may be run that violates some or all the conditions. These conditions may be implemented in several ways and may require adjustments depending on the research question under investigation (Guala, 2005).

6.3 Behavioral Experiments in Single-Agent Problems and Extensions to Humanitarian Operations

In this section, I review single-agent BeExs in operations management. I focus on newsvendor and forecasting studies since they concentrate most of the contributions from BeOps in single-agent problems. For each stream, I provide normative benchmarks, show how the results from BeExs compare against those benchmarks and provide suggestions to extend the reviewed results to HuOps.

6.3.1 Behavioral Newsvendors

The newsvendor problem is a single-period ordering problem under stochastic demand, where the decision maker orders a quantity q before customer demand D realizes. He procures each unit at a cost c and sells each unit at a price p. When the selling season ends and he still has units in inventory (leftovers), he can salvage $q - D$ units at a unit salvage price s ($s < c$). On the other hand, when he runs out of inventory before the selling season ends (shortage), he loses profit from not selling $D - q$ units at a unit rate $p - c$ (depending on the formulation, he could also pay a penalty cost). Calling $c_o = c - s$ the cost of leftovers and $c_u = p - c$ the cost of shortages, the newsvendor problem solution is given by the well-known critical fractile (*CF*):

$$F(q^*) = \frac{c_u}{c_u + c_o}, \qquad (6.1)$$

where F is the cumulative distribution function of D and q^* is the optimal order. The *CF* is commonly used to classify products: a product is considered as high-profit when $CF \geq 1/2$ and as low-profit otherwise (Schweitzer & Cachon, 2000).

Schweitzer and Cachon (2000)'s newsvendor problem experiment (newsvendor experiment) is one of the pioneering studies in BeOps. One of their seminal results shows that individuals tended to order few high-profit products and many low-profit products. This systematic deviation from q^* is also known as anchoring (to the expected demand or μ) and insufficient adjustment (toward q^*) or the pull-to-center effect (pulling orders toward μ).[2] These two expressions have underlying assumptions about the behavioral mechanisms at play. A more neutral term for this behavioral regularity is "level bias" (Rudi & Drake, 2014). Since then, researchers have tested several de-biasing strategies and/or offered several behavioral explanations.

6.3.1.1 Reducing the Level Bias

Several newsvendor experiments have provided participants with multiple learning opportunities (e.g., Benzion, Cohen, Peled, & Shavit, 2008;

Bolton & Katok, 2008). They have shown that although orders tend to get closer to q^*, the level bias remains. A reason why learning may not overcome the level bias is the flatness of Eq. (6.1) around q^*. Given this flatness, the small differences in expected profits between orders close to q^* may slow learning. To address this issue, Bostian, Holt and Smith (2008) made the economic consequences of supply-demand mismatches more severe by doubling p and c, while Bolton and Katok (2008) reduced the set of orders that participants could choose from, from 100 to nine or three options. No significant improvements were observed. Building on extremeness aversion (Simonson & Tversky, 1992), Feng, Keller and Zheng (2011) argued that the ineffectiveness of Bolton and Katok's intervention resulted from the fact that q^* was an extreme option in their reduced order sets. Extremeness aversion posits that extreme options increase the attractiveness of middle options. Feng et al. (2011)'s design reduced the order sets and placed q^* as a middle option, and they found that this intervention reduced the level bias.

Several newsvendor experiments have tested the effects of feedback interventions. The rationale is that feedback interventions can improve information processing, which should reduce the level bias (Bolton & Katok, 2008). Bolton and Katok (2008) provided participants with information about either payoffs from orders not chosen (forgone payoffs) or moving averages of actual and forgone payoffs, or the economic consequences of every supply-demand mismatch realization. None of these feedback interventions reduced the level bias.

Other feedback interventions include reducing the frequency of decisions. By reducing the decision frequency, individuals should be less prone to making inferences from few pieces of information and the level bias should be consequently reduced (Bolton & Katok, 2008). Following this approach, Bolton and Katok (2008) constrained participants to order a fixed quantity for a sequence of 10 demand periods, but showed the outcome feedback for each of the 10 periods. Bostian et al. (2008) also reduced decision frequency, this time to five demand periods, while Lurie and Swaminathan (2009) did so to three or six periods. While the intervention by Bostian et al. was ineffective, Bolton and Katok as well as Lurie and Swaminathan found a reduction of the level bias.

In a further test, Bostian et al. (2008) not only 'tied participants' hands for five periods, but also provided outcome feedback only after five periods. Lurie and Swaminathan (2009) also reduced outcome feedback frequency, this time to every two, six or 10 periods. Again, the intervention from Bostian et al. did not reduce the level bias, but Lurie and Swaminathan showed that reducing outcome feedback frequency is more effective than reducing decision frequency in reducing the level bias.

Another related intervention is that of Bolton, Ockenfels and Thonemann (2012), who trained participants on the newsvendor problem by explaining in detail the rationale behind the calculation of q^* and the detrimental consequences of the level bias on performance. In a further test, they also provided participants with information on q^*. Although both training and providing q^* did reduce the level bias, it was not fully eliminated.

6.3.1.2 Behavioral Explanations of the Level Bias

As the evidence above suggests, the level bias is pervasive. Several behavioral models have been proposed to explain its underlying causes. These models assume that the decision maker's utility function incorporates some behavioral preferences. A model of *anchoring and insufficient adjustment* posits that individuals anchor their orders on μ and insufficiently adjust them toward q^* (Benzion et al., 2008). The model's formulation is as follows:

$$q^* = (1-\alpha) F^{-1}\left(\frac{c_u}{c_u + c_o}\right) + \alpha\mu, \tag{6.2}$$

where α captures the degree of anchoring to μ. The range for α is [0, 1], with values closer to one indicating higher degrees of anchoring. However, values above one are feasible and indicate that individuals overshoot μ, that is, order below it for high-profit products or above it for low-profit products. Values closer to zero indicate that individuals place orders closer to q^*. However, values below zero are feasible and indicate that individuals overshoot q^*, that is, order above it for high-profit products or below it for low-profit products. Typical ordering behavior in newsvendor experiments is consistent with anchoring, that is, with values of α greater than zero (e.g., Benzion et al., 2008; Bostian et al., 2008; Feng et al., 2011).

A model of *loss aversion to the cost of excess inventory* posits that individuals are averse to having leftovers (Becker-Peth, Katok, & Thonemann, 2013). The model's formulation is as follows:

$$q^* = F^{-1}\left(\frac{c_u}{c_u + \beta c_o}\right), \tag{6.3}$$

where β (≥ 0) captures the degree of loss aversion to the cost of leftovers. Values of β greater than one indicate aversion to leftovers and orders below q^*, while values lower than one indicate aversion to shortages and orders above q^*. Values closer to one indicate that individuals place orders closer to q^*. Typical ordering behavior in newsvendor experiments is consistent with either aversion to leftovers for high-profit products, that is, with values of β greater than one, or aversion to shortages for low-profit products, that is, with values of β lower than one (e.g., Becker-Peth et al., 2013; Davis, Katok, & Santamaría, 2014; Ho & Zhang, 2008; Schiffels, Fügener, Kolisch, & Brunner, 2014).

A model of *reference dependence* posits that individuals use D as a reference to evaluate the effectiveness of their orders, assigning psychological disutilities to leftovers and shortages in addition to their financial costs (Ho, Lim, & Cui, 2010). The model's formulation is as follows:

$$q^* = F^{-1}\left(\frac{c_u + \delta_u}{c_u + c_o + \delta_u + \delta_o}\right), \tag{6.4}$$

where δ_o (≥ 0) is the psychological disutility of leftovers and δ_u (≥ 0) is the psychological disutility of shortages. If $\delta_o > \delta_u$, leftovers have a greater impact than shortages on ordering behavior. If $\delta_u > \delta_o$, shortages have a greater impact than leftovers. The level bias for high-profit products suggests that $\delta_o > \delta_u$, whereas for low-profit products it suggests that $\delta_u > \delta_o$. When $\delta_o \approx \delta_u \approx 0$, individuals place orders close to q^*. Often, newsvendor experiments have reported an asymmetric level bias, where the bias is stronger for low than for high-profit products (e.g., Bolton & Katok, 2008; Bostian et al., 2008; Kremer, Minner, & Van Wassenhove, 2010; Moritz, 2010; Schweitzer & Cachon, 2000). Estimating the disutility parameters merging ordering data from high and low-profit products would thus result in $\delta_u > \delta_o$. This model complements the anchoring and aversion to leftovers models as it provides a rationale for the level bias (Becker-Peth et al., 2013; Villa & Castañeda, 2018). However, it has not been explored as much as anchoring and aversion to leftovers, with mixed evidence in terms of the level bias asymmetry (e.g., Ho et al., 2010; Villa & Castañeda, 2018).

6.3.1.3 Applications in Humanitarian Operations Research

Under some simplifying assumptions, the structure of the newsvendor problem could be transferred to a HuOps setting to study prepositioning decisions. For example, instead of working with a selling price, a prepositioning problem could work with an additional expediting cost for each item in short supply. This cost can be regarded as a deprivation cost or a proxy related to the achievement of humanitarian goals (Holguín-Veras, Jaller, Van Wassenhove, Pérez, & Wachtendorf, 2012). While in the profit-based problem the leftover and shortage costs can be interpreted as forgone profits, in the prepositioning problem such costs can be interpreted as forgone savings. An optimal prepositioning policy would be thus modeled by Eq. (6.1).

Since the level bias is pervasive, one could expect to also observe it in prepositioning decisions (Gonçalves & Castañeda, 2013). However, the greater emphasis that HuOps place on service level (*SL*) (Harmer, Cotterrell, & Stoddard, 2004) could lead to some level bias nuances. For example, for a low-cost relief supply (high-profit product in the profit-based problem), the *SL* emphasis could push orders closer to q^*, reducing the level bias, while for a high-cost relief supply (low-profit product in the profit-based problem), the *SL* emphasis could push orders farther away from q^*, strengthening the level bias. Figure 6.1's panels (A) and (B) offer a graphical description of these effects.

In terms of the behavioral explanations, the *SL* emphasis would imply low degrees of anchoring for low-cost supplies and high degrees of anchoring for high-cost supplies, that is, $\alpha \approx 0$ and $\alpha \approx 1$, respectively. The *SL* emphasis would favor an aversion to shortages rather than an aversion to leftovers rationale for both low and high-cost supplies, that is, $\beta < 1$. Similarly, the *SL* emphasis would lead to a greater disutility of shortages for both low and high-cost supplies, that is, $\delta_u > \delta_o$.

Baseline BeExs on prepositioning decisions could test whether the *SL* emphasis leads to differences with respect to traditional newsvendor experiments in (i) ordering behavior and (ii) the behavioral explanations put forward in Eqs. (6.2)–(6.4), as suggested above. Once baseline prepositioning behaviors are established, further BeExs could test which de-biasing strategies deliver improved prepositioning behaviors. However, care is needed when transferring the de-biasing mechanisms to the prepositioning task. For example, the forgone payoffs intervention from Bolton and Katok (2008) would have to be framed in terms of forgone savings. While Bolton and Katok (2008)'s intervention was not effective, a savings frame could induce a different behavior (Schiffels et al., 2014).

Moreover, for high-cost supplies, a de-biasing strategy would conflict with the strong *SL* emphasis of HuOps: de-biasing pushes orders toward q^*, while the *SL* emphasis would move them farther away from q^*, as shown in Fig. 6.1's panel (A). In this setting, rather than eliminating the level bias, one could think of making it more salient to move orders upward and improve *SL* (Castañeda & Gonçalves, 2015). For example, drawing on the reference dependence explanation in Eq. (6.4), one could design interventions to make δ_u more salient and increase orders. Ho et al. (2010) show an opposite example: they made δ_o more salient and reduced orders.

Newsvendor experiments usually assume rather stable demand environments by modeling demand as either uniformly or normally distributed. While baseline BeExs on prepositioning decisions, including initial BeExs of de-biasing strategies, could also assume such stable demand environments to start laying the ground for further research, this further research should increasingly improve on external validity. This

Behavioral Experiments in Single-Agent Operational Problems

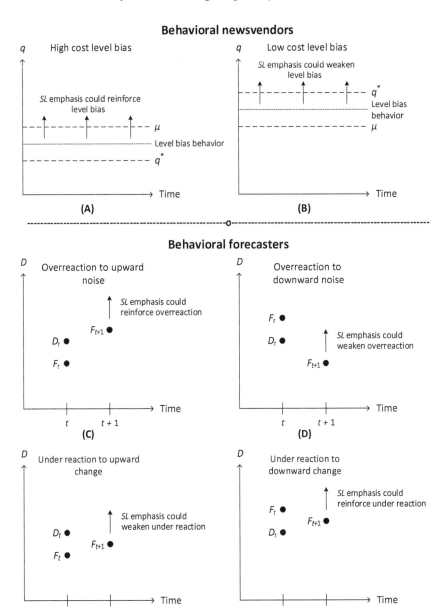

Fig. 6.1 *SL* emphasis impact on behavioral newsvendors and forecasters

external validity could be represented in, for example, the high levels of uncertainty of future demand in HuOps (Holguín-Veras et al., 2012).

This is relevant since such demand uncertainty could pose some challenges to experimental design. For example, uniform and normal demand distributions could no longer be adequate to represent future demand in HuOps. Using distribution-free newsvendor approaches (e.g., Gallego & Moon, 1993; Lan, Ji, & Li, 2015; Natarajan, Sim, & Uichanco, 2018) could help to address this issue.

6.3.2 Behavioral Forecasters

In a simple demand forecasting process, individuals make demand forecasts for the upcoming period (F_{t+1}) after observing the demand of the current period (D_t). The demand process is given by:

$$D_t = \mu_t + \varepsilon_t, \qquad (6.5a)$$

$$\mu_t = \mu_{t-1} + v_t, \qquad (6.5b)$$

where $\varepsilon_t \sim N(0, no^2)$ and $v_t \sim N(0, ch^2)$ are independent random variables. ε_t captures temporary shocks to the demand time series, that is, changes that last only one period, while μ_t captures permanent shocks to the demand time series, that is, changes that persist in subsequent periods. By varying the noise (no) and change parameter (ch), the model in Eq. (6.5) can describe a wide range of different environments, from somewhat stable to highly unstable. The optimal forecasting mechanism for Eq. (6.5) is the well-known exponential smoothing mechanism:

$$F_{t+1} = F_t + \alpha (D_t - F_t), \qquad (6.6)$$

where F_{t+1} is a function of the observed forecast error $D_t - F_t$ and the weight α placed on this error ($0 \leq \alpha \leq 1$). α, known also as the exponential smoothing constant, depends on the change-to-noise ratio $W = ch^2/no^2$. A forecast should thus be revised according to W: with low values of W or stable environments (i.e., $no > ch$), forecast errors should have a low influence on the forecast, while with high values of W or unstable environments (i.e., $ch > no$), forecast errors should have a high influence on the forecast. Thus, α should be low in stable environments and high in unstable environments. The optimal α is given by:

$$\alpha^*(W) = \frac{2}{1 + \sqrt{1 + \frac{4}{W}}}. \tag{6.7}$$

Replacing Eq. (6.7) in Eq. (6.6) gives the optimal forecasts for the demand process in Eq. (6.5) (Kremer, Moritz, & Siemsen, 2011).

Kremer et al. (2011) explored how individuals make forecasts for a demand process like the one in Eqs. (6.5)–(6.7). They observed that while forecasts were somewhat consistent with exponential smoothing (i.e., behavioral estimations of α [BEα] fell between zero and one), the actual forecasting behavior deviated from the optimal forecasting behavior (i.e., BEα were different from $\alpha^*(W)$). They also observed that while participants were prone to overreaction to noise in stable environments (i.e., BEα were greater than $\alpha^*(W)$), they were also prone to under-reaction to change in unstable environments (BEα were lower than $\alpha^*(W)$).

Since the newsvendor problem can be decomposed into a demand forecasting task and an ordering task, some newsvendor experiments are related to demand forecasting. For example, Ren and Croson (2013) tested whether overconfidence can explain the level bias. In this context, overconfidence is operationalized as over-precision, which refers to the belief that one's estimates are more accurate than they truly are (Moore & Healy, 2008). In the newsvendor problem, over-precision can lead to an underestimation of D's variance, which leads to orders below q^* for high-profit products, and above q^* for low-profit products (Ren & Croson, 2013). They measured over-precision with either out-task (unrelated to the ordering task) or in-task (related to the ordering task) measures and observed that both over-precision measures correlate with the level bias.

In a more systematic task decomposition test, Lee and Siemsen (2017) decomposed the ordering task into three components: making a point forecast, estimating D's standard deviation and making an in-stock probability or *SL* decision. The three components can be combined into an order q. Decomposition simplifies the task and this simplification is argued to be beneficial for decision making; however, the evidence is mixed (Lee & Siemsen, 2017). Although they found evidence of overprecision in the estimation of D's standard deviation, the decomposed task reduced the level bias for a high-profit product when D had a relatively low standard deviation. The forecasting task in Ren and Croson (2013) and Lee and Siemsen (2017) was different from the task described in Eqs. (6.5)–(6.7); however, the underestimation of D's variance indicates that participants under-reacted to the demand process, a suboptimal forecasting behavior also reported in Kremer et al. (2011).

6.3.2.1 Applications in Humanitarian Operations Research

Demand in humanitarian response is many times deemed unpredictable (e.g., Balcik & Beamon, 2008; Lodree & Taskin, 2008; Van Wassenhove, 2006). However, Dieckhaus, Heigh, Leonard, Jahre, and Navangul (2011) show that traditional demand forecasting methods can be applied to forecast demand during the initial response of a humanitarian crisis.

Thus, one could potentially explore demand forecasting biases in HuOps using the task described in Eqs. (6.5)–(6.7). Demand unpredictability could be captured to some extent by designing environments with relatively high values of the change parameter (ch). Like with the level bias, the *SL* emphasis of HuOps could influence the overreaction to noise and under-reaction to change patterns documented by Kremer et al. (2011).

When the noise is upward (the forecast error signals that more was needed, i.e., $D_t - F_t > 0$), an overreaction to noise implies that the next forecast will be greater than the current D (i.e., $F_{t+1} > D_t$). The *SL* emphasis could strengthen such overreaction. On the other hand, when the noise is downward (the forecast error signals that less was needed, i.e., $D_t - F_t < 0$), the overreaction to noise implies that the next forecast will be lower than the current D (i.e., $F_{t+1} < D_t$). The *SL* emphasis could reduce such overreaction. With respect to change, when this is upward, an under-reaction to change implies that the next forecast will be lower than the current D ($F_{t+1} < D_t$). The *SL* emphasis could reduce such under-reaction. On the other hand, when the change is downward, the under-reaction to change implies that the next forecast will be greater than the current D ($F_{t+1} > D_t$). The *SL* emphasis could strengthen such under-reaction.

Figure 6.1's panels (C)–(F) offer a graphical description of these effects. If such *SL*-influenced forecasts are used as inputs for, for example, prepositioning decisions, the behaviors in panels (C) and (F) could lead to supply surges, while the behaviors in panels (D) and (E) could prevent supply shortages. Baseline BeExs on demand forecasting in HuOps could test whether the *SL* emphasis leads to differences with respect to Kremer et al.'s results in (i) overreaction to noise and (ii) under-reaction to change, as suggested above.

The overconfidence study by Ren and Croson (2013) shows that over-precision in demand forecasts explains the level bias. The *SL* emphasis of HuOps could also influence over-precision. However, Ren and Croson's in-task over-precision measure could provide insights on how individuals believe that demand in HuOps behaves, which could potentially affect the relation between *SL* emphasis and confidence. For example, if individuals know that future demand in HuOps is highly uncertain (Holguín-Veras et al., 2012), they could perhaps be less confident or precise about their forecasts. Thus, one should initially assess confidence levels in demand forecasts for HuOps. Then, further research could explore how the relation between *SL* emphasis and confidence plays out in demand forecasting in HuOps by adapting the experimental designs from Ren and Croson (2013) and/or Lee and Siemsen (2017) to a HuOps setting.

Adapting these designs could complement prepositioning experiments and one could explore whether the hypothesized supply surges and shortages implied from Fig. 6.1's panels (C)–(F) materialize. Moreover, Lee and Siemsen (2017)'s task decomposition design could provide a cleaner test of the impact of the *SL* emphasis on prepositioning decisions since their design specifically asks participants to make a *SL* decision that is later combined into an order q.

Finally, as further research increasingly improves on external validity, care is needed when considering the demand data for forecasting experiments. For example, although similar types of emergencies generate similar needs, demand could vary by region and the frequency of occurrence and/or the strength of the emergencies (Dieckhaus et al., 2011). Data-driven newsvendor approaches (e.g., Ban & Rudin, 2018; Levi, Perakis, & Uichanco, 2015; Saghafian & Tomlin, 2016) could help inform the design of forecasting experiments considering more realistic demand scenarios.

6.4 Conclusion

This chapter described the BeEx methodology. It then surveyed the BeOps literature that focuses on newsvendor and forecasting studies and suggested extensions for research in HuOps. These extensions should study how individuals decide on prepositioning levels and demand forecasts for future emergencies, analyzing also how particular aspects of HuOps, like their SL emphasis and/or demand features, impact the typical decision-making biases reported in the BeOps literature. In addition, BeExs should study strategies that move prepositioning and forecasting behaviors in intended directions according to HuOps goals, and also analyze how individuals balance cost-effectiveness when meeting such goals.

Notes

1. Some authors differentiate between control and randomization. For example, in Morton and Williams (2010), control refers to techniques other than randomization used to sidestep confounding problems. In this chapter, the term control is used in a broader sense and includes randomization.
2. Schweitzer and Cachon (2000) also showed that participants tended to minimize ex-post inventory errors by adjusting the current q toward the prior D, a pattern known as demand chasing. In this chapter, we focus on level bias since newsvendor experiments have focused more on studying this ordering pattern.

References

Balcik, B., & Beamon, B. M. (2008). Facility location in humanitarian relief. *International Journal of Logistics: Research and Applications, 11*(2), 101–121.

Ban, G.-Y., & Rudin, C. (2018). The big data newsvendor: Practical insights from machine learning. *Operations Research*, in press.

Becker-Peth, M., Katok, E., & Thonemann, U. W. (2013). Designing buyback contracts for irrational but predictable newsvendors. *Management Science, 59*(8), 1800–1816.

Benzion, U., Cohen, Y., Peled, R., & Shavit, T. (2008). Decision-making and the newsvendor problem: An experimental study. *Journal of the Operational Research Society, 59*(9), 1281–1287.

Bolton, G. E., & Katok, E. (2008). Learning by doing in the newsvendor problem: A laboratory investigation of the role of experience and feedback. *Manufacturing & Service Operations Management, 10*(3), 519–538.

Bolton, G. E., Ockenfels, A., & Thonemann, U. W. (2012). Managers and students as newsvendors. *Management Science, 58*(12), 2225–2233.

Bostian, A. A., Holt, C. A., & Smith, A. M. (2008). Newsvendor "pull-to-center" effect: Adaptive learning in a laboratory experiment. *Manufacturing & Service Operations Management, 10*(4), 590–608.

Castañeda, J. A., & Gonçalves, P. (2015). Kicking the "mean" habit: Joint prepositioning in debiasing pull-to-center effects. In E. Bendoly, W. van Wezel, & D. G. Bachrach (Eds.), *The handbook of behavioral operations management: Social and psychological dynamics in production and service settings* (pp. 238–250). Oxford: Oxford University Press.

Davis, A. M., Katok, E., & Santamaría, N. (2014). Push, pull, or both? A behavioral study of how the allocation of inventory risk affects channel efficiency. *Management Science, 60*(11), 2666–2683.

Dieckhaus, D., Heigh, I., Leonard, N. G. T., Jahre, M., & Navangul, K. A. (2011). *Demand forecasting in international humanitarian response*. Paper presented at 23rd Annual Nordic Logistics Research Network Conference, Harstad, Norway.

Fatás, E., & Roig, J. M. (2004). Una introducción a la metodología experimental en economía. *Cuadernos de Economía, 27*(75), 7–36.

Feng, T., Keller, L. R., & Zheng, X. (2011). Decision making in the newsvendor problem: A cross-national laboratory study. *Omega, 39*(1), 41–50.

Gallego, G., & Moon, I. (1993). The distribution free newsboy problem: Review and extensions. *Journal of the Operational Research Society, 44*(8), 825–834.

Gino, F., & Pisano, G. (2008). Toward a theory of behavioral operations. *Manufacturing & Service Operations Management, 10*(4), 676–691.

Gonçalves, P., & Castañeda, J. A. (2013). Impact of joint decisions and cognitive dissonance on prepositioning (newsvendor) decisions. *MIT Sloan Research Paper No. 5021-13*, MIT, Cambridge, MA.

Guala, F. (2005). *The methodology of experimental economics*. Cambridge: Cambridge University Press.

Harmer, A., Cotterrell, L., & Stoddard, A. (2004). From Stockholm to Ottawa: A progress review of the Good Humanitarian Donorship initiative. *Briefing Paper*, Humanitarian Policy Group, Overseas Development Institute, London, UK.

Ho, T.-H., Lim, N., & Cui, T.-H. (2010). Reference dependence in multilocation newsvendor models: A structural analysis. *Management Science, 56*(11), 1891–1910.

Ho, T.-H., & Zhang, J. (2008). Designing pricing contracts for boundedly rational customers: Does the framing of the fixed fee matter? *Management Science, 54*(4), 686–700.

Holguín-Veras, J., Jaller, M., Van Wassenhove, L. N., Pérez, N., & Wachtendorf, T. (2012). On the unique features of post-disaster humanitarian logistics. *Journal of Operations Management, 30*(7–8), 494–506.

Katok, E. (2010). Using laboratory experiments to build better operations management models. *Foundations and Trends in Technology, Information and Operations Management, 5*(1), 1–84.

Kremer, M., Minner, S., & Van Wassenhove, L. N. (2010). Do random errors explain newsvendor behavior? *Manufacturing & Service Operations Management, 12*(4), 673–681.

Kremer, M., Moritz, B. B., & Siemsen, E. (2011). Demand forecasting behavior: System neglect and change detection. *Management Science, 57*(10), 1827–1843.

Lan, C., Ji, H., & Li, J. (2015). A distribution-free newsvendor model with balking penalty and random yield. *Journal of Industrial Engineering and Management, 8*(3), 1051–1068.

Lee, Y. S., & Siemsen, E. (2017). Task decomposition and newsvendor decision making. *Management Science, 63*(10), 3226–3245.

Levi, R., Perakis, G., & Uichanco, J. (2015). The data-driven newsvendor problem: New bounds and insights. *Operations Research, 63*(6), 1294–1306.

Loch, C. H., & Wu, Y. (2007). Behavioral operations management. *Foundations and Trends in Technology, Information and Operations Management, 1*(3), 121–232.

Lodree, E. J., Jr., & Taskin, S. (2008). An insurance risk management framework for disaster relief and supply chain disruption inventory planning. *Journal of the Operational Research Society, 59*(5), 674–684.

Lodree, E. J., Jr., & Taskin, S. (2009). Supply chain planning for hurricane response with wind speed information updates. *Computers & Operations Research, 36*(1), 2–15.

Lurie, N. H., & Swaminathan, J. M. (2009). Is timely information always better? The effect of feedback frequency on decision making. *Organizational Behavior and Human Decision Processes, 108*(2), 315–329.

Moore, D. A., & Healy, P. J. (2008). The trouble with overconfidence. *Psychological Review, 115*(2), 502–517.

Moritz, B. B. (2010). *Cognition and heterogeneity in supply chain planning: A study of inventory decision making.* PhD dissertation, Carlson School of Management, University of Minnesota, Minneapolis, MN.

Morton, R. B., & Williams, K. C. (2010). *Experimental political science and the study of causality: From nature to the lab.* Cambridge, UK: Cambridge University Press.

Natarajan, K., Sim, M., & Uichanco, J. (2018). Asymmetry and ambiguity in newsvendor models. *Management Science, 64*(7), 2973–3468.

Ren, Y., & Croson, R. (2013). Overconfidence in newsvendor orders: An experimental study. *Management Science, 59*(11), 2502–2517.

Rudi, N., & Drake, D. (2014). Observation bias: The impact of demand censoring on newsvendor level and adjustment behavior. *Management Science, 60*(5), 1334–1345.

Saghafian, S., & Tomlin, B. (2016). The newsvendor under demand ambiguity: Combining data with moment and tail information. *Operations Research, 64*(1), 167–185.

Sankaranarayanan, K., Castañeda, J. A., & Villa, S. (2018). Future research in humanitarian operations: A behavioral operations perspective. In G. Kovács, K. M. Spens, & M. Moshtari (Eds.), *The Palgrave handbook of humanitarian logistics and supply chain management* (pp. 71–117). London, UK: Palgrave Macmillan.

Schiffels, S., Fügener, A., Kolisch, R., & Brunner, O. J. (2014). On the assessment of costs in a newsvendor environment: Insights from an experimental study. *Omega,* 43 (March), 1-8.

Schweitzer, M. E., & Cachon, G. P. (2000). Decision bias in the newsvendor problem with a known demand distribution: Experimental evidence. *Management Science, 46*(3), 404–420.

Siemsen, E. (2011). The usefulness of behavioral laboratory experiments in supply chain management research. *Journal of Supply Chain Management, 47*(3), 17–18.

Simonson, I., & Tversky, A. (1992). Choice in context: Tradeoff contrast and extremeness aversion. *Journal of Marketing Research, 29*(3), 281–295.

Smith, V. L. (1976). Experimental economics: Induced value theory. *American Economic Review, 66*(2), 274–279.

Smith, V. L. (1982). Microeconomic systems as an experimental science. *American Economic Review, 72*(5), 923–955.

Smith, V. L. (1994). Economics in the laboratory. *Journal of Economic Perspectives, 8*(1), 113–131.

Taskin, S., & Lodree, E. J., Jr. (2010). Inventory decisions for emergency supplies based on hurricane count predictions. *International Journal of Production Economics, 126*(1), 66–75.

Van Wassenhove, L. N. (2006). Humanitarian aid logistics: Supply chain management in high gear. *Journal of the Operational Research Society, 57*(5), 475–489.

Villa, S., & Castañeda, J. A. (2018). Transshipments in supply chains: A behavioral investigation. *European Journal of Operational Research, 269*(2), 715–729.

7

Behavioral Operations in Multi-agent Settings and Humanitarian Operations

Sebastián Villa

7.1 Introduction

Experiments in operations are used to better understand the factors that affect performance in real operations (Donohue & Croson, 2002). The use of experiments has focused on understanding decision-making biases and deriving heuristics that aim to explain those biases either in multi-agent supply chains (Croson, Donohue, Katok, & Sterman, 2014; Sterman, 1989a; Sterman & Dogan, 2015) or under a unique actor framework (Bolton & Katok, 2008; Schweitzer & Cachon, 2000). General results show how humans display poor performance, even when decision-makers have the opportunity to identify and correct errors (Einhorn & Hogarth, 1981). In particular, decision-makers perform poorly in environments with significant feedback complexity (Diehl & Sterman, 1995; Schweitzer & Cachon, 2000; Sterman, 1989a, 1989b), and changing conditions (Kleinmuntz & Thomas, 1987).

S. Villa (✉)
School of Management, Universidad de los Andes, Bogotá, Colombia
e-mail: s.villab@uniandes.edu.co

Biases might be explained by subjects' bounded rationality. The strong bounds observed in human rationality derive from two basic and related deficiencies in our mental maps (Sterman, 2000). First, our mental maps often capture a simplified and flawed representation of the actual causal structure of systems; i.e., the misperception of feedback structure. Second, even when we perfectly understand the structure of a system, we are unable to infer how the system evolves over time; i.e., the misperception of feedback dynamics (Gonçalves & Villa, 2016). Research on cognitive psychology allows us to conclude that people often adopt an open-loop (event-based) perspective and that they subconsciously use different mechanisms that worsen their understanding of system structure (Axelrod, 1976; Dörner, 1980).

The main objective of this chapter is to build on the concepts of bounded rationality in order to highlight some behavioral factors that influence subjects' decisions in multi-agent supply chains, and to discuss how different behavioral results may be applied to humanitarian operations. Problems in both for-profit and humanitarian operations are characterized by the interaction of multiple actors within a modern information technology environment (Axsäter, 2003). Therefore, a better understanding of the behavioral interactions among different agents may improve coordination in real operations. The following section discusses important mechanisms affecting subjects' behavior. Following that, Sect. 7.3 provides an introduction to the humanitarian sector. Section 7.4 shows general behavioral results within multi-agent settings and provides some implications for the humanitarian sector. Finally, I present the conclusion in Sect. 7.5.

7.2 Behavioral Mechanisms in Supply Chains

Behavioral operations now constitute a mature field of research in operations and supply chain management. Given that the execution of any operation involves decision-makers (e.g., managers, employees and customers), biases and errors in decision-making have a negative impact on operational performance. Behavioral operations can inform models and frameworks to account for such shortcomings. Biases might be explained by two related deficiencies in our mental maps (Sterman, 2000): misperception of feedback structure, and misperception of feedback dynamics (Gonçalves & Villa, 2016). Based on subjects' flawed understanding of the actual causal structure and dynamics of systems, four important mechanisms have been proposed to explain sub-optimal decision-making: heuristics, biases, motivation and the fundamental attribution error (Gonçalves & Villa, 2016).

Heuristics: mental shortcuts or rule-of-thumb strategies that shorten decision-making time and allow people to come up with decisions quickly and efficiently, without regularly stopping to evaluate different alternatives of action (Tversky, 1972). One of the most commonly used heuristics in the literature on behavioral operations is the anchoring and adjustment heuristic (Tversky & Kahneman, 1974).

Cognitive biases: limitations in human thinking that lead to deviations from full rationality (Tversky & Kahneman, 1974). They are often a result of our attempt to simplify information processing using simple heuristics. However, in other cases, they are the result of either judgmental factors, such as overconfidence (Moore & Healy, 2008), or situational factors, such as framing (Tversky & Kahneman, 1974).

Motivation: is a psychological factor that may consciously or unconsciously affect our mental models, through the effort we make to understand systems and our persistence in attempting to reduce the discrepancies between model predictions and outcomes (Gonçalves & Villa, 2016; Latham & Locke, 1991).

Fundamental attribution error: attributing the cause of unexpected outcomes to external factors. Misunderstanding the causes that generate perceived effects stops people from obtaining better information about the system structure, and from creating policies that may lead to better performance (Forrester, 1961).

In order to explain subjects' behavior under operational settings, different structural models have been estimated by building upon the four mechanisms mentioned above (Bostian, Holt, & Smith, 2008; Croson & Ren, 2013; Ho, Lim, & Cui, 2010; Schweitzer & Cachon, 2000; Sterman, 1989a). For example, Bostian et al. (2008) use an anchoring and adjustment model to explain subjects' behavior. Ho et al. (2010) use a reference dependence model that includes asymmetric psychological costs of leftovers and shortages in a multi-location newsvendor setting. Becker-Peth, Katok, and Thonemann (2013) explore a behavioral model that includes anchoring, loss aversion and mental accounting for designing better buyback contracts. Orders are modeled as replacements for (expected) incoming orders modified by an adjustment to bring inventory in line with the target. Croson and Donohue (2005) use a decision rule that regresses the orders placed by subjects in a given period against the initial effective inventory level, total incoming orders, shipments received from the supplier, and retailer's total outstanding orders. All these different models help us to better understand how different behavioral factors manifest under different situations.

7.3 Humanitarian Operations

Over the years, natural and man-made disasters have increased in frequency and impact due to global population growth, climate change and technological complexity (Starr & Van Wassenhove, 2014). Dealing with such disasters lies at the heart of the foundation of humanitarian organizations (HOs). HOs need to design and implement programs aimed at alleviating human suffering. The implementation of these programs requires decision-makers to make important operational decisions following the three fundamental humanitarian principles: humanity, impartiality and neutrality (Van Wassenhove, 2006). However, there might be some clear biases during the implementation of these principles. For example, Nunnenkamp, Öhler and Sosa (2017) show that aid allocation by the World Bank in India is not based on merit, and that some regions receive more aid if the World Bank is already involved in neighboring regions.

During the implementation of the programs, HOs need to interact with multiple actors (see Fig. 7.1) to obtain the required financial resources, information, relief items, logistics support, and visibility to distribute relief items at the right time and place, and to the right people. However, this is not an easy task given challenges such as high environmental uncertainty, a large number of actors, high dependence on donors,

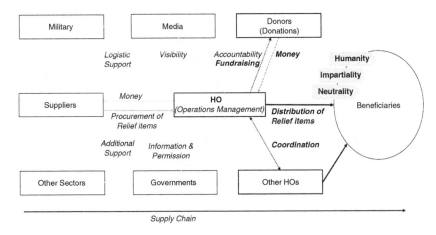

Fig. 7.1 Interactions and flows of a humanitarian supply chain

high decentralization, time pressures, delays, and feedback loops (Besiou, Stapleton, & Van Wassenhove, 2010; Pedraza-Martinez & Van Wassenhove, 2012; Starr & Van Wassenhove, 2014). Results that shed light on the difficulties of managing the limited resources can be interpreted as inefficiencies of the HOs, which may, in turn, affect both access to future donations and the proper execution of operations (Van Wassenhove, 2006). Therefore, decision-makers are required to show that they are making the best use of the resources, with fair allocation of aid among those in need (Halachmi, 2002).

Humanitarian logistics and operations are generally misinterpreted. According to Holguín-Veras, Jaller, Van Wassenhove, Pérez, and Wachtendorf (2012), researchers tend to overlook the fact that humanitarian and commercial activities are somewhat different and that these contrasting worlds may affect decision-making processes. In their work, Holguín-Veras et al. (2012) identify at least seven differences between commercial and humanitarian logistics, including the dissimilarities of the (1) objectives being pursued, (2) origin of commodity flows, (3) knowledge of demand, (4) decision-making structure, (5) periodicity and volume of logistics activities, (6) state of social fabric and networks, and (7) support systems. Is there a common trait among these differences? The fact that there are different contextual characteristics between commercial and humanitarian organizations implies that researchers need to (i) identify similar structures so that we can build on insights from the commercial sector, and (ii) identify those differences to properly address the needs in each independent sector.

In this sense, some of the literature available on decision-making processes in operations may apply to the humanitarian sector. For example, behavioral results show that decision-makers do not behave optimally even when they have perfect information and knowledge of the system structure and that decision-makers tend to ignore the relationship between a cause and a delayed effect (Gonçalves & Villa, 2016; Sterman, 1989a; Villa, Gonçalves, & Arango, 2015). However, the actual impact of subjects' biases in humanitarian operations must be tested for each specific setting and not just directly generalized from commercial operations.

7.4 Behavior in Multi-agent Supply Chains and Extensions to the Humanitarian Sector

In this section, I provide some examples and applications in four important multi-agent settings within behavioral operations literature. In addition, I provide some potential extensions and interpretations to the humanitarian setting.

7.4.1 The Beer Game and the Bullwhip Effect

The Beer Game (BG) is a role-playing simulation of a four-echelon supply chain (developed at MIT) that is characterized by uncertainty and long delays (Forrester, 1961). The game is played for several periods, during which subjects need to decide how many units to order from their immediate supplier in order to satisfy their downstream customer demand. Each player has good local information but limited global information. Sterman (1989a, 2001) finds that in any BG session, subjects display poor performance relative to the optimum and that the systematic underperformance can be understood due to a pervasive misperception of the delays involved in the experimental systems. The bullwhip effect is a particular outcome observed in any BG session. It is a typical supply chain problem that occurs when the variability of orders increases as we move up in the supply chain. This pattern of behavior takes place because decision-makers distort the information they receive from their immediate downstream customer and send it (distorted) to the upstream supplier. This distortion of information from customers to suppliers leads to high operational inefficiencies such as high inventory levels and unnecessary capital investment (Chen & Lee, 2011; Croson et al., 2014; Lee, Padmanabhan, & Whang, 1997a).

Studies of the bullwhip effect have shown that both operational and behavioral causes can provide explanations on its origin (Lee et al., 1997a; Sterman, 1989b). The operational causes suggest that even if managers were fully rational, supply chain instability may persist due to the actual structure of the system. Lee, Padmanabhan, and Whang (1997b) identified four typical operational causes of the bullwhip effect (or order amplification), which should be controlled to improve process design. The four operational causes are: (i) order batching, (ii) price fluctuations, (iii) rationing and shortage gaming, and (iv) demand forecast updating. However, behavioral causes predict that due to subjects' bounded rationality, the bullwhip effect will take place even if we control for the four operational causes. Thus, behavioral causes emphasize how limitations in a subject's rationality lead to behavior that diverges from theoretical predictions (Diehl & Sterman, 1995; Schweitzer & Cachon, 2000; Sterman & Dogan, 2015; Villa et al., 2015). To provide some insights into the decision-making process during a BG, authors have proposed different decision rules based on operational variables and simple heuristics (e.g., Croson et al., 2014; Sterman, 1989a; Sterman & Dogan, 2015).

7.4.1.1 Insights for Research into Humanitarian Operations

In case of uncertainty and delays between causes and effects, decision-makers make mistakes and deviate from optimal decisions due to biases and lack of information. Since humanitarian contexts suffer more than commercial ones from uncertainty and lack of information, actors in the humanitarian sector will be more prone to make sub-optimal decisions.

According to Holguín-Veras et al. (2012), the high level of uncertainty of future demand in humanitarian contexts is a primary difference between humanitarian logistics and commercial logistics. In this sense, automating inventory decisions might not completely apply to humanitarian contexts for two reasons: (i) in humanitarian contexts, every disaster has its own characteristics, so a single automated means of deciding inventory levels would not be optimal to every circumstance, and (ii) in commercial contexts, stock-outs and excess of inventory affect profit margins; however, in humanitarian contexts a mistake in inventory management could impact human lives directly. Therefore, having forecasts (at an aggregated level) is important because they enhance better preparation and rapid response when an event occurs. Similarly, the lack of training is a factor that increases the chances of sub-optimal decision-making. Training is frequently an uncertain and costly activity that requires long-term investment for HOs. However, the development of decision-making training programs in HOs could decrease the effect of biases on operational performance.

7.4.2 Horizontal Coordination in Supply Chains

Horizontal coordination among retailers is usually achieved by the use of transshipments. Transshipments are known as the monitored movement of material among multiple locations at the same echelon level (Herer, Tzur, & Yücesan, 2006). Transshipments are a common practice in many industries (both intra- and inter-firm) as a mechanism to alleviate the problem of localized demand shocks, and encourage independent retailers to coordinate and share their inventories to achieve a better match between supply and demand (Dong & Rudi, 2004; Netessine, Rudi, & Wang, 2001; Sošić, 2006). Therefore, accurate transshipment decisions may improve stock polices, reduce costs, and create better customer service by gaining a source of supply whose reaction time is quicker than that of the regular suppliers (Herer et al., 2006). Rudi, Kapur, and Pyke (2001) study transshipments between two independent newsvendors and show that, in general, maximizing the profit of each retailer will not lead to maximizing the system's profit. However, Hu, Duenyas, and Kapuscinski (2007) formulate the conditions under which the system can be coordinated. These emerging interactions among retailers can be modeled as a game among independent actors (newsvendors), and the game can be analyzed using Nash equilibria (Rudi et al., 2001). Analyzing these interactions, the collective action among multiple subjects and subjects' behaviors requires an understanding of the difficulty faced by people in reaching common goals (Olson, 1965). Ostrom (1990, 2000) explains that individuals neither apply nor learn Nash equilibrium strategies when they face different kinds of dilemmas; rather, they use other types of (behavioral) models that usually lead to non-cooperative behaviors (Cárdenas, 2000). However, biases within these behavioral models can be reduced by including face to face communication as a coordination mechanism that creates a trusting environment that reduces non-cooperative behaviors (Ahn, Ostrom, & Walker, 2011; Castillo & Saysel, 2005; Ostrom, 1998).

From a behavioral perspective, Villa and Castañeda (2018) use a mathematical model to characterize a system formed by two identical newsvendors that place decentralized orders to a unique supplier. They show that in transshipment settings (i) there is persistence of biases common to newsvendor problems (pull-to-center, demand chasing, loss aversion, and psychological disutility), (ii) communication can improve coordination and may reduce demand chasing behavior, and (iii) supply chain performance increases with the use of dynamic heuristics embedded within a traditional optimization model. More recently, Villa and Katok (2018) use laboratory experiments to understand how retailers negotiate transfer prices and make ordering decisions, and how these decisions deviate from the theoretical channel-coordinating benchmarks. They find no significant differences in transfer price negotiations even when subjects face different profitability conditions. Similarly, Zhao, Xu, and Siemsen (2016) examine inventory sharing effectiveness under different transshipment prices. Their results show that without a carefully designed system, inventory sharing may neither be effective nor provide a route to enhanced profitability. In general, decision-makers do not stock enough to benefit from sharing.

7.4.2.1 Insights for Research in Humanitarian Operations

HOs need to coordinate their operations to provide relief to the most vulnerable people when a humanitarian crisis occurs. When organizations coordinate their efforts with others, they can reduce operational costs and gain flexibility to improve more rapidly (Kaatrud, Samii, & Van Wassenhove, 2003; Leiras, de Brito, Queiroz, Rejane, & Yoshida, 2014). However, this coordination is difficult and uncertain. It is hard to know the distribution of needs of the affected population and the total relief capacity, which makes it challenging for HOs to effectively coordinate their efforts to satisfy the needs of such populations (Stauffer, Pedraza-Martinez, & Van Wassenhove, 2016; Tomasini & Van Wassenhove, 2009; Urrea, Villa, & Gonçalves, 2016). Studies on inventory management have raised concerns about the importance of horizontal coordination and information sharing among HOs in relief operations (Ergun, Karakus, Keskinocak, Swann, & Villarreal, 2010).

A common strategy managers use to improve humanitarian response is to pre-position some critical commodities in various locations prior to disasters. In fact, dozens of organizations manage hundreds of distinct items in multiple warehouses globally in order to respond to events that vary in location, type, and size (Acimovic & Goentzel, 2016). Given the stochastic demand and typically long lead times faced by HOs, it is often beneficial to use transshipments as a mechanism to alleviate the problem of localized demand shocks (Herer et al., 2006; Netessine et al., 2001). Transshipments encourage independent HOs to coordinate, share their inventories, and decide on proper strategies to achieve a better match between humanitarian needs and supply (Dong & Rudi, 2004; Herer et al., 2006; Netessine et al., 2001; Sošić, 2006). Therefore, the typical behavioral biases in inventory management under demand uncertainty are also expected to occur in humanitarian operations. Similarly, Bhattacharya, Hasija, and Van Wassenhove (2014) argue that the participation of a central coordination entity that receives and distributes goods and donations reduces the inefficiencies in operations and makes better use of earmarked funds. Hence, it is important to consider the behavioral biases and heuristics that subjects follow within a humanitarian context and integrate them with behavioral models that can provide (i) further insights and generalizations to behavioral operations theorists, and (ii) some managerial implications to HOs.

7.4.3 Competition in Supply Chains

Given the growing number of industries worldwide, more and more companies frequently battle their competitors for customers' attention by offering lower prices, higher service levels, and higher product quality. Given this fierce retailer competition, retailers need to define ordering strategies with their suppliers to get the desired quantities of their products. As a result, retailers amplify their orders, especially when there is limited supplier capacity. Empirical studies have claimed that when we account for non-serial and competitive supply chains, in addition to inflating orders, customers may duplicate their orders with a certain probability by placing additional orders with multiple retailers (Armony & Plambeck, 2005). In addition, in an attempt to guarantee higher service levels, retailers' inventory levels may be increased as the probabilities of duplication and retail competition increase (Cachon & Olivares, 2009).

Similarly, retailers may order differently depending on the allocation scheme chosen by the supplier. Therefore, some specific allocation mechanisms may lead retailers to make decisions that are closer to the theoretical predictions, while others may induce them to strongly deviate from the theoretical predictions in an effort to gain better allocation. Villa (2018) studies how different factors (supplier capacity, level of competition among retailers, supply shortage magnitudes, and different allocation mechanisms) may both independently and in combination influence orders in a system with two retailers facing supply competition. The author shows that the order amplification persists even when subjects do not have incentives to deviate and that order amplification does not disappear over time.

Similarly, Lippman and McCardle (1997) use a two-retailer competition problem to show that under mild conditions, in equilibrium, retailers increased their order quantity in anticipation of the possible overflow from stocked-out competitors. A recent behavioral study by Ovchinnikov, Moritz, and Quiroga (2015) builds on a newsvendor setting to explore behavioral aspects of newsvendor competition. Main results show the newsvendor behavioral regularities remain in competitive newsvendor environments. In addition, they provide a behavioral model that extends the standard theory of newsvendor competition, providing guidance that leads to significant improvements in market share and service levels.

7.4.3.1 Insights for Research in Humanitarian Operations

From a humanitarian perspective, HOs should coordinate with others to create strategic alliances for a fairer distribution of resources and aid following the three fundamental humanitarian principles (humanity, impartiality and neutrality). However, HOs could distribute their resources, pursue their own interests and aim at maximizing visibility and media attention (Fehr & Schmidt, 1999), which may then be transformed into future donations. According to Lindenberg and Bryant (2001), HOs face great competition for resources, especially during the early phases of the response, when there is a lot of media attention and financial resources are readily available (Stephenson & Schnitzer, 2006). The urge for financial resources to cope with the increasing number of disasters, together with the need to demonstrate effective and efficient results to potential donors have led HOs to compete fiercely not only for media and donor attention (Oloruntoba & Gray, 2006; Van Wassenhove, 2006), but also for qualified human resources, local infrastructure and even for recipients of their services. The problem with this competition for resources is that it can lead to negative effects, such as hampering coordination and reducing overall performance. Individualistic behavior can be detrimental to the fair allocation of resources among people in need as it leads to a duplication of efforts and to a lack of information and resource sharing (Kaatrud et al., 2003; Leiras et al., 2014). For instance, HOs may duplicate efforts during the response or hide important information from their counterparts if they believe that sharing will hinder their own efforts at attracting media and donor attention (Kent, 1987;

Lessmann & Markwardt, 2016; Stephenson, 2005). More recently, Urrea, Villa, and Quintane (2018) show that HOs need to define better strategies in order to obtain funds due to the high competition for donations and the lack of available funding to cover everyone's needs. They further show that decision-makers try to reduce the uncertainty surrounding access to scarce funding for disaster response by following two main strategies: finding alternative donors and developing long-term relationships.

Decision-makers in humanitarian contexts often make decisions based on their own experience and knowledge rather than a critical decision-making process (Charles, Lauras, Van Wassenhove, & Dupont, 2016). Behavioral operations support the idea that decision-makers often tend to overestimate their knowledge, creating biases and heuristics in the decision-making process. Future research should focus on finding and estimating behavioral models aiming to explain the biases of humanitarian decision-makers dealing with horizontal competition.

7.4.4 Vertical Coordination in Supply Chains

Decision-makers usually focus their decisions on optimizing their own objectives, which usually results in poor supply chain performance. By using contracts, firms can align their own objectives with the supply chain's objectives and, as such, improve the overall performance. There are many types of contract (Cachon, Graves, & Kok, 2003). Three of the most commonly used are: wholesale-price contract, buyback contract, and revenue-sharing contract. The wholesale-price contract is the simplest type of contract. In this, the supplier sets a fixed wholesale price, which is paid by the retailer for each unit ordered. The wholesale-price contract usually coordinates the supply chain only if the supplier earns a non-positive profit. Therefore, this type of contract is frequently not considered a coordinating contract (for further details on wholesale-price contract see Lariviere and Porteus, 2001). In a buyback contract, the retailer pays the supplier a price w per unit purchased, but receives from the supplier b per unit unsold at the end of the season, with $b < w$. Coordinating the channel requires the simultaneous adjustment of both w and b, which is often identified from first-order conditions (for further details on the wholesale-price contract see Pasternack, 1985). In a revenue-sharing contract, the supplier charges w per unit purchased and the retailer gives the supplier a percentage of his revenue. There is a close connection between revenue-sharing and buyback contracts. In fact, in many settings, they are equivalent (Cachon et al., 2003).

Katok and Wu (2009) studied the effectiveness of wholesale-price, buyback and revenue-sharing contracts to coordinate a two-echelon supply chain. Participants assume the role of either a retailer to decide the order quantity (retailer game) or a supplier to decide the contract parameters (supplier game). The authors observed that although the retailers make better ordering decisions under the buyback and revenue-sharing contracts than the wholesale-price contract, these improvements are smaller than the theoretical predictions. They also observed that suppliers do not offer contracts that coordinate the channel as much as the theory predicts, and, finally, that the mathematically equivalent buyback and revenue-sharing contracts induce different behaviors among inexperienced participants, which tend to disappear with experienced participants.

Davis, Katok, and Santamaría (2014) focus on different versions of wholesale-price contracts. They study the effectiveness of push, pull and advance purchase discount (APD) contracts to coordinate a two-echelon supply chain. In the push contract, the retailer assumes the inventory risk; the supplier sets a wholesale price while the retailer decides whether to accept it and places an order. In the pull contract the supplier assumes the inventory risk; the retailer sets a wholesale price while the supplier decides whether to accept it and produces an order. In the APD contract both parties share the inventory risk; the supplier proposes two wholesale prices (regular and discount wholesale prices), while the retailer decides whether to accept them. If he does, he places an order in advance of realized demand (a prebook) and pays the discount price. The supplier then produces an order and the retailer pays the regular price. The retailer assumes the risk for the prebook, while the supplier assumes the risk for the difference between his production and the prebook. Davis et al. (2014) observe that the pull contract leads to higher channel coordination when compared to the push contract.

However, they also observe that under-ordering was persistent, that wholesale prices systematically favored the party who assumed the inventory risk and that some profitable (unprofitable) contracts were rejected (accepted). In addition, and contrary to theoretical predictions, they observed that the APD contract did not lead to higher channel coordination in comparison to the pull contract. However, it did lead to the most equitable profit distribution.

Finally, Becker-Peth et al. (2013) analyze how buyback contracts affect channel efficiency in a two-stage supply chain. They show that buyback contracts with the same expected profit maximizing order quantity but different contract parameters result in different order quantities. Building on this insight, authors develop a behavioral model to predict ordering behavior and design supply contracts that incentivize subjects to place first-best orders. The behavioral model explains subjects' decisions, building on the concepts of prospect theory and mental accounting (Kahneman & Tversky, 1979).

7.4.4.1 Insights for Research on Humanitarian Operations

When preparing for emergencies, humanitarian organizations usually stock supplies so that when an emergency strikes, these supplies can be shipped quickly to the emergency response area. Supply chain contracts could be tested on these pre-positioning decisions. HOs would assume the role of the retailer, while the supplier would be the agent from whom the humanitarian organization procures its supplies. Care is needed when translating the contracting problem to a humanitarian context, since this context is not about optimizing profit. The chapter on framing effects in this book discusses some alternatives.

Contracts that lead to greater pre-positioned quantities could be preferred for urgent supplies since greater availability could help minimize the loss of lives and suffering, while contracts that lead to relatively low levels of pre-positioned quantities could be preferred for non-urgent supplies since less availability could help minimize expenses and/or material convergence issues. Stocking many supplies could be risky for a humanitarian organization operating with limited funds, especially if the supplies are highly perishable and/or there are no horizontal cooperation agreements to transship excess supply. Buyback contracts could help alleviate some of this risk since unused supplies would be bought back by the supplier. APD contracts could also help alleviate some of this risk since a humanitarian organization could pre-position some quantities at discounted prices.

7.5 Conclusion

Behavioral studies on humanitarian operations are scarce (Sankaranarayanan, Castañeda, & Villa, 2017). Therefore, developing experiments focused on the humanitarian context and building on the four mechanisms described in Sect. 7.2 provides an interesting trend for future research. Future experiments within the humanitarian setting should test how subjects balance coordination and competition when deciding on the best way to satisfy people's needs. In addition, experiments should explore how subjects' strategies deviate from optimal coordinated strategies.

References

Acimovic, J., & Goentzel, J. (2016). Models and metrics to assess humanitarian response capacity. *Journal of Operations Management, 45*, 11–29.

Ahn, T. K., Ostrom, E., & Walker, J. (2011). Reprint of: A common-pool resource experiment with postgraduate subjects from 41 countries. *Ecological Economics, 70*(9), 1580–1589.

Armony, M., & Plambeck, E. L. (2005). The impact of duplicate orders on demand estimation and capacity investment. *Management Science, 51*(10), 1505–1518.

Axelrod, R. (1976). *Structure of decision: The cognitive maps of political elites*. Princeton, NJ: Princeton University Press.

Axsäter, S. (2003). A new decision rule for lateral transshipments in inventory systems. *Management Science, 49*(9), 1168–1179.

Becker-Peth, M., Katok, E., & Thonemann, U. W. (2013). Designing buyback contracts for irrational but predictable newsvendors. *Management Science, 59*(8), 1800–1816.

Besiou, M., Stapleton, O., & van Wassenhove, L. N. (2010). *Exploring the known and the unknown: Future possibilities of system dynamics for humanitarian operations*. Fontainebleau.

Bhattacharya, S., Hasija, S., & Van Wassenhove, L. N. (2014). Designing efficient infrastructure investment and asset transfer mechanisms in humanitarian supply chains. *Production and Operations Management, 23*(9), 1511–1521.

Bolton, G. E., & Katok, E. (2008). Learning by doing in the newsvendor problem: A laboratory investigation of the role of experience and feedback. *Manufacturing & Service Operations Management, 10*(3), 519–538.

Bostian, A. A., Holt, C. A., & Smith, A. M. (2008). Newsvendor "Pull-to-Center" effect: Adaptive learning in a laboratory experiment. *Manufacturing & Service Operations Management, 10*(4), 590–608.

Cachon, G. P., Graves, S. C., & Kok, A. G. D. (2003). Supply chain coordination with contracts. *Handbooks in Operations Research and Management Science, 11*, 227–339.

Cachon, G. P., & Olivares, M. (2009). Competing retailers and inventory: An empirical investigation of General Motors' dealerships in isolated U.S. markets. *Management Science, 55*(9), 1586–1604.

Cárdenas, J. C. (2000). How do groups solve local commons dilemmas? Lessons from experimental economics in the field. *Environment, Development and Sustainability, 2*(3–4), 305–322.

Castillo, D., & Saysel, A. K. (2005). Simulation of common pool resource field experiments: A behavioral model of collective action. *Ecological Economics, 55*(3), 420–436.

Charles, A., Lauras, M., van Wassenhove, L. N., & Dupont, L. (2016). Designing an efficient humanitarian supply network. *Journal of Operations Management, 48*, 58–70.

Chen, L., & Lee, H. L. (2011). Bullwhip effect measurement and its implications. *Operations Research, 60*(4), 771–778.

Croson, R., & Donohue, K. (2005). Upstream versus downstream information and its impact on the bullwhip effect. *System Dynamics Review, 21*(3), 249–260.

Croson, R., Donohue, K., Katok, E., & Sterman, J. D. (2014). Order stability in supply chains: Coordination risk and the role of coordination stock. *Production and Operations Management, 23*(2), 176–196.

Croson, R., & Ren, Y. (2013). Overconfidence in newsvendor orders: An experimental study. *Management Science, 59*(11), 2502–2517.

Davis, A. M., Katok, E., & Santamaría, N. (2014). Push, pull, or both? A behavioral study of how the allocation of inventory risk affects channel efficiency. *Management Science, 60*(11), 2666–2683.

Diehl, E., & Sterman, J. D. (1995). Effects of feedback complexity on dynamic decision making. *Organizational Behavior and Human Decision Processes, 62*(2), 198–215.

Dong, L., & Rudi, N. (2004). Who benefits from transshipment? Exogenous vs. endogenous wholesale prices. *Management Science, 50*(5), 645–657.

Donohue, K. L., & Croson, R. (2002). Experimental economics management supply-chain. *Interfaces, 32*(5), 74–82.

Dörner, D. (1980). On the difficulties people have in dealing with complexity. *Simulation Games, 11*(1), 87–106.

Einhorn, H. J., & Hogarth, R. M. (1981). Behavioral decision theory: Processes of judgement and choice. *Annual Review of Psychology, 32*(1), 53–88.

Ergun, O., Karakus, G., Keskinocak, P., Swann, J., & Villarreal, M. (2010). Operations research to improve disaster supply chain management. In *Wiley encyclopedia of operations research and management science*. Hoboken, NJ: John Wiley & Sons.

Fehr, E., & Schmidt, K. M. (1999). A theory of fairness, competition, and cooperation. *The Quarterly Journal of Economics, 114*(3), 817–868.

Forrester, J. W. (1961). *Industrial dynamics*. Cambridge, MA: MIT Press.

Gonçalves, P., & Villa, S. (2016). Implications of misperception of feedback on behavior in operations. In M. Kunc, J. Malpass, & L. White (Eds.), *Behavioural operational research: Theory, methodology and practice*. London, UK: Palgrave Publishers.

Halachmi, A. (2002). Performance measurement and government productivity. *Work Study, 51*(2), 63–73.

Herer, Y. T., Tzur, M., & Yücesan, E. (2006). The multi-location transshipment problem. *IIE Transactions, 38*(3), 1–33.

Ho, T. H., Lim, N., & Cui, T. H. (2010). Reference dependence in multilocation newsvendor models: A structural analysis. *Management Science, 56*(11), 1891–1910.

Holguín-veras, J., Jaller, M., Wassenhove, L. N. Van, Pérez, N., & Wachtendorf, T. (2012). On the unique features of post-disaster humanitarian logistics. *Journal of Operations Management, 30*(7–8), 494–506.

Hu, X., Duenyas, I., & Kapuscinski, R. (2007). Existence of coordinating transshipment prices in a two-location inventory model. *Management Science, 53*(8), 1289–1302.

Kaatrud, D. B., Samii, R., & van Wassenhove, L. N. (2003). UN joint logistics centre: A coordinated response to common humanitarian logistics concerns. *Forced Migration Review, 18*(1), 11–18.

Kahneman, D., & Tversky, A. (1979). Prospect theory: An analysis of decision under risk. *Econometrica: Journal of the Econometric Society, 47*(3), 263–291.

Katok, E., & Wu, D. Y. (2009). Contracting in supply chains: A laboratory investigation. *Management Science, 55*(12), 1953–1968.

Kent, R. C. (1987). *Anatomy of disaster relief: The international network in action.* London, UK: Pinter Publishers.

Kleinmuntz, D. N., & Thomas, J. B. (1987). The value of action and inference in dynamic decision making. *Organizational Behavior and Human Decision Processes, 39*(3), 341–364.

Lariviere, M., & Porteus, E. L. (2001). Selling to the newsvendor: An analysis of price-only contracts. *Manufacturing & Service Operations Management, 3*(4), 293–305.

Latham, G., & Locke, E. (1991). Self-regulation through goal-setting. *Organizational Behavior and Human Decision Making, 50*, 212–247.

Lee, H. L., Padmanabhan, V., & Whang, S. (1997a). Information distortion in a supply chain: The bullwhip effect. *Management Science, 43*(4), 546–558.

Lee, H. L., Padmanabhan, V., & Whang, S. (1997b). The bullwhip effect in supply chains. *Review, 38*(3), 93–102.

Leiras, A., de Brito, I., Jr., Queiroz, E., Rejane, T., & Yoshida, H. T. (2014). Literature review of humanitarian logistics research: Trends and challenges. *Journal of Humanitarian Logistics and Supply Chain Management, 4*(1), 95–130.

Lessmann, C., & Markwardt, G. (2016). Aid, growth, and devolution: Considering aid modality and different types of decentralization. *World Development, 84*, 118–130.

Lindenberg, M., & Bryant, C. (2001). *Going global: Transforming relief and development NGOs.* Bloomfield, CT: Kumarian Press.

Lippman, S. A., & McCardle, K. F. (1997). The competitive newsboy. *Operations Research, 45*, 54–65.

Moore, D. A., & Healy, P. J. (2008). The trouble with overconfidence. *Psychological Review, 115*(2), 502.

Netessine, S., Rudi, N., & Wang, Y. (2001). *Dynamic inventory competition and customer retention.* Philadelphia, PA.

Nunnenkamp, P., Öhler, H., & Sosa Andrés, M. (2017). Need, merit and politics in multilateral aid allocation: A district-level analysis of World Bank projects in India. *Review of Development Economics, 21*(1), 126–156.

Oloruntoba, R., & Gray, R. (2006). Humanitarian aid: An agile supply chain? *Supply Chain Management: An International Journal, 11*(2), 115–120.

Olson, M. (1965). The logic of collective action. Cambridge, Mass.: Harvard University Press.

Ostrom, E. (1990). *Governing the commons: The evolution of institutions for collective action* (p. 271). Cambridge: Cambridge University Press.

Ostrom, E. (1998). A behavioral approach to the rational choice theory of collective action: Presidential address, American Political Science Association, 1997. *The American Political Science Review, 92*(1), 1–22.

Ostrom, E. (2000). Collective action and the evolution of social norms. *Journal of Economic Perspectives, 14*(3), 137–158.

Ovchinnikov, A., Moritz, B., & Quiroga, B. F. (2015). How to compete against a behavioral newsvendor. *Production and Operations Management, 24*(11), 1783–1793.

Pedraza-Martinez, A. J., & van Wassenhove, L. N. (2012). Transportation and vehicle fleet management in humanitarian logistics: Challenges for future research. *EURO Journal on Transportation and Logistics, 1*, 185–196.

Rudi, N., Kapur, S., & Pyke, D. F. (2001). A two-location inventory with transshipment and a local decision making. *Management Science, 47*(12), 1668–1680.

Sankaranarayanan, K., Castañeda, J. A., & Villa, S. (2017). Future research in humanitarian operations: A behavioral operations perspective. In G. Kovács, K. Spens, & M. Moshtari (Eds.), *Handbook of humanitarian logistics and supply chain management*. London, UK: Palgrave Publishers.

Schweitzer, M. E., & Cachon, G. P. (2000). Decision bias in the newsvendor problem with a known demand distribution: Experimental evidence. *Management Science, 46*(3), 404–420.

Sošić, G. (2006). Transshipment of inventories among retailers: Myopic versus farsighted stability. *Management Science, 52*(10), 1493–1508.

Starr, M. K., & van Wassenhove, L. N. (2014). Introduction to the special issue on humanitarian operations and crisis management. *Production and Operations Management, 23*(6), 925–937.

Stauffer, J. M., Pedraza-Martinez, A. J., & Van Wassenhove, L. N. (2016). Temporary hubs for the global vehicle supply chain in humanitarian operations. *Production and Operations Management, 25*(2), 192–209.

Stephenson, M., Jr. (2005). Making humanitarian relief networks more effective: Operational coordination, trust and sense making. *Disasters, 29*(4), 337–350.

Stephenson, M., Jr., & Schnitzer, M. H. (2006). Interorganizational trust, boundary spanning, and humanitarian relief coordination. *Nonprofit Management and Leadership, 17*(2), 211–232.

Sterman, J. D. (1989a). Misperceptions of feedback in dynamic decision making. *Organizational Behavior and Human Decision Processes, 43*(3), 301–335.
Sterman, J. D. (1989b). Modeling managerial behavior: Misperceptions of feedback in a dynamic decision making experiment. *Management Science, 35*(3), 321–339.
Sterman, J. D. (2000). *Business dynamics: Systems thinking and modeling for a complex world*. Chicago, IL: Irwin-McGraw Hill.
Sterman, J. D. (2001). System dynamics modeling: Tools for learning in a complex world. *California Management Review, 43*(4), 8–25.
Sterman, J. D., & Dogan, G. (2015). "I'm not hoarding, I'm just stocking up before the hoarders get here." Behavioral causes of phantom ordering in supply chains. *Journal of Operations Management, 39–40*(C), 6–22.
Tomasini, R., & van Wassenhove, L. N. (2009). *Humanitarian logistics* (Vol. 20, 1st ed.). London, UK: Palgrave Macmillan.
Tversky, A. (1972). Elimination by aspects: A theory of choice. *Psychological Review, 79*(4), 281–299.
Tversky, A., & Kahneman, D. (1974). Judgment under uncertainty: Heuristics and biases. *Science, 185*(4157), 1124–1131.
Urrea, G., Villa, S., & Gonçalves, P. (2016). Exploratory analyses of relief and development operations using social networks. *Socio-Economic Planning Sciences, 56*, 27–39.
Urrea, G., Villa, S., & Quintane, E. (2018). *In need of aid: Accessing financial resources for humanitarian operations*. Working paper, University of Los Andes.
van Wassenhove, L. N. (2006). Humanitarian aid logistics: Supply chain management in high gear. *Journal of the Operational Research Society, 57*(1), 475–489.
Villa, S. (2018). *Behavioral analysis of the effect of order duplications in single-supplier multi-retailer supply chains*. Working paper, University of Los Andes.
Villa, S., & Castañeda, J. A. (2018). Transshipments in supply chains: A behavioral investigation. *European Journal of Operational Research, 269*(2), 715–729.
Villa, S., Gonçalves, P., & Arango, S. (2015). Exploring retailers' ordering decisions under delays. *System Dynamics Review, 31*(1), 1–27.
Villa, S., & Katok, E. (2018). *Negotiating transfer prices for improving supply chain transshipments*. Working paper, University of Texas at Dallas.
Zhao, H., Xu, L., & Siemsen, E. (2016). *A behavioral perspective on inventory sharing*. Working paper, Wisconsin School of Business.

8

Quantal Theory in Operations Management

Yefen Chen and Yanan Song

8.1 Introduction

Ample evidence revealing the significant and growing impact of natural disasters or unpredictable crises on human well-being and economics points to the importance of humanitarian operations. For example, the Great Wenchuan earthquake in southwest China left about 4.8 million people homeless, over 69,000 people lost their lives, 374,176 were reported injured, and 18,222 people were listed as missing in July 2008. After the earthquake, there were approximately 15 million people living in the affected area with a massive and urgent need for supplies of medicine, food and basic needs, which were tragically disrupted. Such situations require immediate response in order to provide relief and aid for the vulnerable people. However, such operations are not exempt

---

Y. Chen (✉)
Cainiao Smart Logistics Network, Hangzhou, China

Y. Song
Academy of Mathematics and System Sciences, Chinese Academy of Sciences, Beijing, China

from difficulties, such as, for example, how to alleviate suffering and prevent loss of lives, how to reconstruct the facilities, and how to reduce social vulnerability (Van Wassenhove, 2006). They also usually engage very different participants, who may be more heterogeneous in terms of culture, purposes, interests, mandates, capacity, and logistics expertise (Balcik, Beamon, Krejci, Muramatsu, & Ramirez, 2010). Operational goals and management strategies vary across different organizations, meaning that participants' decisions are usually accompanied by various behavioral preferences, which have a profound influence on operational outcomes.

The humanitarian focus is on ensuring human well being, e.g., relieving people's pain, and improving their satisfaction and happiness. As such, humanitarian operations deal with the management and distribution of medical supplies for routine disease prevention, food supplies to fight hunger, and critical supplies in the aftermath of a disaster (Holguín-Veras et al. 2012). Compared with commercial operations, the situation and demand of humanitarian operations is more unpredictable and emergent, and deals with unpredictable crises such as earthquakes, tsunamis, terrorist attacks, etc. The purpose of the former is to minimize the operational cost and maximize the system profit in a relatively stable environment, whereas the latter seeks to minimize the social costs including the operational costs and the deprivation costs in a more variable and more complex situation, especially in post-disaster humanitarian operations.

The human being is central to humanitarian operations, whereby the preferences and choices determine the effectiveness and the efficiency of the operational outcomes. A human being's behavioral standard is generally guided by his personal values, which are in turn formulated based on ethical and social norms, moral rules, beliefs, etc. (Fehr & Fischbacher, 2004). People do not only care about the monetary pay-offs, they also have other preferences, which also help determine their choices. Human actions are usually accompanied by error, which may not exactly follow utility optimization from their personal valuations. Many researchers in the fields of psychology, economics, and social science have shown that people's cognitive and computational capabilities are limited so that they do not behave like perfect optimizers (e.g., Fey,

McKelvey, & Palfrey, 1996; McKelvey & Palfrey, 1992; Goeree & Holt, 2001). In practice, the forecasting of human activities by assuming perfect rationality usually fails to describe the realized behavior, which has profound implications on humanitarian operations. Let us take an example of a soldier in combat to illustrate this. An armed terrorist, who has killed many people, takes a woman from the crowd and uses her as a human shield while he continues to shoot people from behind her. An anti-terrorist commando tries to target the terrorist behind the woman without hurting the woman. The anti-terrorist team fails to target the terrorist, and some additional people are killed. Finally, the terrorist is shot but so is the woman. If you were the judge, how would you judge the anti-terrorist team? If you deem that people can optimize their decisions, you probably find the anti-terrorist team guilty because it should have shot the terrorist sooner to avoid other deaths. But, if you understand that the anti-terrorist team is not innately perfectly rational, you would probably judge it not guilty. This example shows us that understanding the behavioral rules followed by human beings is crucial to managing human society.

In this chapter, we introduce a quantal theory, which takes humans' innate characteristics of decision error into account and provides a mathematical model to capture the decision error in human decision-making processes. The model provides three advantages. First, the quantal choice model is concise, and includes only one behavioral parameter, which can be varied from zero to infinity to obtain predictions with different degrees of rationality. Second, the quantal choice model can be integrated with other behavioral models, which can be embedded into the quantal choice structure to obtain the corresponding predictions with multiple behavioral factors. Third, the quantal choice model fits the data well in existing laboratory experiments. There is evidence showing that the quantal choice model is powerful in accounting for the decision error and to describe subjects' subsequent choices in most commercial operations problems. Although its application to humanitarian problems is not, so far, widespread, future studies can employ the model in analyzing victims' decisions to obtain a more accurate description of human nature.

8.2 Quantal Response Equilibrium

We describe quantal theory through operations management, which plays an important role in improving effectiveness and efficiency in various areas. In humanitarian operations, players from multiple organizations are frequently engaged in situations that include strategic interactions to compete/cooperate with each other. Quantal theory provides a mathematical tool to analyze the equilibrium strategy in predicting the choices of each player when decision errors are considered. We further introduce the quantal theory in the context of its versatility in interpreting and describing human decisions in solving operational problems. Generally, we introduce five representative operations problems, which can be categorized into three types. The first type is the single-period inventory problem with demand uncertainty, known as the newsvendor problem, which presents the economic tradeoff of different inventory costs. The second type involves the strategy interactions between multiple decision-makers in retailer-retailer competition capacity and principle-agent contracts, which respectively present the competition and the cooperation involved between multiple players. The final type involves strategic customer purchasing in advance or waiting behavior, and in terms of the queuing problem, is based on individual choices in planning their consumption.

Quantal theory describes the individuals' probabilistic choice and has been proven as a powerful tool in capturing human decision-making behavior during the past 50 years since Luce (1959). Rather than the assumption of perfect optimizer in standard theory, the quantal theory allows decision errors in the choices made, which is closer to the nature of human beings. When decision-makers face choice alternatives $i \in I$ generating utility u_i, they do not always choose the utility-maximizing alternative $i^* \in \arg\max_i u_i$. Instead, they maximize $u_i + \varepsilon_i$, where ε_i presents the errors in calculating the utilities associated with alternatives. Many reasons in the practical world cause such decision noise; for example, humans' limited cognitive and computational abilities. In quantal theory, the predicted choices that consider decision errors follow a rule that all alternatives have a positive probability of being chosen and that there is a greater probability of more attractive alternatives being chosen (yielding higher utility).

The multinomial logit choice model has received considerable attention in operations management after Su (2008) showed its strength in interpreting the well-known pull-to-center and bullwhip effects. When the noise terms ε_i are independent and identically distributed with an extreme-value distribution (McFadden, 1981), the choice probability can be formulated using a multinomial logit model. The probability of choosing alternative $i \in I$ is

$$\varphi_i = \frac{e^{u_i/\beta}}{\sum_{i \in I} e^{u_i/\beta}}$$

for the discrete alternative set. For the continued alternative set X, the probability of choosing alternative x is

$$\varphi(x) = \frac{e^{u(x)/\beta}}{\int_{x \in X} e^{u(x)/\beta}}.$$

From the above models, we can see that the possibility of choosing alternative x is proportional to the value of $e^{u(x)/\beta}$, where β is a positive parameter reflecting the level of decision errors. Parameter β is a positive value, which is often referred to as a precision parameter and interpreted as the extent of bounded rationality. When parameter β goes to infinity, the choice distribution $\phi(\cdot)$ captures the case that the decision-maker lacks the ability to make any rational judgment and thus randomizes all alternatives with equal probability. When parameter β is zero, the choice distribution $\phi(\cdot)$ captures the case of the perfect optimizer where the decision-maker chooses the payoff-maximizing alternative with certainty. If there is more than one optimal option, these optimal options will be chosen with equal probability.

In the game-theoretical setting, the player's utility depends on her choice and others' choices. So a player has to predict other players' choices, and then choose her best response accordingly. The standard method assumes that each player is a perfect optimizer and employs Nash theory to predict the player's actions. However, sizable laboratory experiments show that human players do not take the actions predicted by the Nash equilibrium. To account for the decision errors, McKelvey and Palfrey (1995) proposed the idea of quantal response equilibrium (QRE) to describe the noisy strategic interactions between multiple players. The QRE model embeds the multinomial logit choice model into each individual player's decision framework so that each player is modeled as a noisy optimizer, which is closer to reality.

QRE distribution is solved from a fixed point function. The probability of choosing alternative x is

$$f(x) = \frac{\exp\{E\pi(x,R)/\beta\}}{\sum_{x' \in X} \exp\{E\pi(x',R)/\beta\}},$$

where $E\pi(x, R)$ is the expected utility giving other players' QRE distribution as R. QRE has two properties. First, players choose stochastic best responses following a multinomial logit model, and the predicted choice is a distribution that all feasible actions are chosen with strictly positive probability. The alternative with higher expected utility is chosen more often. Second, players face uncertainty in terms of their opponents' choices because they recognize that their opponents are also playing stochastic best responses. Similar to the Nash equilibrium, the QRE is internally consistent in the sense that players have rational expectations and possess correct beliefs of the probability distributions over opponents' actions.

8.3 Quantal Theory in Operations Management

To illustrate the strength of quantal theory, we briefly report its applications in five operations management problems: (1) the newsvendor problem; (2) capacity allocation games; (3) the supply chain contract; (4) strategic consumers; (5) the queuing problem.

8.3.1 Single-Period Inventory Problem Under Demand Uncertainty: Newsvendor Problem

The newsvendor model is one of the main building blocks in operations management, which represents a category problem of a decision-maker employing tradeoffs between the pros and cons with uncertainty. The model derives its name from the canonical setting of a newsvendor facing random demand, where the newsvendor has to decide how many newspapers to order: excess quantities that remain unsold have no value, but too few copies means that customers have to be turned away and potential profits are lost. This model has a simple solution—the optimal order quantity is characterized by a critical fractile, which is a ratio of underage cost and overage cost. This solution has extensive applications, including both commercial and humanitarian operations. Yet, does this solution truly describe human decision-makers' decision-making rules? Numerous experimental studies (e.g., Schweitzer & Cachon, 2000; Bolton & Katok, 2008) test this theoretical solution and find some systematic decision biases. As shown in Fig. 8.1, a human newsvendor tends to order too much of the "low-profit" products and too little of the "high-profit" products, producing the so-called "pull-to-center" effect.

Many papers focus on figuring out the behavioral drives behind the "pull-to-center" effect. Decision noise is one of the accepted

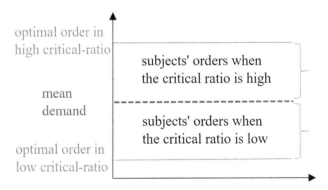

Fig. 8.1 Demand and order quantity in newsvendor experiment

explanations. Su (2008) posits that the quantal choice model taking decision noise into account can generate some of the laboratory observations in newsvendor experiments. They solve the newsvendor's order quantity by embedding the newsvendor's payoff function into the multinomial logit model, as shown in Sect. 8.2. The behavioral solution of order quantity follows a truncated normal distribution over the interval of alternatives when the newsvendor's market demand follows a uniform distribution. The mean of the normal distribution is the standard optimal order solution, but its variance increases with the rational parameter β. This truncated normal distribution fits well with the "pull-to-center" effect. When the profit margin is high enough for the critical fractile to be above 0.5, the expected behavioral solution is below the optimal solution, i.e., under-ordering in high-profit conditions. When the profit margin is low enough for the critical fractile to be below 0.5, the expected behavioral solution is above the optimal solution, i.e., over-ordering in low-profit conditions. These trends coincide well with the experimental data shown in Fig. 8.1. In addition, the level of decision error can further explain the degree of bias. The higher the level of decision error, the more the behavioral solution deviates from the optimal solution. The behavioral parameter β can be manipulated to represent different degrees of decision error.

In after-disaster operations, one of the main challenges faced by humanitarian organizations is to define how many units of food, materials, and medicines should be stocked in order to satisfy the uncertain demand, how many volunteers to recruit to satisfy the uncertain environment, and how many warehouses to build to supply the uncertain demand. These decision problems are essentially newsvendor problems. The existing behavioral studies on the newsvendor problem show us that humanitarian managers incorporate decision errors and the corresponding choices can be described using the multinomial logit choice model. Specifically, the quantities ordered by managers probably exhibit the "pull-to-center" effect. Future research can focus on understanding the behavioral rules and designing behavioral mechanisms to rectify the human decision bias in the specific situations of unpredictable crisis.

8.3.2 Multiple Players Competing for Limited Resource: Capacity Allocation Games

The capacity allocation game is another typical problem in operations management, which represents the competition of limited resources/products between multiple players. This model studies how retailers submit orders to the supplier for competing allocation when the supplier's capacity is not large enough to cover the total demands from downstream retailers. In humanitarian operations, the problem of allocating limited resources occurs frequently; e.g., how to allocate the limited food, material, and medicine supplies to the people with different levels of emergency, how to grant the limited donations to different organizations/applicants, and how to divide the limited service capability to the massive needs of vulnerable people. An accurate understanding of the competing behavior of potential applicants is essential to find an optimal allocation scheme.

The Nash theory is a commonly used tool to analyze the equilibrium choices of multiple players in a game-theoretical setting, in which perfect rationality is common knowledge. When the supplier applies a proportional allocation scheme to divide his capacity, it is a well-known fact that the retailers will submit more orders than they need. To test whether human retailers follow the Nash theory to place their orders, laboratory experiments are conducted. The data shows that human players do not strategize as Nash theory predicts. Chen, Su, and Zhao (2012) experimentally study a capacity allocation game with two retailers facing the same market demand. When there is a supply shortage, Nash theory predicts that the retailers should submit their orders up to the upper bound. In their setting, the Nash equilibrium does not change with the procurement cost. However, the experimental data shows that human subjects' orders are systematically below the Nash equilibrium and vary across different costs. As shown in Fig. 8.2 the data distribute over the interval [0, 100], which goes against the Nash equilibrium 100.

Decision noise can explain why subjects in capacity allocation games place substantially lower order quantities than what is predicted by

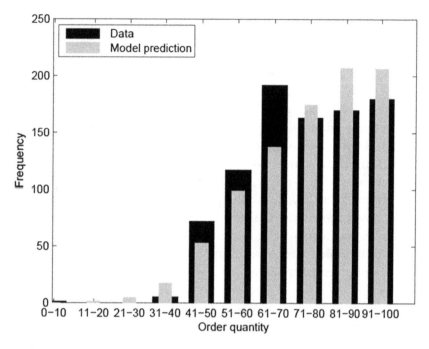

Fig. 8.2 Experimental data vs. quantal response equilibrium predictions in a high-cost condition

Nash theory. With decision noise, the quantal response equilibrium model predicts that orders by human players distribute over a range [0, 100] but that they do not concentrate at 100, which is closer to human actions. Moreover, under the same degree of decision noise, the orders placed in low-cost conditions are, on average, higher than those placed in high-cost conditions, illustrating more subtle descriptions of the data. It was also found that the decision error of human players decreases by repeatedly playing the game. In Fig. 8.2, we can see that the distribution of players' choices are increasingly closer to the Nash equilibrium as the decision round proceeds. The structural estimates show that parameter β presents a decreasing trend with the decision rounds. Finally, their analyses show that the decision error in players' bounded rationality is permanent (i.e., the value of β is always positive) although players are increasingly rational.

The above behavioral studies show us that the players involved in these capacity allocation games present systematic deviations from the standard theoretical predictions. In the practice of humanitarian operations, considering people's decision error in forecasting the applications/orders of funds/materials is important in order to improve the correctness of the optimization model. The QRE model can be a good mathematical tool.

8.3.3 Principle-Agent Interactions: Supply Chain Contract

Supply chain contracts deal with the incentive conflicts of vertical firms. Decentralized decisions made by two firms usually make system performance worse than centralized decisions made by a merged firm (Spengler, 1950). In humanitarian operations, different organizations are frequently engaged in participating contracts to establish cooperative relationships to provide relief and aid for the vulnerable group. Thus, coordination and collaboration among all the actors involved in the humanitarian emergency deserve particular attention (Balcik et al., 2010; Kovács & Spens, 2007, 2009; Maon, Lindgreen, & Vanhamme, 2009; Tomasini & Van Wassenhove, 2009a, 2009b). The studies of supply chain contracts in an inventory context show us how to coordinate two vertical parties to achieve maximum welfare. In the context of inventory management, the decentralized firm has a lower profit margin than the whole system, thus the optimal choice of inventory for the decentralized firm is actually not the best for the system. This conflict of interest between the firm and system is called double marginalization. To resolve this problem, coordination contracts are developed to motivate the firm to take action to maximize system performance. Most of the literature formulates the double marginalization problem as a two-stage Stackberg game between one supplier and one buyer. Usually, the seller is assumed as a leader who moves first and proposes a contract to the buyer. The buyer is a follower and moves second by either accepting the contract by placing a positive order, or rejecting it so that both parties end up with zero earnings. During the past two decades, various contracts have been proposed to make the supply chain coordinate, e.g., revenue sharing, buyback, quantity discount, and fixed fee (Cachon, 2003; Cachon & Lariviere, 2005). The parameters in the coordination contracts are determined by the seller and the buyer making the best choices to optimize system performance.

An important assumption in existing theoretical literature is that the buyer and seller are perfect optimizers who can accurately predict each other's action and implement the best response. However, recent laboratory studies have found that this assumption may not hold in practice. Even if the experiments are conducted with the simplest settings, the human managers under the contract theoretically coordinating the supply chain cannot make the system achieve coordination (Katok & Wu, 2009). On one hand, the followers (buyers) do not respond to the given contracts as theory predicts they should. On the other, the leader (supplier) does not offer the contract parameters coordinating the system. In sum, there are two mainly behavioral explanations in existing literature. First, the contract participants may have some specific behavioral preferences which drive the deviation of their utility function from the stand point theory, e.g., loss-aversion (Lim & Ho, 2007) and fairness (Katok & Pavlov, 2013). Second, the contract participants have to deal with decision noise in maximizing their utility as well as predicting the other's action. For example, Lim and Ho (2007) experimentally study the quantity discount contract and find that the quantal response framework provides a good description of the decision error during the strategic interaction between the supplier and the buyer. Another study by Ho and Zhang (2008) of fix fee contracts, also finds that quantal response equilibrium can capture the supplier/buyer's choice well.

Decision error is innate for human decision-makers although cognitive or computational capability can be improved through experience or training. To better coordinate the system, the contract designer in the supply chain management should take this innate characteristic into account. A recent study by Pavlov, Katok, Haruvy, and Olsen (2016) considers the decision error of human managers, and characterizes a supplier's optimal contract. They compare three types of contract: the wholesale price contract, two-part tariff contract, and minimum order quantity contract. A quantal choice framework is applied to describe the bounded rationality associated with the participant's decision. They show that the supplier's choice of contract parameter depends on the form of the contract as well as the buyer's decision.

The above studies on the inventory contract provide us with insightful evidence to understand the partnerships and collaborative behavior between vertical organizations in humanitarian operations. Although the conflicts of interest in humanitarian operations may not be the same as the double marginalization in the inventory contract, their conflicts will present some similarities and the research method can be shared. Generally, the decision tasks and situations are more complex in humanitarian operations than in commercial ones; thus, we expect more behavioral preferences which impact the social and economic outcomes to appear in the humanitarian context. This encourages us to explore this fruitful area in studying its specific behavioral preferences. It helps to further design proper contracts and partnerships to help reduce pain and deaths (or improve social welfare) in humanitarian crises.

8.3.4 Buy Now or Wait for a Discounted Price: Strategic Customers

Strategic customers are those who strategically choose either to buy a product immediately or to wait for a lower price when there is a possibility of a future discount (Elmaghraby, Gülcü, & Keskinocak, 2008). Strategic customer behavior has been widely studied in operations management. In humanitarian operations, there may be no discount environment for this kind of consumer behavior. However, humanitarian operations often aim at rescuing the victim who may have to make a strategic choice as to whether to stock the goods and materials before the disaster, and whether to save himself or wait for rescue (Lorenz, Schulze, & Voss, 2017; Helsloot & Ruitenberg, 2004; Perry & Lindell, 2003). The study of strategic decision behavior in commercial operations can be a meaningful reference in understanding the victim's behavior in humanitarian operations.

Most existing studies on strategic customer behavior apply standard theory to analyze two different pricing policies: announced fixed-discount and contingent pricing (Cachon & Swinney, 2009). Both are commonly applied in practice. The announced fixed-discount policy requires the seller to commit to its price menu, whereas in the contingent pricing policy, the seller determines the discount price in accordance with the number of leftover products. Under the fixed-discount policy, strategic customers can recognize the prices and the stock quantity of two periods. If they choose to buy immediately, they can obviously obtain the products; if they choose to wait for a discount, they may face competition and the product may be sold out because the stock quantity is limited. Thus, a customer-game arises among multiple customers. Nash theory is a standard method to analyze the equilibrium choices of multiple customers in such a customer-game. Generally, customers make their choices by comparing the expected payoffs of either buying or waiting.

Some recent laboratory experiments have shown that customers do not behave as the standard theory predicts. Song and Zhao (2016) conducted laboratory experiments to investigate the announced fixed-discount policy and explore the decision behavior of human customers, showing that the choices made by human subjects exhibit a deviation from the Nash equilibrium. As shown in Table 8.1, the ratio of waiting observed in experiment $\bar{\alpha}$ is 0.878, which is different from the Nash predictions $\tilde{\alpha}*$. Here, 1 refers to "all-wait" and 0 refers to "all-buy". From columns $V_w(\bar{\alpha})$ (expected payoff of waiting) and V_b (expected payoff of buying), we can see that the best response for each customer is "all-wait", which is the same as the Nash equilibrium. So the results of $\bar{\alpha}$ indicate that subjects would like to have the best response more often instead of fixing on it; thus, the decision behavior of subjects is suitable for the features of QRE. As such, they develop behavioral models using the QRE framework, based on which the extent of bounded rationality is

Table 8.1 Comparison between the experimental data and Nash predictions

Nash predictions			Experimental observations		
$\tilde{\alpha}*$	$V_w(\tilde{\alpha}*)$	V_b	$\bar{\alpha}$	$V_w(\bar{\alpha})$	V_b
1	5	3	0.878	4.896	3

Source: From Song and Zhao (2017)

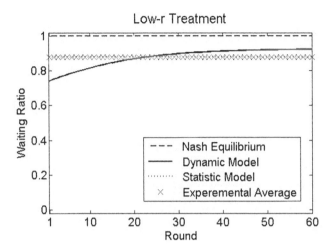

Fig. 8.3 Comparison among the experimental data, Nash predictions and quantal response equilibrium predictions

estimated. The QRE model provides a ratio between the two pure-strategy Nash equilibriums 0 and 1, which is closer to the data. As shown in Fig. 8.3, the QRE models fit the experimental data better than the Nash equilibriums, especially the dynamic model which considers time trends. We can see that the QRE model provides a simple but compelling explanation that describes / predicts the purchasing behavior of strategic customers. Further, Song and Zhao (2017) investigate the influence of bounded rational behavior of strategic customers on newsvendor decisions and profit. They show that the newsvendor should make order decisions considering the bounded rationality of customers.

Their studies show the importance of considering customer behavior in running efficient retailing system. The same happens in the humanitarian system. The bounded rationality of participants should be considered in the optimization model. For example, the strategic behavior of victims influences the practical demand of transportation, which further influences post-disaster logistics planning. It is necessary to consider the bounded rationality of victims when we optimize the transportation capability and routing. One can use QRE to predict the needs and demands of victims, which is helpful in more accurately forecasting and improving system performance.

8.3.5 Customer Queuing Behavior of Estimating Waiting Time

The queuing or service system is an important research area in operations management. Recently, the study of queuing or service system has been paid much attention in humanitarian operations, especially in the area of healthcare (Jiang & Giachetti, 2008; Lakshmi & Sivakumar, 2013). However, few studies on the queuing or service system in humanitarian operations consider the bounded rationality of customers, despite this being an important and meaningful research area. In operations management, some researchers incorporate customer decisions into a queuing model (Naor, 1969). They assume customers to be fully rational and able to perfectly estimate their expected waiting time and expected utility of joining. In other words, it is typical to assume that a customer is perfectly rational in existing queuing literature: if the expected utility is higher than zero, the customer will join the system; otherwise, the customer will balk. However, accurately computing expected waiting and service time is a hard task for customers. Anecdotal evidence and experimental studies show that when a customer queues up for service, he can never accurately and perfectly calculate the benefits and costs of joining before making his decisions.

Huang, Allon, and Bassamboo (2013) study canonical service models with boundedly rational customers. They employ the quantal choice model to describe a random error term in a customer's expected waiting time estimation. This reflects their inability to accurately assess the utility obtained from each action. Furthermore, they investigate the impact of bounded rationality from both a profit-maximizing firm and a social planner's perspective. Their study provides several insightful results on the impact of decision error on system operations. For visible queues (such as a fast food restaurant, a cafe or an ATM), with the optimal price, a little bounded rationality can result in revenue and welfare loss, whereas, with a fixed price, a little bounded rationality can lead to an improvement of social well-being. For invisible queues (such as the call center), bounded rationality benefits the firm when the bounded rationality of customers is sufficient. For both visible and invisible queues, ignoring bounded rationality can result in significant loss of revenue and well-being. Moreover, the loss of revenue and well-being is not necessarily monotone with respect to the level of bounded rationality.

In the queuing system, humanitarian operations advocate for paying attention to consumers' experiences and feelings. The above study shows us that system performance is sensitive to the degree of bounded rationality in customers' choices and that a customer's utility is also sensitive to other customers' rationality. When we formulate the optimal queuing rules after disaster, the bounded rationality of victims will affect the utility function of each victim's experiences and feelings. This reminds us that it is fruitful to integrate human behavioral preferences into humanitarian operations.

8.4 Other Behavioral Theories in Operations Management

In practice, humanitarian organizations face various challenges, including resource planning, traffic design, labor scheduling, etc. These tasks require collaboration and cooperation between multiple organizations. Besides the decision errors, human managers, in solving complex problems, usually present diversified behavioral preferences. The specific type of behavioral preference depends on the context of the problem and the situation in which the human decision-makers are involved. In this section, we introduce several common behavioral theories, which describe salient behavior-determining factors in operations management. These behavioral theories can be broadly applied in humanitarian operations.

8.4.1 Prospect Theory

Prospect theory, proposed by Kahneman and Tversky (1979), has been found to be an influential behavioral drive in operational management problems. We provide a short review on how prospect theory is integrated with quantal theory to describe the economic activities of human beings. Much of the literature shows us that the supply chain can be coordinated by transferring a fixed fee from the buyer to the seller.

Theoretically, there are two equivalent ways to frame the fixed fee. One way is a two-part tariff contract, where there is a fixed fee besides the unit price for each purchase. The other is the quantity discount contract, which offers a unit price, which decreases as the quantity increases. Both frames can coordinate the supply chain and equivalently improve channel efficiency. However, the experimental data by Ho and Zhang (2008) show that the fixed fee contract does not increase channel efficiency as much as the quantity discount contract. The main drive of this result is the loss-aversion and decision error of human managers. One can embed the loss-aversion model into the quantal choice structure to obtain a full model that integrates both behavioral factors.

8.4.2 Fairness (Social Comparison)

Fairness is another prominent type of behavior which influences human managers' choices, especially in the supply chain contract (Anderson & Weitz, 1992; Kahneman, Knetsch, & Thaler 1986). People concerned with fairness not only consider their own incomes but also compare their incomes with other members. People usually dislike unequal shares of total profit and this behavioral preference greatly affects the channel's performance. Fairness appears not only between the supplier and the retailer but also among multiple retailers. A study by Ho, Su, and Wu (2013) presents two types of comparisons in a supply chain with one supplier and two retailers. The concern for fairness in comparisons between vertical channel members is called distributional fairness, and the concern for fairness between horizontal channel members is called peer-induced fairness (Fehr & Schmidt, 1999; Ho & Su, 2009). Further, decision error is also found as another prominent behavioral factor in subjects' choices. The above papers integrate fairness with decision error by embedding the fairness model into the quantal choice model.

8.4.3 Mental Accounting

Mental accounting (or psychological accounting), first referred to as such by Thaler (1985), plays important roles in human choices. People usually categorize the economic outcomes and establish differentiated accounts. In operations management, the mental accounting theory has been applied to explain behavioral anomalies and analyze system performance, including inventory decisions (Chen, Kök, & Tong, 2013; Ho, Lim, & Cui, 2010), supply chain contracts (Becker-Peth & Thonemann, 2016; Ho & Zhang, 2008), and capacity competition (Chen & Zhao, 2015). Chen and Zhao (2015), for example, find that subjects have biased perceptions of the underage cost and overage cost. Also, the decision error is another prominent behavioral factor. They develop a utility function to capture the mental accounting behavior of subjects. Further, the utility function is embedded into the QRE structure to obtain a full model integrating mental accounting with the decision errors. Their results suggest that subjects systematically perceived the underage cost as the same as the overage cost, and the ratio of underage cost to the overage cost increases over time.

8.5 Summary and Future Applications

Quantal theory can be broadly applied in humanitarian operations. Both managers and customers in situations of unpredictable crisis cannot be fully rational. Their choices are usually accompanied by decision errors, which may change the system's operational policy and management strategy. For example, standard optimized queuing rules cannot perform as predicted if people do not follow the choices of fully rational behavior in standard theory. The standard optimization of allocation rules for the emergency supply cannot organize allocations as expected when people present behavioral preferences. Quantal theory can be applied to describe the bounded rationality of both managers and victims in disasters, and to design better operational mechanisms to better respond to the crisis.

Besides decision errors, other behavioral preferences have great influence on humanitarian management, for example, prospect theory, mental accounting, herding effect, scarcity effect, fairness, trust and reciprocity. The incorporation of behavioral science into humanitarian operations offers numerous opportunities for future research. Take fairness for example, the concern for which usually clashes with system optimization.

When disaster strikes, managers have to allocate limited resources to alleviate suffering and prevent the loss of lives. In standard theory, fairness is not considered. The standard optimization algorithm usually allocates resources extremely, to save the most lives by allocating resources to urban rather than rural areas because urban areas have a greater population density. However, such outcomes are not fair for the people living in the rural areas, who will strongly oppose such planning. Thus, the fairness concern should be considered when formulating the optimization model. Allocation schemes should make a tradeoff between system performance and people's fairness concerns. Future research can explore more behavioral factors in different situations of disaster/crisis, and further develop the corresponding behavioral mechanisms to improve our social welfare.

Although quantal theory is versatile, it still presents some disadvantages. First, the prediction of the quantal choice model is always a uniform distribution of all alternatives if the alternatives have the same utility. When there are a huge number of alternatives with the same utility, the quantal choice model cannot differentiate among them, making the prediction uninformative and restricting its predictive power. Second, the mathematical analyses of the quantal choice model are usually untraceable. In most cases, it is hard to obtain a closed-form solution after applying the quantal choice structure to the mathematical analysis, making it unlikely to obtain explicit solutions to some problems using this method.

Acknowledgments The authors wish to thank the editor and two anonymous reviewers for their guidance and constructive comments. The authors would also like to thank the National Natural Science Foundation of China (71501004) for its support.

References

Anderson, E., & Weitz, B. (1992). The use of pledges to build and sustain commitment in distribution channels. *Journal of Marketing Research, 29*(1), 18–34.

Balcik, B., Beamon, B. M., Krejci, C. C., Muramatsu, K. M., & Ramirez, M. (2010). Coordination in humanitarian relief chains: Practices, challenges and opportunities. *International Journal of Production Economics, 126*(1), 22–34.

Becker-peth, M., & Thonemann, U. W. (2016). Reference points in revenue sharing contracts—How to design optimal supply chain contracts. *European Journal of Operational Research, 249*(3), 1033–1049.

Bolton, G. E., & Katok, E. (2008). Learning by doing in the newsvendor problem: A laboratory investigation of the role of experience and feedback. *Manufacturing & Service Operations Management, 10*(3), 519–538.

Cachon, G. P. (2003). Supply chain coordination with contracts. *Handbooks in Operations Research and Management Science, 11*, 227–339.

Cachon, G. P., & Lariviere, M. A. (2005). Supply chain coordination with revenue-sharing contracts: Strengths and limitations. *Management Science, 51*(1), 30–44.

Cachon, G. P., & Swinney, R. (2009). Purchasing, pricing, and quick response in the presence of strategic consumers. *Management Science, 55*(3), 497–511.

Chen, L., Kök, A. G., & Tong, J. D. (2013). The effect of payment schemes on inventory decisions: The role of mental accounting. *Management Science, 59*(2), 436–451.

Chen, Y., Su, X., & Zhao, X. (2012). Modeling bounded rationality in capacity allocation games with the quantal response equilibrium. *Management Science, 58*(10), 1952–1962.

Chen, Y., & Zhao, X. (2015). Decision bias in capacity allocation games with uncertain demand. *Production and Operations Management, 24*(4), 634–646.

Elmaghraby, W., Gülcü, A., & Keskinocak, P. (2008). Designing optimal preannounced markdowns in the presence of rational customers with multiunit demands. *Manufacturing & Service Operations Management, 10*(1), 126–148.

Fehr, E., & Fischbacher, U. (2004). Social norms and human cooperation. *Trends in Cognitive Sciences, 8*(4), 185–190.

Fehr, E., & Schmidt, K. M. (1999). A theory of fairness, competition, and cooperation. *Quarterly Journal of Economics, 114*(3), 817–868.

Fey, M., McKelvey, R. D., & Palfrey, T. R. (1996). An experimental study of constant-sum centipede games. *International Journal of Game Theory, 25*(3), 269–287.

Goeree, J. K., & Holt, C. A. (2001). Ten little treasures of game theory and ten intuitive contradictions. *American Economic Review, 91*(5), 1402–1422.

Helsloot, I., & Ruitenberg, A. (2004). Citizen response to disasters: A survey of literature and some practical implications. *Journal of Contingencies and Crisis Management, 12*(3), 98–111.

Ho, T.-H., Lim, N., & Cui, T. (2010). Reference-dependence in multilocation newsvendor models: A structural analysis. *Management Science, 56*(11), 1891–1910.

Ho, T.-H., & Su, X. (2009). Peer-induced fairness in games. *American Economic Review, 99*(5), 2022–2049.

Ho, T.-H., Su, X., & Wu, Y. (2013). Fairness in supply chain contract design. *Production and Operations Management, 23*(2), 161–175.

Ho, T.-H., & Zhang, J. (2008). Designing price contracts for boundedly rational customers: Does the framing of the fixed fee matter? *Management Science, 54*(4), 686–700.

Holguín-Veras, J., Jaller, M., Van Wassenhove, L. N., Pérez, N., & Wachtendorf, T. (2012). On the unique features of post-disaster humanitarian logistics. *Journal of Operations Management, 30*(7), 494–506.

Huang, T., Allon, G., & Bassamboo, A. (2013). Bounded rationality in service systems. *Manufacturing & Service Operations Management, 15*(2), 263–279.

Jiang, L., & Giachetti, R. E. (2008). A queueing network model to analyze the impact of parallelization of care on patient cycle time. *Health Care Management Science, 11*(3), 248–261.

Kahneman, D., Knetsch, J. D., & Thaler, R. (1986). Fairness as a constraint on profit seeking: Entitlements in the markets. *American Economic Review, 47*(2), 263–291.

Kahneman, D., & Tversky, A. (1979). Prospect theory: An analysis of decision under risk. *Econometrica, 76*(4), 728–741.

Katok, E., & Pavlov, V. (2013). Fairness in supply chain contracts: A laboratory study. *Journal of Operations Management, 31*(3), 129–137.

Katok, E., & Wu, D. Y. (2009). Contracting in supply chains: A laboratory investigation. *Management Science, 55*(12), 1953–1968.

Kovács, G., & Spens, K. M. (2007). Humanitarian logistics in disaster relief operations. *International Journal of Physical Distribution & Logistics Management, 37*(2), 99–114.

Kovács, G., & Spens, K. M. (2009). Identifying challenges in humanitarian logistics. *International Journal of Physical Distribution & Logistics Management, 39*(6), 506–528.

Lakshmi, C., & Sivakumar, A. I. (2013). Application of queueing theory in health care: A literature review. *Operations Research for Health Care, 2*(1), 25–39.

Lim, N., & Ho, T.-H. (2007). Designing price contracts for boundedly rational customers: Does the number of blocks matter? *Marketing Science, 26*(3), 312–326.

Lorenz, D. F., Schulze, K., & Voss, M. (2017). Emerging citizen responses to disasters in Germany. Disaster myths as an impediment for a collaboration of unaffiliated responders and professional rescue forces. *Journal of Contingencies and Crisis Management, 25*(3). https://doi.org/10.1111/1468-5973.12202

Luce, R. D. (1959). *Individual choice behavior: A theoretical analysis*. New York, NY: Wiley.
Maon, F., Lindgreen, A., & Vanhamme, J. (2009). Developing supply chains in disaster relief operations through cross-sector socially oriented collaborations: A theoretical model. *Supply Chain Management: An International Journal, 14*(2), 149–164.
McFadden, D. (1981). Econometric models of probabilistic choice. In C. F. Manski & D. McFadden (Eds.), *Structural analysis of discrete data with econometric applications* (pp. 198–272). Cambridge, MA: MIT Press.
McKelvey, R. D., & Palfrey, T. R. (1992). An experimental study of the centipede game. *Econometrica, 60*(4), 803–836.
McKelvey, R. D., & Palfrey, T. R. (1995). Quantal response equilibria for normal form games. *Games and Economic Behavior, 10*(1), 6–38.
Naor, P. (1969). The regulation of queue size by levying tolls. *Econometrica, 37*, 15–24.
Pavlov, V. Katok, E., Haruvy, E., & Olsen, T. (2016). Bounded rationality in supply chain contracts. *Working Paper*.
Perry, R. W., & Lindell, M. K. (2003). Preparedness for emergency response: Guidelines for the emergency planning process. *Disasters, 27*(4), 336–350.
Schweitzer, M. E., & Cachon, G. P. (2000). Decision bias in the newsvendor problem with a known demand distribution: Experimental evidence. *Management Science, 46*(3), 404–420.
Song, Y., & Zhao, X. (2016). Strategic customer behavior facing possible stockout: An experimental study. *International Journal of Production Economics, 180*, 57–67.
Song, Y., & Zhao, X. (2017). A newsvendor problem with boundedly rational strategic customers. *International Journal of Production Research, 55*(1), 228–243.
Spengler, J. J. (1950). Vertical integration and antitrust policy. *Journal of Political Economy, 58*(4), 347–352.
Su, X. (2008). Bounded rationality in newsvendor models. *Manufacturing & Service Operations Management, 10*(4), 566–589.
Thaler, R. (1985). Mental accounting and consumer choice. *Marketing Science, 4*(3), 199–214.
Tomasini, R., & Van Wassenhove, L. N. (2009a). From preparedness to partnerships: Case study research on humanitarian logistics. *International Transactions in Operational Research, 16*(5), 549–559.
Tomasini, R., & Van Wassenhove, L. N. (2009b). *Humanitarian logistics*. London, UK: Palgrave Macmillan.
Van Wassenhove, L. N. (2006). Blackett memorial lecture. Humanitarian aid logistics: Supply chain management in high gear. *Journal of the Operational Research Society, 57*(5), 475–489.

9

The Framing Effect in Humanitarian Operations

Jaime Andrés Castañeda

9.1 Introduction

Framing effects refer to different responses to different semantic but objectively equivalent descriptions of the same problem. Studies of framing effects originated in judgment and decision-making. They proliferated and expanded to other areas like healthcare, marketing and management, among others. Framing effects have been documented in decisions made by providers and recipients of healthcare, consumer choices, bargaining decisions and many other decision-making contexts (Levin, Schneider, & Gaeth, 1998).

Despite the breadth of applications of framing effects, their study in humanitarian operations is scant. One of the seminal framing effects problems is Tversky and Kahneman's (1981) Asian disease problem, which frames the outcomes of a risky vaccination program in terms of either lives saved or lives lost. Since saving lives is among the main

---

J. A. Castañeda (✉)
School of Management, Universidad del Rosario, Bogotá, Colombia
e-mail: jaime.castaneda@urosario.edu.co

objectives of humanitarian operations, one could ask how emphasizing either lives saved or lives lost affects humanitarian operations decisions.

Framing effects research can be structured using Levin et al.'s (1998) framing effects typology, which organizes the literature into risky choice, goal and attribute framing studies, since many studies deviate from the original implementation of framing effects like the one in the Asian disease problem. Thus, framing effects in humanitarian operations are not restricted to a lives saved/lives lost frame. For example, decisions related to emergency preparedness could incur high costs, but could also help save funds during emergency response. Hence, one could also ask how emphasizing either costs or savings affects humanitarian operations decisions.

This chapter explores the application of framing effects research in humanitarian operations. It describes the origins of framing effects research and Levin et al.'s typology. Following this, the chapter reviews framing effects research in operations management, focusing on inventory and employee productivity studies. For each study, the chapter describes its design, main results and place in Levin et al.'s typology. Based on the reviewed studies, the chapter describes framing effects problems that could be studied in humanitarian operations. The chapter ends with a summary of the work and a discussion of its limitations.

9.2 The Framing Effect

9.2.1 Origins

To understand the original interpretation of the framing effect (Tversky & Kahneman, 1981), it is important to first understand the basic ideas behind the expected utility model, prospect theory and decision frames. In the expected utility model, the overall utility of a prospect is the expected utility of its outcomes. That is, the utility of the prospect $(x_1, p_1; \ldots; x_n, p_n)$, where x_i is outcome i, p_i is the probability that outcome x_i realizes, and $p_1 + \cdots + p_n = 1$, is:

$$U(x_1, p_1; \cdots; x_n, p_n) = p_1 \cdot u(x_1) + \cdots + p_n \cdot u(x_n), \tag{1}$$

where U is the overall utility and u is the utility of a given outcome. Importantly, the domain of the utility function is final states (e.g., final state of wealth) and the function assumes risk aversion (i.e., people prefer a sure prospect of outcome x to a risky prospect with expected value x). Prospect theory (Kahneman & Tversky, 1979) models more realistic assumptions to describe the ways people choose between outcomes that involve risk, departing from the expected utility model in two major ways. First, outcomes are expressed as positive or negative deviations (gains or losses) from the decision-maker's reference point. That is, the domain of the utility function is changes in states (e.g., changes in wealth). This utility (or value) function is normally concave above the reference point and convex below it (i.e., there is a diminishing sensitivity to changes in gains and losses). The value function is normally steeper for losses than for gains (i.e., the response to losses is stronger than the response to gains—loss aversion). Secondly, the utility of gains and losses are multiplied by decision weights $\pi(p_i)$, which are a function of the probabilities of gains and losses. These decision weights capture the idea that people tend to overreact to small probability events and underreact to moderate and large probability events. The overweighting enhances the value of long shots, allowing risk-seeking preferences in gains for low probabilities, while the underweighting attenuates the averseness of negative gambles, allowing risk-seeking preferences in losses for moderate and high probabilities. That is, risk aversion no longer prevails. Figure 9.1 illustrates an example of the (a) value and (b) weighting functions.

Tversky and Kahneman (1981) define a decision problem in terms of "the acts or options among which one must choose, the possible outcomes or consequences of these acts, and the contingencies or conditional probabilities that relate outcomes to acts" (p. 453). A decision frame is the conception that decision-makers have about the options, outcomes and probabilities associated with a particular choice, and the frame they adopt is controlled by the formulation of the problem, and by their norms, habits and personal characteristics (Tversky & Kahneman, 1981).

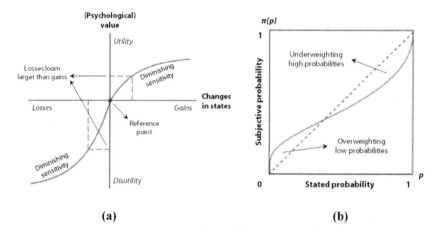

Fig. 9.1 Prospect theory's (a) value and (b) weighting functions. Source: adapted from Slovenia Hotel (http://sloveniahotel.info/)

If the weighting and value functions of prospect theory were linear, choices would be independent of the framing of options, outcomes or probabilities. However, given the nonlinearities of the weighting and value functions, variations in the framing of options, outcomes or probabilities can lead to different choices. The Asian disease problem (Tversky & Kahneman, 1981) illustrates an example of the framing effect by a change in the frame of outcomes. Participants were asked to choose between two vaccination programs to prepare for the outbreak of an unusual Asian disease that was expected to kill 600 people. In the first version of the problem, two possible outcomes are framed in term of lives saved (gains); the first outcome is a sure gain, while the second outcome is a gamble with the same expected value as the first outcome:

- If Program A is adopted, 200 people will be saved.
- If Program B is adopted, there is 1/3 probability that 600 people will be saved, and 2/3 probability that no people will be saved.

In the second version, the two possible outcomes are framed in terms of lives lost (losses); the first outcome is a sure loss, while the second outcome is a gamble with the same expected value as the first outcome:

- If Program C is adopted, 400 people will die.
- If Program D is adopted, there is 1/3 probability that nobody will die, and 2/3 probability that 600 people will die.

The two problems are undistinguishable in real terms. However, in the first problem, most participants (72%) chose the sure gain, while in the second problem, most participants (78%) chose the gamble. In simple terms, changes in the wording of the decision problem led to a preference reversal: choices involving gains are often risk averse and choices involving losses are often risk seeking (Tversky & Kahneman, 1981). Interested readers are referred to the literature that gave rise to framing effects for more details about their original interpretation and more examples (Kahneman & Tversky, 1984; Tversky & Kahneman, 1981, 1986).

9.2.2 Different Framing Effects

According to Levin et al. (1998), framing effects "are often treated as a relatively homogeneous set of phenomena explained by a single theory, namely prospect theory" (p. 150). It is important to recognize that framing effects are not only related to situations involving risk, since many studies deviate from the original implementation of framing effects. To clarify the likely mechanisms behind framing effects, reduce confusion when comparing studies, and organize the framing effects literature, Levin et al. (1998) developed a framing effects typology that considers three types of framing manipulations: risky choice, attribute, and goal framing.

9.2.2.1 Risky Choice Framing

Risky choice framing refers to the "standard" treatment of framing effects. The prototypical example is the Asian disease problem. Decision problems in this category present a decision scenario with two options or prospects: the first prospect has one sure outcome (no risk), while the second prospect has two outcomes, each outcome with a given probability (gamble). The manipulation involves a positive frame, where the outcomes of both prospects are described as gains, and a negative frame, where the outcomes of both prospects are described as losses. Framing effects are measured by comparing choice proportions for the two prospects across frames (Levin et al., 1998).

Levin et al.'s (1998) literature review shows that when there are risky choice framing effects, these indicate risk aversion to realize gains and risk seeking to avoid losses. However, there is heterogeneity in the results since while some studies find a choice or preference reversal, some others find a choice shift. A preference reversal occurs when (i) choices change from the sure outcome in the positive frame to the risky outcome in the negative frame and (ii) the proportion of people who choose the risky outcome is significantly lower than 50% in the positive frame and significantly greater than 50% in the negative frame. A choice shift only meets (i). This heterogeneity could have several sources. For example, decision problems differ along several dimensions like the problem domain, risk features, task features, hedonic tone and sample of participants, among others (Levin et al., 1998).

9.2.2.2 Attribute Framing

In this category, decision problems ask to evaluate an object or an event. Evaluations can be ratings of favorability, yes/no judgements, accept/reject the object or event and other forms of evaluation. The manipulation involves a positive frame, where an attribute of the object or event is framed positively, and a negative frame, where the same attribute is framed negatively. Framing effects are measured by comparing evaluations across frames (Levin et al., 1998).

Levin, Schnittjer and Thee (1988) exemplify attribute framing effects using a medical decision problem. They told participants that a new treatment was developed to treat a kind of cancer. In the positive frame, the treatment was said to have a 50% success rate, while in the negative frame, the treatment was said to have a 50% failure rate. Participants were asked to rate the effectiveness of the treatment and to state the likelihoods of recommending the treatment and encouraging a relative to undergo treatment. The positive frame led to greater ratings of effectiveness and greater likelihoods of recommending the treatment and encouraging a relative to undergo treatment.

Levin et al.'s (1998) literature review shows a consistent attribute framing effect, where the positive framing of attributes leads to more favorable evaluations than the negative framing of the same attributes. These effects occur because the positive labeling of attributes leads to an encoding of the information that evokes favorable associations in memory, while the negative labeling of the same attributes leads to an encoding that evokes unfavorable associations (Levin & Gaeth, 1988; Levin et al., 1998).

9.2.2.3 Goal Framing

In this category, decision problems ask to adopt a behavior. The positive frame stresses the positive consequences (gains) of acting or behaving in a certain way, while the negative frame stresses the negative consequences (losses) of not acting or behaving in that way. Both framing conditions should promote the same act; the question is which frame will have the greater persuasive impact. Framing effects are measured by comparing rates of adoption across frames (Levin et al., 1998).

Levin, Gaeth and Schreiber (2002) exemplify goal framing using a dietary decision problem. Participants had to indicate the extent to which they would recommend reducing or eliminating red meat from the diet. In the positive frame, a message said that doing so would reduce cholesterol and the likelihood of heart disease, while in the negative frame, the message said that failing to do so would not reduce cholesterol and the likelihood of heart disease. Responses did not show framing effects.

Goal framing has greater variation in the way it is implemented than attribute framing since more than one aspect of the message may be manipulated, making goal framing more susceptible to linguistic and contextual variations. This could explain why goal framing effects are less consistent than attribute framing effects (Levin et al., 1998). However, when there are goal framing effects, they show that the negative frame has a stronger persuasive impact than the positive frame (e.g., in the dietary decision problem, the negative frame would have led people to recommend reducing or eliminating red meat from the diet to a greater extent than the positive frame). These effects could be explained by a negativity bias in processing information, where negative information has a stronger impact on judgment than comparable positive information (Meyerowitz & Chaiken, 1987). This is also consistent with loss aversion, which can occur also in the absence of risk, where negative wording that focuses on avoiding a loss may produce a greater impact than comparable positive wording that focuses on obtaining a gain (Levin et al., 1998).

9.3 Framing Effects in Operations Management

Despite the widespread study of framing effects in several domains, operations management research on framing effects seems rather scant. This section reviews several studies of framing effects in inventory management and employee productivity and classifies them following Levin et al.'s (1998) typology. The section also provides details about how the studies implemented their framing manipulations.

The studies reviewed here do not include, for example, the behavioral experiments on contracts of Ho and Zhang (2008), Katok and Wu (2009), Kremer and Van Wassenhove (2014), and Wu and Chen (2014), or the behavioral experiments on pricing of Bendoly (2013). Although they are mentioned in Tokar, Aloysius, Waller and Hawkins' (2016) literature review section on framing effects in operations management, their manipulations go beyond semantic representations, including different mathematical formulations that lead to the same or similar results. Finally, the section does not include Kremer, Minner and Van Wassenhove's (2010) neutral/operations framing study either, since their neutral manipulation does not correspond to an operations problem.

9.3.1 Inventory Management

This section is organized around three topics that reflect what aspects of the inventory problem were subjected to the framing manipulation: the costs of the problem, the metric subject to optimization and the type of purchasing transaction.

9.3.1.1 Costs of the Problem

Schultz, McClain, Robinson and Thomas (2007) explored framing effects in ordering behavior using a newsvendor laboratory (lab) experiment. They framed the decision problem emphasizing either profit or cost. For example, in the positive frame (profit) manipulation, a high-profit item was presented as an item with a unit cost of $3 and a unit selling price of $10, while in the negative frame (cost) manipulation, the same item was presented as an item with a cost of $3 for each leftover unit and a cost of $7 for each shortage unit. These framing manipulations were implemented in the outcome feedback. For example, leftover situations were described in the following way:

- *Positive frame*: "Any inventory left over immediately becomes obsolete and is disposed of at no cost."
- *Negative frame*: "Any inventory leftover immediately becomes obsolete and is disposed of at a cost of $3 per unit."

Shortage situations were described in the following way:

- *Positive frame*: "If demand equals or exceeds the amount you ordered, everything you order is sold."
- *Negative frame*: "If you do not order enough to satisfy demand the company will have to put in a rush order and it will cost $7 per unit."

In addition, the description of the performance of a given decision was also influenced by the framing manipulation. For example, if a participant ordered 50 items and realized demand was 60 items, the outcome feedback in the positive frame would tell the participant that he earned $350, while in the negative frame it would tell the participant that he lost $70.

Drawing on prospect theory, Schultz et al. (2007) expected a stronger influence of the negative frame on ordering behavior across their two profit (high and low) conditions. However, orders were not greater in the negative frame condition, even though opportunity costs were explicit (cost of rush order).

Schultz et al.'s (2007) framing manipulation contains elements of both attribute and goal framing. Attribute framing materializes in the description of the costs of the item and the financial performance, while elements of goal framing materialize in the description of the consequences of leftovers and shortages.

In a newsvendor system, shortage costs are usually represented as either opportunity or penalty costs. Schiffels, Fügener, Kolisch and Brunner (2014) explored whether these different representations lead to differences in ordering behavior in a newsvendor lab experiment. Assuming p as the retail price, c as the wholesale cost and s as the penalty cost, in the opportunity cost manipulation, the unit shortage cost corresponds to forgone profit ($p - c$), while in the penalty cost manipulation, the unit shortage cost corresponds to the additional costs of the reorder to satisfy excess demand ($s - c$). These framing manipulations were implemented in the written instructions given to participants. For example:

- *Opportunity cost frame*: "If the demand exceeds your order quantity, the unsatisfied demand expires."
- *Penalty cost frame*: "If the demand exceeds your order quantity, you have to reorder products instantly at a higher price."
- *Opportunity cost frame*: "For each product sold, you will receive a price of … from your customers (the opportunity costs for each product ordered too little corresponds to …)."
- *Penalty cost frame*: "For each product ordered too little, you have to pay a price of … to the wholesaler (the additional costs for each product ordered too little correspond to …)."
- *Opportunity cost frame*: "At the end of the experiment, the gains/losses in … incurred in all rounds are added together. Your payoff is the resulting amount …"
- *Penalty cost frame*: "At the end of the experiment, the costs in … incurred in all rounds are added together. These costs will be deducted from a fixed budget of …, which is available to fulfill the task. Your payoff is the resulting amount…"

Schiffels et al. (2014) observed that penalty costs led to increased orders compared with opportunity costs across their three profit (high, medium and low) conditions. Schiffels et al.'s (2014) framing manipulation contains elements of both attribute and goal framing. Attribute framing materializes in the description of the shortage cost and the reward mechanism, while elements of goal framing materialize in the description of the consequences of shortages.

9.3.1.2 Optimization Metric

Tokar et al. (2016) presented a thorough examination of framing effects in ordering behavior. First, they tested Levin et al.'s (1998) typology using three simple inventory problems in the form of vignettes or situational experiments. For example, to test attribute framing effects, they asked participants to evaluate a new inventory policy. In the positive frame, the policy was described as providing a 90% in-stock rate, while in the negative frame, the same policy was described as providing a 10% out-of-stock rate. They observed framing effects across all three typologies.

After establishing the efficacy of the typology in simple inventory problems, Tokar et al. (2016) ran two lab experiments in more complex inventory problems focusing on goal framing. Experiment one was set in a single-echelon inventory system. The negative frame manipulation asked participants to minimize the total cost they incurred, tracking lost sales (shortage costs), while the positive frame manipulation asked them to maximize the total profit they earned, tracking actual sales (revenues). These framing manipulations were implemented in the written instructions given to participants. For example (emphasis from the original text):

- *Negative frame*: "Your goal is to <u>minimize</u> your <u>Total Cost</u> in the game. Cost will be assessed as follows:
  – In each period, the *cost* of a lost sale is *$10.00/unit.*
  – The cost of leftover inventory (carrying inventory from one period to the next) is $1/unit[.]"

- *Positive frame*: "Your goal is to <u>maximize</u> your <u>total profit</u>. Profit (the difference between revenue and cost) will be assessed as follows:
  - In each period, the *revenue* for demand that is filled is *$10.00/unit*.
  - The cost of leftover inventory (carrying inventory from one period to the next) is *$1/unit*."

Tokar et al. (2016) observed greater orders and inventory in the negative frame. Experiment two was set in a four-echelon supply chain system. Like in experiment one, the negative frame led to greater orders and inventory.

Tokar et al.'s (2016) situational experiments were designed to test Levin et al.'s (1998) typology. Thus, there is one situational experiment for each type of framing. While their lab experiments were designed focusing on goal framing, the framing manipulation also contains elements of attribute framing. By framing the problem in terms of either profits or costs, attribute framing comes already into play.

9.3.1.3 Purchasing Transaction

Finally, Chen, Kök and Tong (2013) tested the effect of three different payment schemes or purchasing transactions on ordering behavior in a newsvendor lab experiment. In the standard scheme, the retailer pays a unit wholesale cost (c) when placing the order and receives a unit selling price (p) after the demand realizes (e.g., purchasing items with own capital). In the credit scheme, the retailer pays nothing when placing the order, receives $p - c$ per unit sold after the demand realizes, and pays the creditor the unit wholesale cost c per leftover (e.g., purchasing items on account, paying the supplier later). In the loan scheme, the retailer receives $p - c$ per unit ordered when placing the order and pays the unit selling price p per leftover to the loaner after the demand realizes (e.g., raising money from investors to purchase items, paying investors a share of the business' revenues).

All payment schemes are equivalent since they all produce the same profits or losses for any given order and demand realization. However, purchasing transactions are different. In the standard scheme, there is an outgoing purchasing transaction when placing the order; in the credit scheme, there is not a purchasing transaction when placing the order; and in the loan scheme, there is an incoming purchasing transaction when placing the order. These framing manipulations were implemented in the written instructions given to participants. For example:

- *Standard frame*: "At this time you pay $1 per unit and place the units in your store (…). [You] receive $2 per unit that you sell."
- *Credit frame*: "Your supplier sends you these units and you place them in your store (…). You receive $1 profit per unit that you sell, but you must pay a penalty of $1 for each leftover unit."
- *Loan frame*: "At this time you actually receive $1 per unit that you place [in] your store (advanced payment.) (…). You receive $0 for each unit that you sell, but you must pay a penalty of $2 for each extra unit you have leftover."

Since outgoing and incoming payments are analogous to negative and positive utilities, respectively, prospective accounting (Prelec & Loewenstein, 1998) predicts that orders would be greater in the standard (negative utility frame) than in the credit scheme and that orders would be greater in the credit than in the loan scheme (positive utility frame). Consistent with this, Chen et al. (2013) observed that the orders were greater in the standard than in the credit scheme, thus getting closer to the optimum in a high-profit setting, while they were lower in the loan than in the credit scheme, thus getting closer to the optimum in a low-profit setting.

Chen et al.'s (2013) framing manipulation contains elements of both attribute and goal framing. The attribute is the timing or type of transaction, which is interpreted as either positive if it is an incoming transaction or negative if it is and outgoing transaction. Elements of goal framing materialize in the description of the consequences of sales and leftovers. Table 9.1 shows a summary of the reviewed studies.

Table 9.1 Summary of framing effects research in operations management

Study	Framing	Manipulation	Results[a,b]
Inventory management			
Schultz et al. (2007)	Attribute	– Costs of the item – Financial performance	No framing effects[a]
	Goal	– Leftover and shortage consequences	
Schiffels et al. (2014)	Attribute	– Shortage cost – Reward mechanism	Penalty costs led to greater orders than opportunity costs[b]
	Goal	– Shortage consequences	
	Situational tasks		
	Risky choice	– Outcomes of actions to prepare for a given demand scenario	The losses frame led to risk seeking, while the gains frame led to risk aversion[b]
	Attribute	– Attribute of an inventory policy	The positive frame led to a better evaluation of the policy[b]
Tokar et al. (2016)			
	Goal	– Consequences of an inventory policy	The negative frame led to a greater intention of implementing the policy[b]
	Experimental tasks		
	Attribute	– Costs of the item – Objective metric	The cost frame led to greater orders and inventory than the profit frame[b]
	Goal	– Leftover and shortage consequences	
Chen et al. (2013)	Attribute	– Timing of transactions – Sales and leftover consequences	Outgoing transactions led to greater orders than incoming transactions[b]
	Goal		
Employee productivity			
Hannan et al. (2005)	Attribute	– Performance incentive – Consequences of whether a high outcome is achieved	The penalty frame led to greater employee effort than the bonus frame[b]
	Goal		
Hossain and List (2012)	Attribute	– Performance incentive – Consequences of whether a productivity target is met	For teams, the punishment frame led to greater productivity increases than the reward frame[b]
	Goal		

[a] Not as expected
[b] As expected

9.3.2 Employee Productivity

Hannan, Hoffman and Moser (2005) tested whether the frame of contracts affects employee effort allocation, assessing bonus (gains) and penalty (losses) contracts. In their lab experiment, participants were assigned to either the bonus or the penalty contract manipulation. They assumed the role of an employee of a fictitious company and were asked to choose an effort level to achieve the company's performance goal. The effort level ranged from 1 to 13, with the cost of effort rising in $0.50 increments from $0.50 (effort level = 1) to $6.50 (effort level = 13). The probability of achieving the performance goal increased with the effort level, rising in 5% increments from 30% (effort level = 1) to 90% (effort level = 13).

The implementation of the contract manipulation was done in the description of the contract given to participants. The bonus contract paid a salary of $20 plus a bonus of $10 if the performance goal was achieved, while the penalty contract paid a salary of $30 with a penalty of $10 if the performance goal was not achieved. Both contracts are economically equivalent because under both the employee would receive $30 if the goal is achieved and $20 if the goal is not achieved. The contract terms and the parametrization of effort levels and probabilities of achieving the performance goal were used to determine participants' final payments.

A table with the effort costs and the probabilities of achieving the performance goal was also manipulated. The headings of two columns containing the probabilities were framed as follows:

- *Bonus frame*: "Probability of Achieving a High Outcome and Receiving the $10 Bonus" and "Probability of <u>not</u> Achieving a High Outcome and Not Receiving the $10 Bonus".
- *Penalty frame*: "Probability of Achieving a High Outcome and Avoiding the $10 Penalty" and "Probability of <u>not</u> Achieving a High Outcome and Paying the $10 Penalty".

Hannan et al. (2005) observed that the penalty contract led to greater employee effort than the bonus contract. Before determining final payments, they also asked participants to rate how disappointed they would be if the outcome were low and therefore they did not receive the bonus (or had to pay the penalty, according to the contract frame). The disappointment was greater in the bonus contract frame, reflecting loss aversion. In addition, this disappointment mediated the effect of contract frame on effort level, suggesting that participants chose greater effort levels in the penalty contract because they are more averse to having to pay the penalty than they are to not getting the bonus.

Hannan et al.'s (2005) framing manipulation contains elements of both attribute and goal framing. Attribute framing materializes in the description of the performance incentive, while elements of goal framing materialize in the description of the consequences of whether the performance goal is achieved.

Hossain and List (2012) extended Hannan et al.'s (2005) results by running a natural field experiment in a high-tech Chinese company to test whether the frame of incentive schemes affects worker productivity, assessing reward (gains) and punishment (losses) schemes. All workers who took part in the experiment experienced both incentive schemes; however, they were not aware that an experiment was taking place and did not know that they were going to work under both incentive schemes. Before starting working under an incentive scheme, they received a letter informing them that they had been chosen to participate in a short-term program. The relevant portion of the letter read as follows:

- *Punishment frame*: "[F]or every week in which the weekly production average of your team is below K units/hour, the salary enhancement will be reduced by RMB 80…"
- *Reward frame*: "[Y]ou will receive a salary enhancement of RMB 80 for every week the weekly production average of your team is above or equal to K units/hour…"

In the reward frame, the workers started with a bonus of zero and could potentially earn RMB 80 in each of the four weeks under the scheme, while in the punishment frame, they started with a bonus of RMB 320 and could potentially lose RMB 80 in each week under the scheme.

Hossain and List (2012) ran the experiment across teams and individuals. They observed that both incentive schemes increased productivity. In addition, for teams, they also observed that the punishment scheme led to greater productivity increases than the reward scheme.

Hossain and List's (2012) framing manipulation contains elements of both attribute and goal framing. Attribute framing materializes in the description of the performance incentive, while elements of goal framing materialize in the description of the consequences of whether the productivity target is met. Table 9.1 shows a summary of the reviewed studies.

The reviewed designs include elements of attribute and goal framing. As mentioned above, goal framing manipulations are more complex than those of other frames. Overall, one could think that the reviewed designs correspond to goal framing manipulations intertwined with attribute framing manipulations that help to more clearly align the description of the task with the intended frame. It is thus difficult to isolate the framing effects observed (or the lack of them) to a particular type of frame. In inventory management, for example, if one focuses on the costs of the problem and the consequences of leftovers and shortages, one would need at least three different designs to disentangle the framing effect: (i) an attribute framing design could manipulate the description of the costs of the problem, while fixing the way the consequences of shortages and leftovers are described; (ii) a goal framing design could manipulate the description of the consequences of shortages and leftovers, while fixing the description of the costs of the problem; and (iii) an attribute-goal framing design could manipulate the description of the costs of the problem and the consequences of shortages and leftovers.

9.4 Applications in Humanitarian Operations Research

This section discusses potential applications of framing effects research in humanitarian operations. It discusses research problems that are based on the studies cited above and mentions particularities of humanitarian operations that must be considered when designing framing manipulations.

9.4.1 Prepositioning Decisions

This section is organized around three topics that are based on the studies reviewed in inventory management and the particularities of humanitarian operations. The topics are the costs of the problem, lives saved/lives lost framing and the type of purchasing transaction.

9.4.1.1 Costs of the Problem

When framing the information of a prepositioning problem (stockpiling supplies before an emergency response), the profit/cost frame has little application since humanitarian operations do not optimize a profit metric.

However, a cost-based problem could still be tested for some framing effects. By properly framing the costs, Schiffels et al.'s (2014) framing manipulation could be tested in a prepositioning problem. For example, assuming a wholesale cost (c) for each item and an additional expediting cost (e) for each item that is not initially prepositioned and has to be rushed to the emergency response area, the newsvendor derivation would result in a unit shortage cost of e. Under this setting, an opportunity cost frame would emphasize forgone savings—with magnitude of e times the difference between the realized demand (D) and the quantity prepositioned (Q). The growing pressure for a cost-effective use of funds in humanitarian operations indicates that this could be a reasonable approach (Van der Laan, de Brito and Vergunst, 2009; Van Wassenhove, 2006). On the other hand, a penalty cost frame would emphasize the additional costs of the rushed order—with magnitude $e(D - Q)$.

Tokar et al.'s (2016) lab experiments could be adapted to test goal framing effects in prepositioning problems. Their framing manipulation asked participants to track either lost (shortage cost) or actual sales (revenue). Their shortage cost corresponds to a penalty cost. Under the same cost structure assumed above, the penalty costs would be the additional costs of the rushed order, while the revenues would correspond to the wholesale costs of the prepositioned items. Thus, a negative frame would ask participants to track the costs of rushed orders, while a positive frame would ask participants to track the wholesale costs of the prepositioned items.

Note that both frames would ask participants to minimize costs. The translation of revenues into a metric that has a financial appeal for a prepositioning problem is less straightforward, but one could think, for example, about the actual money savings that a prepositioning decision generates when there is no need to rush orders. Thus, a positive frame would ask participants to track the savings of not having to rush orders.

9.4.1.2 Lives Saved/Lives Lost Framing

The lives saved/lives lost frame of the Asian disease problem could add more elements to this kind of research. Like in Schultz et al. (2007) and Schiffels et al. (2014), the framing of supply-demand mismatches could be manipulated. For example, shortages could be framed emphasizing either lives saved or lives lost, considering that whether one uses an opportunity or a penalty cost influences the description of shortages. Using an opportunity cost, under the lives saved frame, shortages could be downplayed by mentioning that the prepositioned quantity helped saving lives, while under the lives lost frame, shortages could be emphasized by mentioning that the lack of items led to lives lost.

Using a penalty cost, under the lives saved frame, shortages would be downplayed by mentioning that the rush order led to lives saved. However, under the lives lost frame, emphasizing shortages in terms of lives lost would conflict with the idea of a penalty cost since this cost is associated with a rush order that can help saving lives. Table 9.2 summarizes this framework.

Table 9.2 Framing shortages under lives saved/lives lost frames

	Lives saved	Lives lost
Opportunity cost	Shortages are downplayed – Prepositioned quantity helped saving lives	Shortages are emphasized – Lack of items led to lives lost
Penalty cost	Shortages are downplayed – Rush order helped saving lives	–

When using a lives saved/lives lost frame, one must carefully think about how to translate the number of items prepositioned into lives saved and the lack of items into lives lost. The wording of both frames needs to be carefully designed as well; following the Asian disease problem could provide some guidance. As with framing effects in inventory management, one could test what frame leads to either greater or lower prepositioned items. Results from this kind of research could help inform framing interventions. For example, if some relief supplies are critical and need to be readily accessible, a framing intervention that leads to greater prepositioned quantities could be preferred. Alternatively, if some relief supplies are non-urgent, a framing intervention that leads to lower prepositioned quantities could be preferred.

Tokar et al.'s (2016) situational experiments could be run to test Levin et al.'s (1998) typology in a simple prepositioning problem. If one thinks about testing the lives saved/lives lost frames, the risky choice framing task would be very similar to the original Asian disease problem after adapting the problem description, which would not be about a vaccination program but about a prepositioning plan or policy. For the attribute framing task, one must think about how to translate in-stock and out-of-stock rates into lives saved and lives lost, respectively. For the goal framing task, one must think about how to translate the chances of getting better results into chances of saving lives or chances of avoiding losing lives. An example of Tokar et al.'s (2016) goal framing task looks as follows:

- *Gain focus*: "By implementing policy A, you get a 50% chance of getting better results."
- *Loss focus*: "By not implementing policy A, you give up a 50% chance of getting better results."

To disentangle the lives saved/lives lost framing effect, one would need two versions of this task. The first version would have to translate *getting a certain chance* (and *giving up a certain chance*) *of getting better results* into *getting a certain chance* (and *giving up a certain chance*) *of saving lives*, while the second version would have to translate *getting a certain chance* (and *giving up a certain chance*) *of getting better results* into *getting a certain chance* (and *giving up a certain chance*) *of avoiding losing lives* (alternatively, instead of thinking on *giving up a certain chance of avoiding losing lives*, one could think in terms of *getting a certain chance of losing lives*). These situational experiments and/or adaptations of them could serve as a starting point to explore whether particularities of a humanitarian context can bias choices, which could inform the design of more complex experiments like the ones described earlier.

9.4.1.3 Purchasing Transaction

Although at first glance one could think about manipulating payment schemes to increase or decrease prepositioning quantities, a closer look suggests that the loan scheme as studied by Chen et al. (2013) would not apply in prepositioning. For example, after a humanitarian organization fundraises money to preposition supplies, they would not pay donors a share of whatever economic output could result from prepositioning, if any. Prepositioning starts like a loan scheme, but after demand realizes, it works like a standard scheme. At best, one could think about comparing this mixed scheme against a credit scheme to explore whether one of them leads to greater prepositioning quantities. If one of them does, it could be useful for critical relief supplies, which must be readily available during emergency response to prevent the loss of lives. On the other hand, if one of them leads to lower prepositioning quantities, it could be useful for non-urgent relief supplies to avoid material convergence issues that could result from a large flow of these supplies to emergency response areas (Holguín-Veras, Jaller, Van Wassenhove, Pérez and Wachtendorf, 2014). Care must be taken when translating Chen et al.'s (2013) revenue metric into a more appropriate metric for prepositioning; the discussion in *Costs of the Problem* could provide some guidance.

9.4.2 Humanitarian Workers' Productivity

The experiments on employee productivity reviewed above study the effect of awarding financial bonuses or financially penalizing employees based on whether they met performance targets. However, applying related designs to study financial incentives based on the performance of humanitarian workers could be counter-productive. People often work in humanitarian organizations to fulfill personal or social values, which provide a powerful intrinsic motivator to do the job. However, providing financial incentives for performance can crowd out intrinsic motivation and hurt performance (Osterloh & Frey, 2002; Perry, Mesch, & Paalberg, 2006).

Several humanitarian organizations have performance evaluation policies (ALNAP, 2016; IFRC, 2011; UN, 2010). However, these policies do not have sections instructing on awarding financial bonuses or financially penalizing humanitarian workers based on the results of evaluations. Financially speaking, evaluations could be used to grant salary increments at best (e.g., UN, 2010). This reinforces the difficulties of studying framing effects in financial incentives based on the performance of humanitarian workers.

On the other hand, many humanitarian workers receive a hardship and/or danger pay in addition to their base salary. Hardship and danger pays are allowances established for humanitarian workers who are required to work in places where living and working conditions are difficult and very dangerous conditions prevail, respectively. Attribute framing research could explore framing alternatives for these allowances. For example, one could manipulate the frame of the allowance in terms of the degree of either hardship or comfort of the working environment and ask people to evaluate, for instance, the attractiveness of such allowance. One could thus test what frame leads to either greater or lower attractiveness. Findings from this kind of research could be useful to design the arrangements of these allowances to, for example, increase the recruitment of humanitarian workers for some locations.

Table 9.3 summarizes the applications discussed above, showing the activity subject to framing effects, the variables that are manipulated, the frame applied to them and its implementation.

Table 9.3 Summary of applications of framing effects research in humanitarian operations

Activity	Variable	Frame	Implementation
Prepositioning	Shortage cost	Opportunity cost	Forgone savings
		Penalty cost	Expediting costs
	Shortage consequences	Negative	Costs of rush orders
		Positive	Savings from not rushing orders
		Lives saved	See Table 9.2
		Lives lost	
	Purchasing transaction	Neutral	Credit scheme
		Mixed	Standard/loan schemes
Recruitment	Hardship allowance	Negative	Degree of hardship
		Positive	Degree of comfort
	Danger allowance	Negative	Degree of danger
		Positive	Degree of safety

9.5 Conclusion

This chapter discussed framing effects research in operations management and how it could be applied to study related problems in humanitarian operations. It reviewed studies in inventory management and employee productivity. In inventory management, framing manipulations are present in the costs of the problem, the metric subject to optimization and the type of purchasing transaction. In employee productivity, framing manipulations are present in incentive schemes.

Most of the reviewed studies reported framing effects in the expected directions, showing that decision-makers in operations management are prone to framing effects. Based on the reviewed studies and the particularities of humanitarian operations, the chapter proposed potential research topics to explore framing effects in humanitarian operations.

In prepositioning problems, the proposed topics revolved around the idea of manipulating the costs of the problem, the consequences of shortages and leftovers and the type of purchasing transaction to either increase or decrease stockpiles of relief supplies. In humanitarian workers' productivity, the proposed topics revolved around the idea of manipulating hardship and danger allowances to improve recruitment efforts.

The chapter has some limitations. The review did not include behavioral contracting or pricing studies. For example, future research could explore how different (but mathematically equivalent) supply chain contracts can be transferred to procurement problems in humanitarian operations and propose research agendas to explore their effectiveness and behavioral differences among them. Volunteer management was not mentioned in humanitarian workers' productivity. Since volunteers are not under contractual obligation, one cannot talk about framing allowances. However, employee volunteering programs could be within the scope of framing research. Employee volunteering refers to volunteering organized and/or supported by employers through financial incentives, special rewards or other means of direct support (EC, 2014). For example, framing research could explore framing options for these incentives and/or rewards to increase employee involvement in volunteering initiatives. Based on the reviewed studies, the chapter considered only two activities within humanitarian operations that could be affected by framing effects. More activities could be affected by framing effects (e.g., funding, needs assessment). Future research should hypothesize what other activities within humanitarian operations could be prone to framing effects and propose research agendas to explore them.

Finally, the research designs outlined in this chapter are exploratory. Researchers may adapt them to the research questions (framing effects) they intend to study. Behavioral experiments are a reasonable research method to start exploring these designs before trying to implement them in the field. Given the humanitarian context of the proposed designs, caution is suggested when applying the method. Sankaranarayanan, Castañeda and Villa (2018) discuss different challenges that a humanitarian context brings to behavioral experiments.

References

ALNAP. (2016). *Evaluation of humanitarian action guide. ALNAP guide*. London, UK: ALNAP/ODI.

Bendoly, E. (2013). Real-time feedback and booking behavior in the hospitality industry: Moderating the balance between imperfect judgment and imperfect prescription. *Journal of Operations Management, 31*(1–2), 62–71.

Chen, L., Kök, A. G., & Tong, J. D. (2013). The effect of payment schemes on inventory decisions: The role of mental accounting. *Management Science, 59*(2), 436–451.

EC. (2014). *Employee volunteering and employee volunteering in humanitarian aid in Europe*. Brussels: EC.

Hannan, R., Hoffman, V., & Moser, D. (2005). Bonus versus penalty: Does contract frame affect employee effort? In A. Rapoport & R. Zwick (Eds.), *Experimental business research* (pp. 151–169). Dordrecht, The Netherlands: Springer.

Ho, T.-H., & Zhang, J. (2008). Designing pricing contracts for boundedly rational customers: Does the framing of the fixed fee matter? *Management Science, 54*(4), 686–700.

Holguín-Veras, J., Jaller, M., Van Wassenhove, L., Pérez, N., & Wachtendorf, T. (2014). Material convergence: Important and understudied disaster phenomenon. *Natural Hazards Review, 15*(1), 1–12.

Hossain, T., & List, J. A. (2012). The behavioralist visits the factory: Increasing productivity using simple framing manipulations. *Management Science, 58*(12), 2151–2167.

IFRC. (2011). *IFRC framework for evaluation*. Geneva: IFRC.

Kahneman, D., & Tversky, A. (1979). Prospect theory: An analysis of decision under risk. *Econometrica, 47*(2), 263–291.

Kahneman, D., & Tversky, A. (1984). Choices, values, and frames. *American Psychologist, 39*(4), 341–350.

Katok, E., & Wu, D. Y. (2009). Contracting in supply chains: A laboratory investigation. *Management Science, 55*(12), 1953–1968.

Kremer, M., Minner, S., & Van Wassenhove, L. N. (2010). Do random errors explain newsvendor behavior? *Manufacturing & Service Operations Management, 12*(4), 673–681.

Kremer, M., & Van Wassenhove, L. N. (2014). Willingness to pay for shifting inventory risk: The role of contractual form. *Production and Operations Management, 23*(2), 239–252.

Levin, I. P., & Gaeth, G. J. (1988). How consumers are affected by the framing of attribute information before and after consuming the product. *Journal of Consumer Research, 15*(3), 374–378.

Levin, I. P., Gaeth, G. J., & Schreiber, J. (2002). A new look at framing effects: Distribution of effect sizes, individual differences, and independence of types of effects. *Organizational Behavior and Human Decision Processes, 88*(1), 411–429.

Levin, I. P., Schneider, S. L., & Gaeth, G. J. (1998). All frames are not created equal: A typology and critical analysis of framing effects. *Organizational Behavior and Human Decision Processes, 76*(2), 149–188.

Levin, I. P., Schnittjer, S. K., & Thee, S. L. (1988). Information framing effects in social and personal decisions. *Journal of Experimental Social Psychology, 24*(6), 520–529.

Meyerowitz, B. E., & Chaiken, S. (1987). The effect of message framing on breast self-examination attitudes, intentions, and behavior. *Journal of Personality and Social Psychology, 52*(3), 500–510.

Osterloh, M., & Frey, B. S. (2002). Does pay for performance really motivate employees? In A. Neely (Ed.), *Business performance measurement: Theory and practice* (pp. 107–122). Cambridge: Cambridge University Press.

Perry, J. L., Mesch, D., & Paalberg, L. (2006). Motivating employees in a new governance era: The performance paradigm revisited. *Public Administration Review, 66*(4), 505–514.

Prelec, D., & Loewenstein, G. (1998). The red and the black: Mental accounting of savings and debt. *Marketing Science, 17*(1), 4–28.

Sankaranarayanan, K., Castañeda, J. A., & Villa, S. (2018). Future research in humanitarian operations: A behavioral operations perspective. In G. Kovács, K. M. Spens, & M. Moshtari (Eds.), *The Palgrave handbook of humanitarian logistics and supply chain management* (pp. 71–117). London, UK: Palgrave Macmillan.

Schiffels, S., Fügener, A., Kolisch, R., & Brunner, O. J. (2014). On the assessment of costs in a newsvendor environment: Insights from an experimental study. *Omega, 43*(March), 1–8.

Schultz, K. L., McClain, J. O., Robinson, L. W., & Thomas, L. J. (2007). The use of framing in inventory decisions. *Johnson School Research Paper Series #02–07*, Cornell University, Ithaca, NY.

Tokar, T., Aloysius, J., Waller, M., & Hawkins, D. L. (2016). Exploring framing effects in inventory control decisions: Violations of procedure invariance. *Production and Operations Management, 25*(2), 306–329.

Tversky, A., & Kahneman, D. (1981). The framing of decisions and the psychology of choice. *Science, 211*(4481), 453–458.

Tversky, A., & Kahneman, D. (1986). Rational choice and the framing of decisions. *Journal of Business, 59*(4), S251–S278.

UN. (2010). *Performance management and development system*. New York, NY: United Nations.

Van der Laan, E. A., de Brito, M. P., & Vergunst, D. A. (2009). Performance measurement in humanitarian supply chains. *International Journal of Risk Assessment and Management, 13*(1), 22–45.

Van Wassenhove, L. N. (2006). Humanitarian aid logistics: Supply chain management in high gear. *Journal of the Operational Research Society, 57*(5), 475–489.

Wu, D. Y., & Chen, K.-Y. (2014). Supply chain contract design: Impact of bounded rationality and individual heterogeneity. *Production and Operations Management, 23*(2), 253–268.

Part III

Dynamics

10

Modeling Disaster Operations Management Problems with System Dynamics

Carlos A. Delgado-Álvarez and Yris Olaya-Morales

10.1 Introduction

The aim of this chapter is to illustrate the potential use of System Dynamics (SD) to study Humanitarian operations management (HOM) problems. Before and after a disaster, there are several complex decision-making issues that humanitarian agencies and governments have to deal with in the short, medium, and long term. Managing inflows of population, volunteers, resources, and funds are some examples of complex tasks that humanitarian managers have to address routinely during an emergency. To perform these tasks, managers need to estimate impact at the

---

C. A. Delgado-Álvarez (✉)
Faculty of Business, Politécnico Colombiano Jaime Isaza Cadavid,
Medellín, Colombia
e-mail: cadelgado@elpoli.edu.co

Y. Olaya-Morales
Department of Computing and Decision Sciences, Universidad Nacional de Colombia, Medellín, Colombia
e-mail: yolayam@unal.edu.co

© The Author(s) 2019
S. Villa et al. (eds.), *Decision-making in Humanitarian Operations*,
https://doi.org/10.1007/978-3-319-91509-8_10

mitigation and preparedness phases, plan service capacity, and make operational decisions during the immediate response phase, among other actions. However, during a disaster, decision-making is subject to uncontrollable and uncertain factors including social behaviors, changing operating conditions, conflicting interests, and unpredictable and interrelated impacts.

Lack of planning and preparation before an emergency, and lack of coordination for immediate response have devastating consequences as observed in the aftermath of hurricane Katrina in 2005 (Farazmand, 2007) or the Haiti earthquake in 2010 (IASC, 2010). Hurricane Katrina evidenced the importance of adequate mitigation and preparedness for disasters. The response when the storm landed was slow and only 80% of the New Orleans population had evacuated when the levees failed (DOT, n.d.). Nearly 90,000 people remained in the city with need of assistance but delivery of supplies was tardy, and there was not a clear plan for receiving, storing and distributing donations (Sebbah, Boukhtouta, Berger, & Berger, 2013).

In the Haiti case, the airport and harbors were not operational immediately after the emergency which created logistical challenges for initial response. Delivery of aid was further delayed for lack of coordination between logistics partners. Humanitarian organizations were overwhelmed by a large influx of volunteers with no previous experience and skills, and of inappropriate in-kind donations (Patrick, 2011). The cholera epidemic that spread after the earthquake evidenced the difficulties of the recovery phase and the importance of reducing vulnerability during recovery and mitigation phases.

System dynamics is a suitable method to analyze complex decisions under dynamic and uncertain conditions, to model the soft variables involved in coordinating multiple decision-makers in uncertain environments, and to anticipate the unintended consequences of actions. The system thinking approach of SD helps with problem formulation by identifying cause and effect relationships and feedback cycles. SD models built from these relationships are useful for understanding accumulation processes and complex dynamic behaviors and once validated, for generating scenarios and testing alternative policies.

As discussed in following sections SD has been applied to study a variety of HOM problems such as: service capacity and delivery of humanitarian supplies, customs clearance procedures, resource allocation (e.g. volunteer and personnel training, hiring personnel, trucks, fleet vehicles), and staff learning and training process.

This chapter is organized as follows: The next section describes the humanitarian operations (HO) associated with the phases of the disaster management cycle. Section 10.3 discusses the complexity of decision-making during disasters, while Sect. 10.4 presents a summary of OR/MS methods for supporting decision-making in HOM. Section 10.5 describes the system dynamics methodology and Sect. 10.6 illustrates the application of an SD model for understanding a simple HO problem.

10.2 Humanitarian Operations Management and the Disaster Cycle

Natural and man-made disasters endanger or devastate human life, properties and environment (Nikbakhsh & Zanjirani Farahani, 2011). Humanitarian relief operations seek to reduce loss of life, ease suffering, and advance human dignity through research on planning and responding to disasters (Ergun, Keskinocak, & Swann, 2011; Van Wassenhove, 2006). Four phases: mitigation, preparedness, response and recovery make up the disaster management cycle (Altay & Green, 2006; Van Wassenhove, 2006).

10.2.1 Mitigation

Mitigation and preparedness take place before disaster events. Mitigation seeks to prevent hazards or reduce the impact of disasters through long-term planning and investments. Structural mitigation measures apply technological advances while nonstructural measures like legislation, land-use planning and insurance create conditions for preventing disasters and reducing risk (Nikbakhsh & Zanjirani Farahani, 2011).

10.2.2 Preparedness

Preparedness involves making plans to respond to a disaster and ensuring that five key elements: human and financial resources, knowledge and process management, and community are in place (Van Wassenhove, 2006). These elements are interrelated as explained by Van Wassenhove (2006).

Selection and training of human resources (HR) helps to develop planning, coordination and execution capabilities in local and international teams. Knowledge management, which consists of capturing, codifying and transferring operations knowledge about operations learned from previous disasters, aids in developing HR capabilities. Operations and process management involve logistics decisions such as setting up goods, agreements and means to move resources quickly. Operations can be improved by developing agreements with other humanitarian organizations, governments, military, and business (community). Finally, sufficient funds and financial resources allow preparation and a smooth response.

10.2.3 Response

In the response phase resources, personnel and equipment are immediately dispatched to the disaster area and emergency procedures are employed. In this phase, the quality and speed of logistics impacts the ability of local communities to reconstruct themselves after a disaster (Leiras et al., 2014) and successful response requires a plan for coordination of relief forces and operations (Altay & Green, 2006).

10.2.4 Recovery

Finally, recovery includes rehabilitation and reconstruction activities to restore affected areas to their previous state (Van Wassenhove, 2006), as well as community self-sufficiency and local/national governance (Goldschmidt & Kumar, 2016). During recovery there are opportunities to reduce future risks by implementing mitigation techniques while, ideally, lessons learned after the disaster inform mitigation and preparedness phases (Ergun et al., 2011; Kovács & Spens, 2009; Zeimpekis, Minis, & Ichoua, 2013).

10.3 Decision Context in Humanitarian Operations Management

HOM deals with unpredictable impacts of disasters, complex operating conditions and changing needs (Overstreet, Hall, Hanna, & Kelly Rainer, 2011; Van Wassenhove, 2006). HO decisions depend on environmental, economic and social contexts (Kunz & Reiner, 2012) and decision-making in each part of the disaster cycle involves multiple parties and organizations with sometimes conflicting objectives. Interaction of local and international humanitarian organizations (IHO), private sector companies, governments, military, and individuals is complex, as these organizations face uncertain and dynamic conditions, time pressure, resource constraints, and rigid funding structures (Besiou, Stapleton, & Van Wassenhove, 2011; Kovács & Spens, 2009; Van Wassenhove, 2006).

Van Wassenhove (2006) highlights how diverse and interacting factors hide the nature of problems, and increase complexity of disaster operation management. Ignored factors, and ambiguous cause-effect relationships further complicate disaster management. Multiple feedback loops arise as bad crisis management triggers new phenomena and actors and operations interact.

10.4 Research for Decision Support in HOM

HOM is an emerging research field in operations management (OM) and supply chain management (SCM) that has gained increasing attention of many OM researchers (Altay & Green, 2006; Ergun et al., 2011; Goldschmidt & Kumar, 2016; Kovács & Spens, 2009).

Most studies in HOM focus on the response, preparedness and mitigation phases of a disaster (Altay & Green, 2006; Kunz & Reiner, 2012). Despite its importance in mitigating risks (Goldschmidt & Kumar, 2016), the recovery phase is less studied (Kunz & Reiner, 2012).

OR/MS methods, including decision analysis, mathematical programming, expert systems and simulation, have been applied to support decision-making in HO. (Kunz & Reiner, 2012; Simpson & Hancock,

2009; Overstreet et al., 2011; Özdamar & Ertem, 2015; Kovács & Spens, 2011). Planning of delivering systems and inventory control during the response and preparedness phase are the most commonly addressed problems (Kunz & Reiner, 2012; Goldschmidt & Kumar, 2016). Facility location, inventory management, and network flows problems are formulated and solved using mathematical programming and heuristics while uncertain disaster impacts are studied using stochastic programming and scenario analysis models (Altay & Green, 2006; Leiras et al., 2014; Overstreet et al., 2011; Özdamar & Ertem, 2015).

Mathematical programming models and the normative solutions they provide rely on data and strong assumptions about resources availability. Thus, simulation methods, including discrete event, agent-based and SD models, have been applied to manage uncertainty and incomplete knowledge characterizing HOM (Altay & Green, 2006).

Among the applications of simulation to HOM are traffic (Özdamar & Ertem, 2015) and mass evacuation (Swamy, Kang, Battam, & Chung, 2016), understanding of chain events (Santella, Steinberg, & Parks, 2009), and training for understanding the complexity of resources planning (Albores & Shaw, 2008; Rauner, Schaffhauser-Linzatti, & Niessner, 2012). SD and its applications for strategic planning and complex systems analysis are underrepresented in HO literature (Altay & Green, 2006).

Table 10.1 summarizes the range of applications of SD in HOM. These applications include systems thinking for problem formulation, generic models for learning and understanding complex dynamics issues and models for supporting strategic decision-making. Most SD applications in Table 10.1 relate to planning for the preparedness and mitigation phases of the disaster cycle.

Planning for human-made and natural disasters is, in some aspects, a wicked problem as each disaster is unique and its impacts and solutions depend on social conditions and political decisions. IHO's, for instance, need to coordinate their actions with multiple stakeholders from private sector companies to governments and donors in order to assist victims of human-made and natural disasters that develop in complex environments (Besiou et al., 2011). Systems thinking and SD has been useful for identifying causal relationships and structuring complex problems such as coordination of partnerships (Heaslip, 2013) or the vicious cycle

Table 10.1 Applications of system dynamics and systems thinking to HOM

Systems thinking	
Problem structuring and understanding	
Mitigation	Causal diagrams are used to represent causal relationships between system components and to identify the disruptive variables and feedback mechanisms that can amplify disruptions, thus creating risks (Powell, Mustafee, Chen, & Hammond, 2016).
	A system dynamics framework is used to propose and perform econometrics tests of causal and feedback relationships between disasters occurrence and economic and population vulnerability (Sodhi, 2016).
Preparedness	Dynamics of risk potential in mass-gathering events and its implications for policy (Handel, Biedermann, Kielar, & Borrmann, 2014).
Response	Coordination and partnership selection in logistics operations involving military and aid organizations. Uses systems analysis and design techniques (SADT) and system dynamics for identifying causal relationships (Heaslip, 2013)
	Flow of financial resources from different donors and with different constraints (Burkart, Besiou, & Wakolbinger, 2016)
Generic models for learning and understanding dynamic complexity	
	Feedback loops and delays
	Uncertainty
	Accumulation dynamics
Mitigation	Models the relationship between the quantity of non-novel events and organizational crises. The rate of interruptions resolution decreases as incoming interruptions arrive and accumulate (Rudolph & Repenning, 2002).
Preparedness	A model for the 1992 Westrey mine disaster in Nova Scotia, Canada shows that accidents are outputs of a complex system in which organizational and personal commitment is needed to create a safety culture (Cooke, 2003).
	State of preparedness increases with technology changes, attitudes to prevent risk, and resource state availability (Kwesi-Buor, Menachof, & Talas, 2016).
Response	Model for the evacuation process includes evacuees and relief units conducting evacuation and installing mobile protections during a flood (Berariu, Fikar, Gronalt, & Hirsch, 2016).
Recovery	Labor availability limits the ability for housing reconstruction after a disaster. Labor management model to support housing construction after a disaster (Kumar, Diaz, Behr, & Toba, 2015).
	Flow of materials during reconstruction (Diaz, Kumar, & Behr, 2015).

(continued)

Table 10.1 (continued)

	Models for supporting strategic decisions *Resource allocation* *Capacity building* *Impact of capacity and information delays on lead times*
Mitigation	Flood relief costs in the U.S. continue to rise, despite the availability of federal policies. A generic system dynamics model is developed to show how policies can increase vulnerability in flood-prone areas (Deegan, 2006). The Critical Infrastructure Protection Decision Support System (CIPDSS) is a system dynamics model of the interdependences between critical infrastructures in a disaster. A scenario for road and telecommunications damage is examined (Santella et al., 2009).
Preparedness	Mitigation and preparation for urban disasters, focusing on preparation of urban subsystems: population, industry, transportation, public facilities, housing, life-support and environmental protection (Ho, Chienhao, & Hsiao-Lin, 2006). A model of field vehicle fleet management for international humanitarian organizations is developed and applied to study the impact of donations and media attention on humanitarian relief operations (Besiou et al., 2011) Field vehicle management in international humanitarian organization. SD model for long-term planning of 4WD vehicles under management and funding scenarios (Besiou, Pedraza-Martinez, & Van Wassenhove, 2014)
Response	The delivery of ready to use therapeutic food items for immediate response phase is modeled using system dynamics. Scenarios of developing disaster management capabilities and prepositioning inventory are compared. The impact of developing management capabilities in custom clearance lead times is estimated (Kunz, Reiner, & Gold, 2014). Impact of dynamic road conditions and information delays on on-time transportation rate (Min Peng, Peng, & Chen, 2014). Dynamic lead-time prediction after an earthquake considering dynamic road conditions and information delays (M Peng, Chen, & Zhou, 2014).
Recovery	Identify temporary debris management sites and evaluate debris removal under different scenarios using SD and GIS (Kim, Deshmukh, & Hastak, 2018).

(continued)

Table 10.1 (continued)

Models for policy support	
	Policy evaluation
	Potential impacts evaluation
Preparedness	Social and psychological factors, including awareness of risk and knowledge of disasters, affect population acceptances of evacuation orders (Simonovic & Ahmad, 2005).
	Disaster planning in remote rural communities, specifically hospital's surge capacity (Hoard et al., 2005).

linking disaster impacts with increased economic and population vulnerability (Sodhi, 2016).

Regarding dynamic complexity, generic SD models have been developed to increase learning and understanding of the effect of feedback loops, delays, and accumulation dynamics in HO such as evacuees and resources flows (Berariu et al., 2016; Diaz et al., 2015; Kumar et al., 2015) and on risk (Cooke, 2003; Rudolph & Repenning, 2002) and preparedness (Kwesi-Buor et al., 2016).

Other SD models applications aim at supporting strategic decisions, such as capabilities development, and resources allocation, considering information and transportation delays. Finally, other models are developed to analyze operative policies affecting evacuations (Simonovic & Ahmad, 2005) and hospital surge capacity (Hoard et al., 2005).

10.5 System Dynamics in HO

SD is a policy-oriented quantitative systems approach classified within the problem-structuring methods and soft systems approaches. It emerged as a system modeling and simulation methodology to capture, understand, and analyze the dynamics of complex systems. The system complexity is determined by non-linear interactions among the elements of the system, multiple feedback processes, time delays, and stock and flow structures (Sterman, 2000).

Feedback means that problems are consequences of our previous decisions and actions. That is, assuming that managers see problems as discrepancies between the current situation and their goals, solving these problems entails decisions leading to actions and results that change the current situation alleviating the current problem, but generating new discrepancies with our next goals (Morecroft, 2015). Feedback processes are represented by closed loops formed by the interaction among variables and describe the way a decision can determine the state of the system in the short or long term. In feedback processes, a change in a variable leads either to counteracting (i.e., balancing or negative feedback loop) or reinforcing (i.e., reinforcing or positive feedback loop) the change when the effects of that change are followed around the loop (Morecroft, 2015). The dynamics of the system arises from the interaction between feedback loops.

Feedback is often delayed. Time delays between actions and their impact on the state of the system make long-term responses different from short-term responses and increase dynamic complexity (Sterman, 2000). As discussed by Sterman (2000) time delays reduce our ability to accumulate experience by cycling around learning loops, and cause interventions to continue well after they are needed, producing instability and oscillations.

Managers usually make decisions based on their experience and intuition considering problems as event-oriented systems, even in complex situations, and ignoring feedback (Sterman, 2000). The SD methodology facilitates the comprehension of problems and allows gaining relevant insights into the feedback processes which determine the system behavior.

A logical and intuitive process is used to capture key complexities of a system (Kumar et al., 2015) and analysis tools allow managers to evaluate the short and long-term effects of their decisions. SD is useful to learn about system complexity, understand the source of policy resistance, and design better operating policies to improve systems' performance (Sterman, 2000). SD is also used as a systems thinking tool for analyzing HOM problems as complex systems formed by interconnected elements with the same purpose (e.g., Powell et al., 2016). Through SD we can construct broad-brush models to capture a holistic view of the system and understand cause-and-effect relationships.

10.5.1 System Dynamics Modeling Process

System dynamics modeling is a continuous and iterative learning process which involves articulating the problem, formulating a dynamic hypothesis, building, testing, and reviewing a simulation model, and designing and evaluating policies (Sterman, 2000). Problem articulation implies defining the issue under investigation, the key variables and factors that must be considered to address such issues, the time horizon, and the reference modes (i.e., the historical and future behavior of key variables). Stakeholders associated with the problem play an important role in this step. During problem articulation, the modeling team must keep in touch with stakeholders to gather information about the issues that concern them the most and their purpose with the model (Sterman, 2000). The modeling team must capture enough information for building a model aimed at addressing a specific problem rather than an entire system.

10.5.1.1 Dynamic Hypothesis Formulation

The dynamic hypothesis is a preliminary theory, developed by the modeling team together with the client, to account for the structure that yields the system behavior through time. This hypothesis provides the modeling team with an endogenous explanation for the behavioral patterns of the system generated by the interaction of the variables (Sterman, 2000). SD offers a set of diagramming tools to facilitate developing and understanding this hypothesis. The most used are causal loop diagrams (CLDs) and stock and flow (S&F) maps.

10.5.1.2 Causal Loop Diagrams

A CLD is a flexible and visual tool useful for capturing our mental models about the dynamic hypothesis of the system by diagramming the cause and effect relationships between variables that depict the feedback structure (Morecroft, 2015; Sterman, 2000). A CLD is drawn by connecting variables through links (arrows), indicating that a variable has influence on another. Each link is assigned a polarity, either positive or negative, to denote the effect the causing variable has on the influenced variable. A link with positive '+' polarity implies that effect moves in the same direction than the cause (i.e., as the cause increases, the effect increases as well; or, as the cause decreases, the effect decreases too), whereas a negative '−' polarity entails that effect moves in the opposite direction than the cause (i.e., as the cause increases, the effect decreases; or, as the cause decreases, the effect increases). Feedback loops are easily identified in a CLD by tracing the effect of a change in a variable. We have a feedback loop when that effect propagates across the arrows linking the variables and arrives at the variable which originally effects the change. If that effect strengthens the original change, there is a positive (i.e., reinforcing) feedback loop; otherwise, if the effect contrasts with the original change, there is a negative (i.e., balancing) feedback loop (Sterman, 2000).

10.5.1.3 Stock and Flows Maps

CLDs are very useful for capturing mental models and communicating feedback structure. However, they do not differentiate between the S&F structure of dynamic systems. Complex problems are modeled using SD under a S&F structure where stocks represent state variables that describe the state of the system and change over time depending on the flows. Subjects' decisions are based on information generated by the stocks and the resulting actions are reflected in the flow rates.

In an S&F map, tanks (rectangles) represent stocks, while pipes controlled by valves represent flows. Flows can be inflow or outflow variables. Inflow and outflow variables control stock levels by increasing and decreasing them. Tangible (e.g., material and goods) and intangible (e.g., information) items flow through S&F structures. Stocks perform as a kind of memory which stores the results of past decisions (Morecroft, 2015). For example, stocks can represent inventory levels, people waiting to be evacuated, a backlog of patients, humanitarian supplies waiting for the clearance certificate and warehouse capacity levels, among others. Inflow variables include incoming humanitarian aid, allocation rate of relief units, injured people and capacity-acquisition rate, among others. Outflow variables could be humanitarian aid delivery rate, surgery rate, medical service rate and evacuation rate, among others. Flows originating outside the boundary of the model surge from a source, while flows leaving the model drain into a sink. Both sources and sinks are represented by a cloud (Sterman, 2000).

In addition to the stock and flow variables, a SD model contains auxiliary variables. Such variables enable different S&F structures communicate among them. These can be endogenous (i.e., as functions of stocks or other auxiliary variables) or exogenous variables (i.e., parameters or constants).

10.5.1.4 Formalization of the Model

The model requires equation formulation, parameterization and simulation for understanding the structure/behavior relationship (Lane & Husemann, 2008). Equation (10.1) is the mathematical expression for a S&F structure. This equation determines the way stock variables accumulate according to the net flow—inflow rate minus outflow rate.

$$\text{Stock level}(t) = \int_{t_0}^{t} \left[\text{Inflow}(t) - \text{Outflow}(t) \right] dt + \text{Stock level}(t_0) \tag{10.1}$$

The S&F's structure and equations allow us to transform the qualitative feedback loops of the CLD into quantitative dynamic models useful for diagnosing performance problems, testing policies and strategies, and designing experiments for learning from the complexity of the systems (Morecroft, 2015).

The next step after clearly defining the structure of the system behavior is to formalize it by building a computer simulation model. Building a simulation model includes specifying its structure in a computer program, allocating constant values to the exogenous variables (parametrization) and validating or testing the model for consistency within its purpose and boundaries (Sterman, 2000). The computer simulation models are used to conduct experiments to test the dynamic hypothesis and assess policies and strategies. To test the dynamic hypothesis, simulated behavior is compared to the actual behavior of the system.

Once built, the formal computer simulation model must be validated by applying different tests described by Sterman (2000) and Barlas (1994). The objective of validation is to establish that the model satisfies its intended purpose. Validation tests include running the model under extreme conditions, verifying that it obeys physical laws, checking dimensional consistency, assessing parameters, performing sensitivity analysis and testing integration errors, among others. For a detailed description of validation tests see Sterman (2000).

10.5.1.5 Policy Analysis

SD methodology allows decision-makers to create alternative what-if scenarios to assess their action policies without taking risks in the real system. When the simulation model is finished and validated, the modeling team interacts with stakeholders to establish a common framework for policy analysis (Hoard et al., 2005). The policy analysis provides decision-makers with a picture of how their ideas or strategies might perform, and enables them to design the best path to success. In the SD context, policies refer to strategies, new structures and decision rules aimed at improving the system behavior. That is, policies can involve changing or adding feedback loops, eliminating time delays, modifying the decisions-making process, and/or changing parameters (Sterman, 2000). By carrying out a policy analysis with a SD model, decision-makers can obtain evidence of how their strategies impact the system performance without losing sight of the control variables of the system and avoiding risks.

10.6 An Illustrative Example: Water Supply after a Disaster

The supply of water to the population affected by a disaster is a relevant dynamic issue during the response phase. Figure 10.1 illustrates a simple S&F diagram for describing the process of delivering and distributing water to an affected community. Tankers deliver water from a nearby location and volunteers in the disaster zone distribute water to the affected population. Two key resources are modeled: tankers and volunteers. A number of tankers and volunteers are available in the first response stage, and the model finds the additional tankers and volunteers needed to deliver water within desired standards.

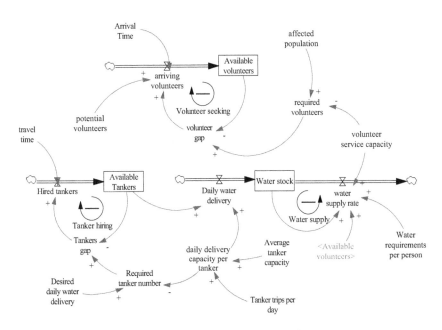

Fig. 10.1 Stock and flow diagram for water delivery after a disaster

10.6.1 The Dynamic Hypothesis of the Problem

Each tanker has a *daily delivery capacity* that depends on its capacity and the number of trips it makes during the day. All tankers are assumed to have the same *average tanker capacity* and make the same number of trips per day (*tanker trips per day*). The variable *required tankers number* is a function of the *desired daily water delivery*, which represents the estimated cubic meters (m^3) per day needed to attend to the community and is assumed to be constant, and of the *daily delivery capacity per tanker*. The *required tankers number* is the goal of the balancing loop *tanker hiring*. Tankers are hired to fill the gap between available and required tankers, and their arrival is delayed by a *travel time*.

The water the tankers deliver is collected for distribution to the population, depending on the service capacity of the available volunteers. *Daily water delivery* depends on the number of *available tankers* and their *daily delivery capacity*. Volunteers distribute water at a *water supply rate* that depends on the number of *available volunteers, volunteer service capacity* and *water requirements per person*.

A balancing loop called "*volunteer seeking*" represents the process of finding volunteers to reach a distribution goal. The number of required volunteers depends on the affected population and on volunteer service capacity. A volunteer gap is defined as the difference between available and required volunteers, and potential volunteers are called and arrive to fill this gap.

10.6.2 Formalization of the Model

Equations (10.2), (10.3), and (10.4) are the mathematical expressions of the S&F structure and determine the dynamics of the system (Sterman, 2000). They represent the way *available tankers, available volunteers, and supplied water*, respectively, accumulate according to their net flow—inflow rate minus outflow rate. An equivalent expression is Eq. (10.5), which describes the net change in the water stock at any time t.

$$\text{Available tankers}(t) = \int_{t_0}^{t} \left[\text{Hired tankers}(t) \right] dt \\ + \text{Available tankers}(t_0) \quad (10.2)$$

$$\text{Available volunteers}(t) = \int_{t_0}^{t} \left[\text{Arriving volunteers}(t) \right] dt \\ + \text{Available volunteers}(t_0) \quad (10.3)$$

$$\text{Water stock}(t) = \int_{t_0}^{t} \left[\begin{array}{l} \text{Daily water delivery}(t) \\ -\text{Water supply rate}(t) \end{array} \right] dt \\ + \text{water stock}(t_0) \quad (10.4)$$

$$\frac{\text{dSupplied water}}{dt} = \text{Daily water supply}(t) \\ - \text{Serving rate}(t) \quad (10.5)$$

Model parameters for this example are based on water delivery recommendations by the World Health Organization (WHO & WEDC, 2011, 2014) and own assumptions, and summarized in Table 10.2.

10.6.3 Simulation Results

The dynamic issue at the water supply problem is coordinating supply capacity given by available tankers and available volunteers with the water requirements of the community. Figure 10.1 shows that the dynamics of both the available tankers and available volunteers is determined by negative feedback loops which act to bring the states of these two stock variables in line with the desired states. Figures 10.2a and b illustrate the resulting behaviors of this negative feedback structure on the available tankers and the available volunteers. Figure 10.2c shows that the water stock increases. This occurs because the *desired daily water delivery* (200 m³/day) is higher than the *desired water supply rate* (150 m³/day)

Table 10.2 Parameters for model formalization

Estimated parameter	Value	Units	Sources/assumptions
Desired daily water delivery	200	m³ per day	Based on (WHO & WEDC, 2014)
Average tanker capacity	5	m³	Based on (WHO & WEDC, 2014)
Tanker trips per day	11	Trips per day	Based on 130 minutes gross turnaround time in (WHO & WEDC, 2014)
Water requirements per person	0.015	m³ per day	Based on 15.2 liters per day requirements for a community during survival phase in (WHO & WEDC, 2011)
Arrival time (volunteers)	2	Days	Assumed
Travel time (trucks)	2	Days	Assumed
Affected population	10,000	Persons	Assumed
Volunteer service capacity	96	Persons/(volunteer-day)	Based on assumption of 5 minutes for supplying water to affected persons

and the gap between the desired and actual available tankers is corrected faster than the gap between the desired and actual available volunteers, as shown in Figs. 10.2a and b. Enough tankers and budget are available to satisfy hiring needs while the arrival of new volunteers depends on whether potential volunteers are willing to travel to the disaster site. Consequently, the success of water delivery depends on how quickly potential volunteers can be engaged. According to Fig. 10.2d, it takes about 17 days for the system to reach the desired water supply. Thus, our analysis suggests that design policies should be focused on attracting new volunteers.

10.6.4 Policy Analysis

The model is used to test an advertising policy to attract potential volunteers. We assume that by advertising volunteer campaigns we can increase,

Modeling Disaster Operations Management Problems... 241

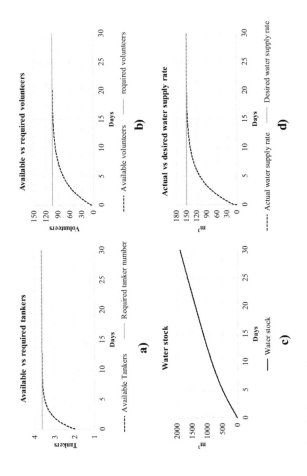

Fig. 10.2 Base case simulation results

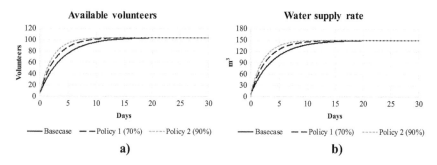

Fig. 10.3 Policy analysis results

to some extent, the impact of potential volunteers on the net inflow volunteers (i.e., arriving volunteers). To illustrate the impact of such a policy, we change the parameter of potential volunteers and again simulate the model with the new values. This parameter represents the effectiveness of campaigns to attract and train new volunteers and is modeled as a percentage of the volunteer gap. Figure 10.3 illustrates the resulting behavior for three different values of the parameter *potential volunteers*: 0.5 (base case), 0.7 (policy 1), and 0.9 (policy 1). Results show that the higher the share of potential volunteers reached by campaigns, the faster the new volunteers arrive, and the quicker the target water supply is achieved. This result reflects the importance of the number of available volunteers for appropriately attending to a catastrophe.

10.7 Conclusions and Future Work

This chapter illustrates how SD can be used as a framework to study HOM problems. The SD simulation and modeling process has been described, as have the kind of HOM issues that can be addressed. Learning is one of the main applications of simulation and SD models in HO. Learning through models allows for continuous improvement of disaster operations management from governments and humanitarian organizations.

SD modeling and simulation provides humanitarian decision-makers with information to make strategic decisions that increase the performance of the entire humanitarian supply chain. By modeling feedback mechanisms, accumulations and delays, system dynamics helps governments to understand the unintended impacts of their policies and to be aware of the long-term performance of plans for mitigating disasters and protecting populations from hazards. Disaster planning includes strategies for vulnerability reduction. These strategies can be tested by simulating SD models under different impact and exposure scenarios that capture disasters' uncertainty and without risking actual resources and lives. SD simulation can also help to reduce risks by educating people about the hazards and threats posed by natural disasters.

SD modeling has the potential to contribute distinctively to HOM issues. It is a useful methodology to simulate a plethora of scenarios to learn from the results and develop strategies and alternative structures for the improvement of the HOM. The humanitarian research community has mainly focused on studying issues at the response and preparedness phases, while the recovery phase is largely unexplored. Actions in the recovery phase are key to reduce risk exposure and vulnerability, but their impact depends on complex social and economic conditions. For its ability to model soft variables of decision environments, SD is a useful tool to devise reconstruction strategies and assess their long-term impacts, especially if combined with other simulation techniques and GIS. SD will be a powerful tool to explore the long-term impacts caused by strategies aimed at developing local capabilities for responding to emergencies.

Integration of SD and AB, DES, and SIG modeling and simulation is a promising area of research. Integration of GIS and SD can, among other applications, model the relationships between the physical, economic and social vulnerability of communities, and explain the interactions between natural systems (e.g., wildland, coastal) and urban areas. Neuwirth, Peck, and Simonovic (2015) propose a framework for using GIS data as initial values for the stock variables of a spatially disaggregated SD model. Modeling of spatial and temporal feedback is proposed for assessing flood risks (Ahmad & Simonovic, 2015), and coastal storm damages (Hartt, 2014). The applications of SD and SIG integrated modeling are not limited to the mitigation phase. For the recovery phase, the integration of spatial information and system dynamics has been proposed to find locations and design resilient debris management systems (Kim et al., 2018).

Some HOM problems such as the mass movement or convergence of people, supplies and information have the structure of a queuing system in which servers (volunteers), donations and messages arrive and are assigned to serve arriving customers (victims) (Lodree & Davis, 2016). Important assumptions of queuing models, such as considering arrival and service rates as exogenously determined and the steady-state condition (i.e., arrival rates do not exceed, on average, service rates), are not usually satisfied in disaster conditions. SD allows for relaxing queuing models' steady-state assumptions, and for modeling arrival and service rates as the result of endogenous processes and as influenced by soft variables such as media coverage and individual impulses.

Finally, many organizations with conflicting objectives interact in humanitarian operations. A combination of system dynamics with multi-criteria decision analysis is proposed to capture decision-makers' priorities and to design policies to achieve several objectives (Pruyt, 2007; Tsaples, Papathanasiou, & Ploskas, 2017)

References

Ahmad, S. S., & Simonovic, S. P. (2015). System dynamics and hydrodynamic modelling approaches for spatial and temporal analysis of flood risk. *International Journal of River Basin Management, 13*(4), 443–461.

Albores, P., & Shaw, D. (2008). Government preparedness: Using simulation to prepare for a terrorist attack. *Computers and Operations Research, 35*(6), 1924–1943.

Altay, N., & Green, W. G. (2006). OR/MS research in disaster operations management. *European Journal of Operational Research, 175*(1), 475–493.

Barlas, Y. (1994). Model validation in system dynamics. *System Dynamics Review, 12*(3), 183–210.

Berariu, R., Fikar, C., Gronalt, M., & Hirsch, P. (2016). Training decision-makers in flood response with system dynamics. *Disaster Prevention and Management, 25*(2), 118–136.

Besiou, M., Pedraza-Martinez, A. J., & Van Wassenhove, L. N. (2014). Vehicle supply chains in humanitarian operations: Decentralization, operational mix, and earmarked funding. *Production and Operations Management, 23*(11), 1950–1965.

Besiou, M., Stapleton, O., & Van Wassenhove, L. N. (2011). System dynamics for humanitarian operations. *Journal of Humanitarian Logistics and Supply Chain Management, 1*(1), 78–103.

Burkart, C., Besiou, M., & Wakolbinger, T. (2016). The funding—Humanitarian supply chain interface. *Surveys in Operations Research and Management Science, 21*(2), 31–45.

Cooke, D. L. (2003). A system dynamics analysis of the Westray mine disaster. *System Dynamics Review, 19*(2), 139–166.

Deegan, M. A. (2006). Exploring U.S. flood mitigation policies: A feedback view of system behavior. In A. Größler, E. A. J. A. Rouwette, R. S. Langer, J. I. Rowe, & J. M. Yanni (Eds.), *Proceedings of the 24th International Conference of the System Dynamics Society, July 23–27, 2006, Nijmegen, The Netherlands* (p. 31). Nijmegen: The System Dynamics Society.

Diaz, R., Kumar, S., & Behr, J. (2015). Housing recovery in the aftermath of a catastrophe: Material resources perspective. *Computers and Industrial Engineering, 8*, 130–139.

DOT. (n.d.). Perspectives on disaster responses. Case study: Hurricane Katrina. U.S. Department of Transportation. Retrieved March 2018, from https://www.transportation.gov/sites/dot.dev/files/docs/7 - Case Study Hurricane Katrina US - English.pdf

Ergun, Ö., Keskinocak, P., & Swann, J. (2011). Introduction to the special issue on humanitarian applications: Doing good with good OR. *Interfaces, 41*(3), 215–222.

Farazmand, A. (2007). Learning from the Katrina crisis: A global and international perspective with implications for future crisis management. *Public Administration Review, 67*(Suppl. 1), 149–159.

Goldschmidt, K. H., & Kumar, S. (2016). Humanitarian operations and crisis/disaster management: A retrospective review of the literature and framework for development. *International Journal of Disaster Risk Reduction, 20*, 1–13.

Handel, O., Biedermann, D. H., Kielar, P. M., & Borrmann, A. (2014). A system dynamics based perspective to help to understand the managerial big picture in respect of urban event dynamics. *Transportation Research Procedia, 2*, 669–674. https://doi.org/10.1016/j.trpro.2014.09.072

Hartt, M. D. (2014). An innovative technique for modelling impacts of coastal storm damage. *Regional Studies, Regional Science, 1*(1), 240–247.

Heaslip, G. (2013). Services operations management and humanitarian logistics. *Journal of Humanitarian Logistics and Supply Chain Management, 3*(1), 37–51.

Ho, Y., Chienhao, L., & Hsiao-Lin, W. (2006). Dynamic model for earthquake disaster prevention system: A case study of Taichung City, Taiwan. In

A. Größler, E. A. J. A. Rouwette, R. S. Langer, J. I. Rowe, & J. M. Yanni (Eds.), *The 24th International Conference of the System Dynamics Society July 23–27, 2006 Nijmegen, The Netherlands* (p. 23). Nijmegen: The System Dynamics Society.

Hoard, M., Homer, J., Manley, W., Furbee, P., Haque, A., & Helmkamp, J. (2005). Systems modeling in support of evidence-based disaster planning for rural areas. *International Journal of Hygiene and Environmental Health, 208*, 117–125.

IASC. (2010). *Response to the humanitarian crisis in Haiti following the 12 January 2010 earthquake*. Retrieved March 2018, from http://www.ifrc.org/docs/IDRL/Haiti/IASC-Haiti_6Mos_Review_USA-2010-005-1.pdf

Kim, J., Deshmukh, A., & Hastak, M. (2018). A framework for assessing the resilience of a disaster debris management system. *International Journal of Disaster Risk Reduction, 28*, 674–687.

Kovács, G., & Spens, K. (2009). Identifying challenges in humanitarian logistics. *International Journal of Physical Distribution & Logistics Management, 39*(6), 506–528.

Kumar, S., Diaz, R., Behr, J. G., & Toba, A.-L. (2015). Modeling the effects of labor on housing reconstruction: A system perspective. *International Journal of Disaster Risk Reduction, 12*, 154–162.

Kunz, N., & Reiner, G. (2012). A meta-analysis of humanitarian logistics research. *Journal of Humanitarian Logistics and Supply Chain Management, 2*(2), 116–147.

Kunz, N., Reiner, G., & Gold, S. (2014). Investing in disaster management capabilities versus pre-positioning inventory: A new approach to disaster preparedness. *International Journal of Production Economics, 157*(1), 261–272.

Kwesi-Buor, J., Menachof, D. A., & Talas, R. (2016). Scenario analysis and disaster preparedness for port and maritime logistics risk management. *Accident Analysis and Prevention*, in press. http://doi.org/10.1016/j.aap.2016.07.013

Lane, D. C., & Husemann, E. (2008). System dynamics mapping of acute patient flows. *The Journal of the Operational Research Society, 59*(2), 213–224.

Leiras, A., De Brito, I., Peres, E. Q., Bertazzo, T. R., Tsugunobu, H., & Yoshizaki, Y. (2014). Literature review of humanitarian logistics research: Trends and challenges. *Journal of Humanitarian Logistics and Supply Chain Management, 4*(1), 95–130.

Lodree, E. J., Jr., & Davis, L. B. (2016). Empirical analysis of volunteer convergence following the 2011 tornado disaster in Tuscaloosa, Alabama. *Natural Hazards, 84*(2), 1109–1135. https://doi.org/10.1007/s11069-016-2477-8

Morecroft, J. D. W. (2015). *Strategic modelling and business dynamics: A feedback systems approach* (2nd ed.). New York, NY: Wiley.

Neuwirth, C., Peck, A., & Simonovic, S. P. (2015). Modeling structural change in spatial system dynamics: A Daisyworld example. *Environmental Modelling & Software, 65*, 30–40.

Nikbakhsh, E., & Zanjirani Farahani, R. (2011). Humanitarian logistics planning in disaster relief operations. In R. Farahani, S. Rezapour, & L. Kardar (Eds.), *Logistics operations and management. Concepts and models* (1st ed., pp. 291–332). Amsterdam: Elsevier Inc.

Overstreet, R. E., Hall, D., Hanna, J. B., & Kelly Rainer, R. (2011). Research in humanitarian logistics. *Journal of Humanitarian Logistics and Supply Chain Management, 1*(2), 114–131.

Özdamar, L., & Ertem, M. A. (2015). Models, solutions and enabling technologies in humanitarian logistics. *European Journal of Operational Research, 244*(1), 55–65.

Patrick, J. (2011). Haiti earthquake response Emerging evaluation lessons. *Evaluation Insights, 1*, 1–13. Retrieved from http://www.oecd.org/dac/evaluation/dcdndep/48321181.pdf

Peng, M., Chen, H., & Zhou, M. (2014). Modelling and simulating the dynamic environmental factors in post-seismic relief operation. *Journal of Simulation, 8*, 164–178.

Peng, M., Peng, Y., & Chen, H. (2014). Post-seismic supply chain risk management: A system dynamics disruption analysis approach for inventory and logistics planning. *Computers and Operations Research, 42*, 14–24.

Powell, J. H., Mustafee, N., Chen, A. S., & Hammond, M. (2016). System-focused risk identification and assessment for disaster preparedness: Dynamic threat analysis. *European Journal of Operational Research, 254*(2), 550–564.

Pruyt, E. (2007). *Dealing with uncertainties? Combining system dynamics with multiple criteria decision analysis or with exploratory modelling*. Retrieved January 2018, from https://pdfs.semanticscholar.org/d5b7/c57804409bf9cd-687b645e45a17318e2d140.pdf

Rauner, M. S., Schaffhauser-Linzatti, M. M., & Niessner, H. (2012). Resource planning for ambulance services in mass casualty incidents: A DES-based policy model. *Health Care Management Science, 15*(3), 254–269.

Rudolph, J. W., & Repenning, N. P. (2002). Disaster dynamics: Understanding the role of quantity in organizational collapse author (s): Jenny W. Rudolph and Nelson P. Repenning Published by: Sage Publications, Inc. on behalf of the Johnson Graduate School of Management, Cornell University. *Administrative Science Quarterly, 47*(1), 1–30.

Santella, N., Steinberg, L. J., & Parks, K. (2009). Decision making for extreme events: Modeling critical infrastructure interdependencies to aid mitigation and response planning. *Review of Policy Research, 26*(4), 409–422.

Sebbah, S., Boukhtouta, A., Berger, J., & Berger, A. (2013). Military logistics planning in humanitarian relief operations. In V. Zeimpekis, S. Ichoua, & I. Minis (Eds.), *Humanitarian and relief logistics. Research issues, case studies and future trends* (1st ed., p. 227). Springer.

Simonovic, S. P., & Ahmad, S. (2005). Computer-based model for flood evacuation emergency planning. *Natural Hazards, 34*(1), 25–51.

Simpson, N. C., & Hancock, P. G. (2009). Fifty years of operational research and emergency response. *The Journal of the Operational Research Society, 60*(Suppl. 1), S126–S139.

Sodhi, M. S. (2016). Natural disasters, the economy and population vulnerability as a vicious cycle with exogenous hazards. *Journal of Operations Management, 45*, 101–113.

Sterman, J. D. (2000). *Business dynamics. Systems thinking and modeling for a complex world* (1st ed.). Boston, MA: McGraw-Hill.

Swamy, R., Kang, J. E., Battam, R., & Chung, Y. (2016). Hurricane evacuation planning using public transportation. *Socio-Economic Planning Sciences, 59*, 1–20.

Tsaples, G., Papathanasiou, J., & Ploskas, N. (2017). Integrating system dynamics with exploratory MCDA for robust decision-making. In I. Linden, S. Liu, & C. Colot (Eds.), *Decision support systems VII. Data, information and knowledge visualization in decision support systems. Lecture notes in business information processing vol. 282* (pp. 179–192). Cham: Springer.

Van Wassenhove, L. N. (2006). Humanitarian aid logistics: Supply chain management in high gear. *Journal of the Operational Research Society, 57*(5), 475–489.

WHO & WEDC. (2011). *How much water is needed in emergencies* (Technical notes on drinking-water, sanitation and hygiene in emergencies No. 9). Geneva. Retrieved March 2018, from http://www.who.int/water_sanitation_health/publications/2011/tn9_how_much_water_en.pdf

WHO & WEDC. (2014). *Delivering safe water by tanker* (Technical notes on drinking-water, sanitation and hygiene in emergencies No. 12). Geneva. Retrieved March 2018, from http://www.who.int/water_sanitation_health/emergencies/WHO_TN_12_Delivering_safe_water_by_tanker.pdf

Zeimpekis, V., Minis, I., & Ichoua, S. (Eds.). (2013). *Humanitarian and relief logistics research issues, case studies and future trends. Operations research/Computer science interfaces series* (1st ed.). New York, NY: Springer London.

11

Collaborative Strategies for Humanitarian Logistics with System Dynamics and Project Management

Diana Carolina Guzmán Cortés, Leonardo José González Rodríguez, and Carlos Franco

11.1 Introduction

Interest in humanitarian operations has increased due to the rising number of natural disasters and the complexities of providing aid to the affected populations. The number of actors involved in providing aid for a disaster situation is high and the interactions among them make up a complex system, making it crucial to develop appropriate tools to coordinate the different types of operations to ensure that they can help to support the affected population.

When a natural or anthropic disaster of great magnitude and impact occurs, many actors come together to provide assistance to the population, generating problems of collaboration and coordination in the

---

D. C. Guzmán Cortés (✉) • L. J. González Rodríguez
Faculty of Engineering, Universidad de La Sabana, Chía, Colombia
e-mail: dianaguco@unisabana.edu.co; leonardo.gonzalez1@unisabana.edu.co

C. Franco
School of Management, Universidad del Rosario, Bogotá, Colombia
e-mail: carlosa.franco@urosario.edu.co

humanitarian logistics system. Coordination is affected by factors such as the number and diversity of actors, donor expectations, unpredictability, scarcity or excess resources and financial costs. This increases response times and, logically, aid provision times, thus decreasing the welfare of the affected population. Additionally, the aid handling and delivery system is highly complex and is affected by factors of randomness and delays in its process, which can be represented by SD.

In this chapter, we use project management theory to propose a combination of different techniques and concepts based on SD to develop strategies to coordinate actors in humanitarian logistics. The chapter explores these concepts in project management, comparing them with humanitarian logistics to shed light on the similarities. Also, a model based on collaboration is defined to visualize the impact on the humanitarian logistics indicators. To do this, the system is characterized by identifying the network of activities, actors and resources, and a definition of collaborative logistics strategy is presented along with some definitions of project management. The response time is determined using a dynamic model that integrates the network of system and supply chain activities to determine the possible impacts.

11.2 Actors and Flows of the Humanitarian Supply Chain

In this section, the actors and flows of the humanitarian logistics system will be presented along with the objectives of the system and an explanation of the performance of the humanitarian logistics system.

According to Van Wassenhove (2006), a disaster can be defined as a perturbation that affects the overall system and becomes a risk for the system's priorities and goals. Therefore, an event can be characterized as a disaster when it occurs in populated areas causing devastation of local infrastructure and affecting the population (Costa, Campos, & Bandeira, 2012).

When a disaster of huge magnitude and multiple impacts occurs—natural or anthropic, a variety of different actors come to the aid of the community and the affected population (Oloruntoba & Gray, 2006). This can lead to coordination problems between actors in the system, affecting response times and increasing complexity.

The Pan American Health Organization (PAHO) has identified the following as actors of the humanitarian logistics system for the local population and the affected community in nearby regions: local governments; national or foreign individuals; non-governmental organizations (NGOs); United Nations organizations; multilateral organizations; governmental agencies; bilateral, private, and commercial sectors; military forces; and organizations specialized in vulnerability analysis, risk evaluation, and needs evaluation. Oloruntoba and Gray (2006) enumerated the same actors identifying governments as donors. Holguín-Veras, Jaller, Van Wassenhove, Pérez, and Wachtendorf (2014) determined that the local community is also part of the humanitarian logistics system. They emphasized the set of social networks that are involved in the affected zone, paying particular attention to the importance of collaboration with these local social networks, their organization, resources, and knowledge to support the micro-distribution and delivery of aid to the victims (Holguín-Veras, Jaller, & Wachtendorf, 2012).

Van Wassenhove (2006) established that a supply chain has three different flows: materials, information, and financial. Each one of these flows requires careful design and close coordination. A fourth flow, referred to as personnel flow is proposed in the literature. Van Wassenhove (2006) defines the three main flows as:

- *Materials*: representing the physical flow of relief items and human resources.
- *Information*: representing the transmission of orders and the control and coordination of the physical flow.
- *Financial*: humanitarian operations are financed by unilateral flows (from donors) through a funding process. This flow is not parallel with the flow of relief items.

Different authors have developed characterizations for the humanitarian supply chain from different points of view. Oloruntoba and Gray

(2006) describe the typical sequence of a humanitarian supply chain, emphasizing the flow of donations. The donations flow in the following order: governments, international agencies, international NGOs, local NGOs, the community (local organizations and partners), and the affected population. Balcik, Beamon, Krejci, Muramatsu, and Ramírez (2010) also develop this concept by emphasizing the flow of donations. They distinguish monetary donations from physical donations and characterize the humanitarian supply chain in functional echelons identifying the following: supplies acquisitions (monetary and physical), warehouses (distribution and intermediate storage centers), local distribution centers or last mile, and beneficiaries.

Complementary to the previous references, Blecken (2010) presents a configuration for humanitarian supply chains that is more complex than those presented by Oloruntoba and Gray (2006) and Balcik et al. (2010). Blecken (2010) provides a configuration based on the flows of materials but combines some actors in the chain, some support systems from the functional point of view, and infrastructure. Hence, he identifies the NGOs, local population, governmental organizations, private sector, specialized institutions and military institutions as suppliers and actors. These actors begin the flow of aid, which is then directed to humanitarian organizations or to providers of logistical services to be delivered to regional warehouses, humanitarian organizations or directly to the affected population.

Finally, Maon, Lindgreen, and Vanhamme (2009) include in their characterization of the humanitarian supply chain the local community, the government, NGOs, military forces, logistics suppliers, and private sector donors, whereas Thomas and Kopczak (2005), while also focusing on the actors, emphasized the importance of financial flows and donations. In all system nodes, there are actors such as public, private, national and international organizations, civil and military organizations, and the community. These are mainly connected through physical flows such as the flows of materials, donations, equipment, and money and information flows that include the characteristics of the victims and their needs (Balcik et al., 2010; Blecken, 2010). In this way, these organizations develop supply operations, transportation, storage, and distribution (PAHO, 2001).

11.3 Phases of Response in the Humanitarian Supply Chain

In this section, some definitions of the response phases in humanitarian logistics developed by different authors are presented.

Kovács and Spens (2009) identified, in their review of humanitarian logistics, different phases in disaster relief. A minimum differentiation is made between the preparation and the events following the disaster (Falasca & Zobel, 2011; Long, 1997; Van Wassenhove, 2006). A greater disaggregation differentiates between the support provided in an emergency, rehabilitation, and development (Ludema & Roos, 2000). Other types of approaches divide the response phases into prevention, transition, and recovery (Safran, 2003); preparation, response, and recovery (Pettit & Beresford, 2006; Van Wassenhove, 2006); mitigation, preparation, response, and recuperation (Altay & Green, 2006); or preparation, immediate response, and reconstruction (Kovács & Spens, 2007).

Kunz (2012) used the model developed by Kovács and Spens (2007) that consists of three stages in the management of disasters. The preparation phase includes evacuation plans, training, and pre-positioning of supplies, among other aspects. The immediate response phase corresponds to the phases of rescue operations, evacuation, coordination and delivery of supplies. Finally, the reconstruction phase involves buildings, infrastructure and economic development, among other aspects. The mitigation phase that is included by some authors is equivalent to the preparation phase since mitigation is carried out before the occurrence of a disaster.

According to Charles and Lauras (2011), the life cycle of the humanitarian operation is activated once the disaster occurs. This is the phase of immediate response that, according to the authors, corresponds to a period of one to five days. Then, the action is reinforced during a support phase that may last between three months to one year and which may end earlier if support is no longer necessary and all the operations are finished.

Cozzolino, Rossi, and Conforti (2012) identified a preparation phase, a response phase, and reconstruction phase. The preparation phase is interrupted by an emergency event, followed by the immediate response phase, which is based on the idea of effective action and conservation of human life (if the response is faster more lives can be saved). Finally, they present the reconstruction phase in which the objective is defined as efficiency and saving lives.

Altay and Green (2006) propose disaster attention phases divided into mitigation, preparation, immediate response, and reconstruction or rehabilitation. Van Wassenhove (2006) does not emphasize the mitigation and rehabilitation phases because he does not consider them to be part of the logistics of the disaster (Besiou, Pedraza-Martinez, & Van Wassenhove, 2014), whereas Kovács and Spens (2007) do not consider the mitigation phase.

It is important to establish that flows in the humanitarian supply chain depend on the event and/or operations. In the response phase, there are huge information flows to the strategic nodes, which activate the flows of personnel, support, and equipment to the affected area. Once this phase is over, it is common to have outgoing flows of rescued, hurt, and dead people and incoming flows of medicines, larger equipment, and provisions necessary to support the operation. Once the operation is over, inverse flows related to the clearance of temporary installations are observed and, finally, the personnel and equipment return to the strategic nodes (Eßig & Tandler, 2010).

11.4 Definition of Collaboration Strategies in the Field of Humanitarian Logistics

In this section, the concepts of collaboration in a supply chain are described along with an adaptation to humanitarian logistics.

As responses to disasters involve different actors, individual goals are not always aligned at the same level and, as the actions are not coordinated, humanitarian action could be invalidated (Balcik et al., 2010; Carroll & Neu, 2009; Chandes & Paché, 2009). This situation transforms the coordination and collaboration between actors in the humanitarian chain into one of the most important aspects that can determine the failure or success of the humanitarian operations (Chandes &

Paché, 2009; Dorasamy, Raman, & Kaliannan, 2013). According to Chandes and Paché (2009), "only a collective strategy can improve the performance of humanitarian supply chains; while its absence will have dramatic consequences for the affected populations."

The concept of collaboration in the supply chain means that two or more independent companies work together for planning and execution of the operations in the chain (Simatupang & Sridharan, 2002). Collaborative relationships can support companies with risk sharing and access to complementary resources (Park, Mezias, & Song, 2004), reduce the costs, improve productivity (Kalwani & Narayandas, 1995), and improve benefits and competitive advantages over time (Mentzer, Foggin, & Golicic, 2000).

Richey, Adams, and Dalela (2012) define collaboration as a mutually shared process in which two or more companies have a unified understanding and shared vision. Additionally, companies integrate human and financial resources. The main objective of collaboration is to allow suppliers to work cooperatively in order to implement better approaches to problem solving so that the co-created value is delivered to customers (Richey et al., 2012).

On the other hand, Cao and Zhang (2011) define collaboration in the supply chain as a function of seven components which can be adapted to humanitarian logistics:

- *Information exchange.* This refers to the fact that a company shares a wide variety of timely, relevant, exact, complete and confidential information with its supply chain partners (Angeles & Nath, 2001; Cagliano, Caniato, & Spina, 2003; Sheu, Yen, & Chae, 2006). In terms of humanitarian logistics, the exchange of information between different actors is important when it comes to providing an adequate and timely response to the affected population. This includes information related to the magnitude of the disaster, the affected area and the population, the needs assessment, resources, storage capacities, transportation and distribution, and available infrastructure.
- *Congruence of objectives.* This consists of the degree of perception of the partner regarding the extent to which its own goals are met by achieving the goals of the supply chain (Angeles & Nath, 2001). In

humanitarian logistics, this is represented when organizations and actors involved in the operations of the disaster work to achieve the same goal.
- *Synchronized decisions.* This refers to the process in which partners of the supply chain agree on decisions related to operations and planning in order to optimize the benefits of the supply chain (Simatupang & Sridharan, 2002). For humanitarian logistics, this is identified when different actors agree on how to conduct operations in the different phases, aiming at carrying out the work in the most efficient and effective way.
- *Aligned incentives.* This occurs when partners share costs, risks, and benefits in the supply chain (Simatupang & Sridharan, 2002). In humanitarian logistics, it corresponds to joint response planning in different phases and between many actors.
- *Shared resources.* This refers to the process of sharing resources and assets (Harland, Zheng, Johnsen, & Lamming, 2004). In humanitarian logistics, actors can share resources such as vehicles, infrastructure, airports and monetary resources.
- *Team communication.* This consists of the contact and processes between partners relating to the chain of transmission of messages and the strategy of influence in terms of frequency, direction and mode. In humanitarian logistics, this occurs when shared communication systems are created.
- *Creation of joint knowledge.* This refers to the case in which partners develop a better understanding of and response to the market by working together (Malhotra, Gosain, & El Sawy, 2005). In humanitarian logistics, this occurs when one or more actors in the chain develop and share methodologies, strategies or models that help the development and control of the joint operations.

Thus, the concept of collaboration adapted to humanitarian logistics consists of cooperative and joint work between different echelons that are involved with the humanitarian operations (Ertem, Buyurgan, & Rossetti, 2010) that seeks out ways to implement better practices in disaster attention, placing team communication and the creation of joint knowledge as main principles in order to benefit the affected population. It is important to establish that collaboration, coordination, and cooperation is made difficult if information is not shared among actors (Váncza et al., 2011).

On the other hand, a logistics strategy in the context of humanitarian logistics can be defined as the set of actions and activities carried out by the humanitarian logistics system within the support systems to provide the vulnerable and affected population with aid (Moreno Valbuena & González Rodríguez, 2011).

Finally, a logistics collaborative strategy in humanitarian logistics is defined as a set of actions carried out by two or more entities (Simatupang & Sridharan, 2002) that work together to provide adequate response to the disaster events in the correct place, at the right time, and in the correct proportions required (Cozzolino et al., 2012; González Rodríguez, Kalenatic, Rueda Velasco, & López Bello, 2012; US Department of Defense, 2000).

11.5 Adaptation of Project Management and System Dynamics to Humanitarian Logistics

In this section, several project management and SD concepts will be introduced and their adaptation to humanitarian logistics defined.

A project can be defined as a unique process consisting of a set of coordinated activities required to reach a goal consisting of specific requirements and which is subject to time, cost, and resource constraints (Lester, 2006). Dobson (2004) relates each of these constraints to specific factors. The time restriction is thus related to deadlines, the occurrence of specific events and urgency. The cost and resource constraints include money, personnel, equipment and supplies as well as general and intangible costs. He also proposes a third set of constraints called performance criteria in which he includes functional requirements, purpose and evaluation criteria.

In the context of humanitarian logistics operations as part of disaster relief, operations can be approached as a project given that each disaster has unique characteristics (PAHO, 2001), which determine the need to execute a set of activities such as the delivery of aid and evacuation of victims. All activities are aimed at the rapid and efficient recovery of the well-being of the affected population.

Slack, Chambers, and Johnston (2010) identified six common elements in projects, which can be identifiable in logistics operations of humanitarian disaster relief. These are shown in Table 11.1.

Meanwhile, Klein (2000) groups the conceptual design and definition phases together and consolidates the structuring, programming and allocation of resources into what he calls the planning phase. These two phases will be taken as a methodological basis, together with a proposed third phase of strategic analysis under uncertain conditions. Thus, it is concluded that disaster relief operations are viewed as projects subject to extremely variable demands and resources.

Therefore, in the context of humanitarian logistics, different actors that are involved in the support systems develop sets of activities that are interconnected, which can be organized and diagrammed as projects, and can be represented by using nodes of activity networks. These networks have common activities that can use shared resources, which are in turn limited and variable. The combined execution of interconnected projects is crucial for the flow of personnel, equipment, information, and support within the humanitarian supply chain because any interruption or any delay of one or more activities can affect or interrupt the aid operations, generating longer response times (see Fig. 11.1).

In this conceptual structure (see Fig. 11.1), the humanitarian supply chain is the part in charge of managing the physical, human, and information flows to and from the affected area. Therefore, while the supply chain is focused on the flows associated with the fulfillment of the mission, the other parts of the logistics system, made up of the transversal support systems, oversee flows and processes that allow supply chain organization, operation and generation of value.

Similar to the logistics system, the supply chain is organized functionally, whereby each functional set of the chain is known as a link and each

Table 11.1 Identification of the common elements of a humanitarian logistics project

Element	In the context of project management (Slack et al., 2010)	In the context of humanitarian logistics
An object or goal	A definable end product, result, or output defined in terms of cost, quality, and time.	Aims to recover the well-being of the affected population (González Rodríguez, Kalenatic, Rueda Velasco, & Sarmiento, 2013).
Uniqueness Complexity	A project is not repetitive. The relationships between the activities are complex.	Each disaster is unique (PAHO, 2001). The interaction of multiple and varied actors with diverse interests (González Rodríguez et al., 2012).
Temporary nature	The projects have a defined beginning and a defined end.	Begins with the occurrence of the disaster and ends when the well-being of the affected population has been partially or totally reestablished (depending on the scope) (Ministerio del Interior y de Justicia & Dirección de Gestión del Riesgo [DGR], 2010).
Uncertainty	The projects are planned before their execution, which implies risk. The nature of a project is associated with uncertainty.	Uncertainty in demand, availability of resources and infrastructure, and sociocultural reactions (Holguín-Veras, Jaller, Aros-Vera, Amaya, Enarnación, & Wachtendorf, 2016).

(continued)

Table 11.1 (continued)

Element	In the context of project management (Slack et al., 2010)	In the context of humanitarian logistics
Life cycle (consists of six phases)	The conceptual design phase identifies (by own initiative or via a third party) the need to carry out the project.	As a result of monitoring, the occurrence of the event is identified, the magnitude of the catastrophe is estimated and compared with the local response capacity, and the aid requirements for the affected area are determined (Unidad Nacional para la Gestión del Riesgo de Desastres [UNGRD], 2016).
	The definition phase involves the definition of what is to be done and how. This translates into project objectives, scope and strategy.	The role and activities that each actor will develop are determined based on the estimated needs and the environmental conditions, the scope of the operations, and the actors to be involved (Federal Emergency Management Agency [FEMA], 2008; UNGRD, 2016).
	The planning phase consists of dividing the project into manageable work packages associated with specific activities. Here the duration and precedence of activities are estimated as well as the controllable and uncontrollable influential variables and the needs and availability of resources.	The need for the application of specific action protocols is estimated, depending on the magnitude and type of disaster or catastrophe, the selected actors, and the resources and donations available (UNGRD, 2016).
	The scheduling phase involves the establishment of a start and end time of each of the activities as well as the resources allocated to each of them.	In order to avoid problems of convergence, the availability of resources, personnel, infrastructure and donations are ordered, especially considering the use of shared resources such as ports and warehouses (Holguín-Veras et al., 2014).
	The implementation phase involves the implementation of activities, progress monitoring and the application of corrective actions if necessary.	Humanitarian assistance activities such as securing the area, search and rescue, relocation, delivery of aid, infrastructure recovery and support services are implemented, among others.
	The end phase consists of the delivery of the project results and project closure.	The area having been normalized and the well-being of the population restored, temporary facilities are dismantled and the different actors are withdrawn (Sistema Nacional para la Prevención y Atención de Desastres [SNPAD] & Dirección de Prevención y Atención de Desastres [DPAD], 2006).

Collaborative Strategies for Humanitarian Logistics...

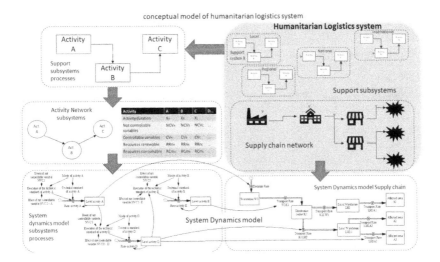

Fig. 11.1 Conceptual model of the humanitarian logistics system

one of these links can be formed of one or multiple actors that develop activities with resources and infrastructure that can be shared or individually owned.

It is important to establish that there must not necessarily be a connection between the support systems and the links. While there are clearly associations between support systems and a particular link of the chain, there is another set of support systems that are transversal to the chain and support more than one link. This also happens with the actors in the chain.

The humanitarian logistics system is identified as the controllable and non-controllable variables that affect the system, renewable and non-renewable resources, main responsible parties for the operations, and order of precedence of the different activities. With this characterization, a network of activities for the different related projects is built, and the dynamic model is built using the information of available resources. Finally, this model is connected with the supply chain model in order to simulate the impacts of operations on the support of different systems and different flows of the chain.

11.5.1 An Applied Case of the Sub-system of Handling and Delivery of Humanitarian Aid

This sub-section illustrates the application of a humanitarian logistics strategy applying the principles of project management and using SD.

The humanitarian system modeled represents a sub-system of handling and delivery of support. Its main goal is the delivery of the necessary support to the affected areas. According to SNPAD and DPAD (2006), its functions are the following:

- Receive, collate, consolidate, organize, and verify requests for support and the demand of physical, human and logistics resources for attention to emergencies.
- Request or confirm the requirements for national and international aid.
- Coordinate and organize the logistics process for the reception, delivery and administration of aid in the affected regions.

These were disaggregated at a tactical-strategic level into five activities. The first two are aimed at coordinating the reception of national and international aid and the other three are aimed at coordinating the delivery of aid in the affected area (González Forero, 2013). These activities are as follows:

- Request and/or confirm the aid requirements.
- Define the plan for the reception of aid.
- Receive national and international aid.
- Define the quantities and resources for the delivery of aid.
- Deliver the aid.

These activities are used to make up the network of activities in the sub-system. This network was designed using an AON representation in which the activities and their execution level (ELA) are represented in levels (nodes), each one with its execution rate (ERA), and the precedence relations are indicated as information flows between the levels of previous activities and the rates of execution of the following activities by means of an auxiliary variable called execution of the technical norm of the activity (ETN) (see Fig. 11.2). Each activity has an associated technical norm (TNA).

The most important activity is 5.5 as it receives the assignment of resources necessary for the delivery of aid. In this case, aid corresponds to food kits, whereby at least one kit is needed for every five members of the family (UNGRD, 2013). This activity has a supply chain of three links. The first one is made up of donors, the second link is made up of entities that are in charge and support the regional areas affected by the disaster, and finally, the aid is delivered to the third link, the affected population.

Reaction times are conditioned by the delays in the supply chain and this can affect the delivery of aid. Activity 5.5 is affected by five delays in the supply chain. The first two delays are represented by aid and personnel affected by the time of activation of the organizations related to these activities (between 3 and 24 hours). The following two are represented by the delivery of kits and personnel that are affected by the number of trips that each vehicle can make per hour as a function of the distance and the available air and ground infrastructure, vehicle capacities, and assigned vehicles. Finally, the delivery of aid depends on the delays in travel times.

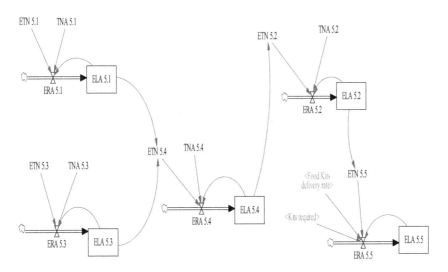

Fig. 11.2 Network of activities

11.5.2 Example of a Collaborative Logistics Strategy in Humanitarian Logistics

Once the sub-system is modeled, a collaborative logistics strategy is proposed. This strategy contemplates the shared use of infrastructure between agents, the sharing of information about quantities required, and it includes a stop order to the aid procurement process when the cumulative level of kit inventory is greater than or equal to the quantity of kits required. This strategy includes three of the seven collaboration components explained above: information exchange, congruence of objectives and shared resources.

As a base strategy, the use of shared infrastructure among the agents is contemplated due to system limitations. For example, agents must share the available airports in the affected city.

Figures 11.3 and 11.4 present the causal loop diagrams. Figure 11.3 represents the base strategy and Fig. 11.4 represents the collaboration

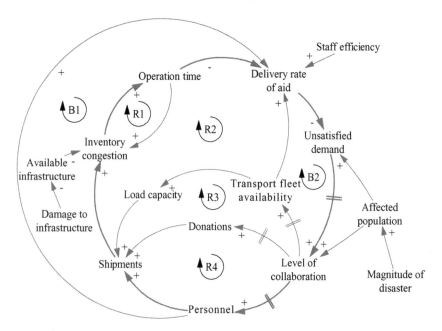

Fig. 11.3 Causal loop diagram of the base strategy

Collaborative Strategies for Humanitarian Logistics...

strategy proposed. In the base strategy, it is considered that the actors only share infrastructure, as explained above. The causal diagram presents four reinforcement cycles (R1, R2, R3 and R4) and two balance cycles (B1, B2).

The greater the magnitude of a disaster, the greater the numbers of the affected population and the greater the amount of unsatisfied demand, leading to the need for a higher level of collaboration. The higher the level of collaboration (the greater number of actors involved), the greater the availability of resources for emergency assistance (transport fleet, donations and personnel), in turn leading to an increase in the number of deliveries. These shipments, coupled with the effect of damage to infrastructure due to the disaster, increase inventory congestion and consequently operation times, negatively affecting the aid delivery rate. In turn, this delivery rate also depends on personnel efficiency in delivering

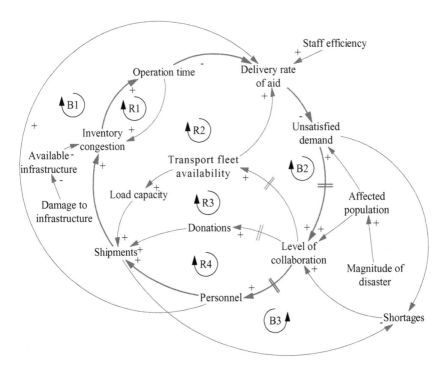

Fig. 11.4 Causal loop diagram of the proposed collaborative strategy

the aid. The lower the rate of aid delivery in the system, the greater the amount of unsatisfied demand.

In general, the system is affected by 3 delays: the first is presented in the population needs assessment whereby, once the disaster has occurred, the personnel who carry out this information survey must be moved to the affected area. The second delay is presented in terms of obtaining aid and in the delivery of resources by the actors considering that distances traveled by local actors are not the same as the distances traveled by international ones. The third delay is represented by the reinforcement cycle R1. Inventory congestion delays the operation of the system.

The reinforcement cycles R2, R3 and R4 represent a greater degree of collaboration and the greater resources available, leading to greater congestion of the system. The balance cycles B1 and B2 represent how the greater availability of operational personnel and transportation fleets should improve the delivery rate and, therefore, decrease the unmet demand.

In the strategy proposed (see Fig. 11.4), a balance loop (B3) is added to the base strategy. The system stops when a shortage occurs as mentioned in the strategy. A greater amount of deliveries, less shortages, and a lower level of collaboration in terms of quantity and type of actors is required.

Using the model described above and the collaborative strategies, we have run the simulation and summarized the results of the average response times (ART). The ART is calculated as a weighted average where the delivery time multiplied by the number of kits delivered is divided by the number of kits delivered.

Figure 11.5 presents the average response times (ART) and the inventory level of kits (IL) for both strategies, considering five levels of disasters: levels 1 and 2 present minimal effect on the population, level 3 has a medium effect, and levels 4 and 5 present a strong effect (Fondo de Prevención y Atención de Emergencias [FOPAE] & Alcaldía Mayor de Bogotá D.C., 2008). Levels 1, 2 and 3 involve the participation of local entities; level 4 includes local and regional entities; and level 5, the two previous entities plus other national and international entities.

As we can see in Fig. 11.5, when the affected population increases, specifically in level 5 (corresponding to a large magnitude disaster),

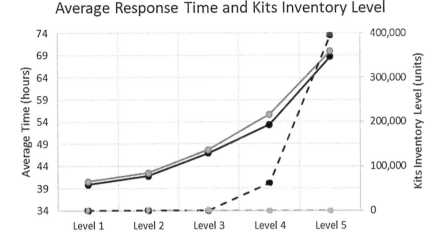

Fig. 11.5 Results of response times

response times increase because at this level, national and international organizations are included and there is a waiting time for the delivered aid to reach the affected population. Delays due to transportation are higher compared to the local and regional actors, thus increasing response times.

Although the response times are similar, the difference lies in the accumulation of kits in inventory. The two strategies satisfy the needs of the population affected by the disaster, but the base strategy accumulates large quantities of kits that are not delivered to the population. For this reason, in addition to response times, it would be necessary to consider the costs that entities would be willing to assume in order to maintain inventory.

11.6 Conclusion

The analysis of the humanitarian supply chain from the project management approach allows its representation from different perspectives: the first focuses on information flows and the second is based on the actors and resources involved.

The project-based approach allows the diagnosis of the humanitarian logistics supply chain from the perspective of its structure, identifying activities that restrict response, the functional allocation of actors and resource constraints in the system. It therefore helps to identify gaps in the allocation of resources that need to be increased for correct functioning.

In addition, the integration of the analysis of the structure of the humanitarian logistics system with simulation models allows us to evaluate the effects of modifications to the system and to identify those parts that are susceptible to improvement given their level of criticality.

Collaboration between actors in humanitarian logistics is identified as a key factor that defines the failure or success of humanitarian operations. For this reason, it is important to design collaborative logistics strategies for humanitarian logistics that contemplate joint and voluntary work between several entities that are willing to share information, resources, infrastructure, and/or personnel in order to provide the best response to the affected population. The SD model allows the representation and evaluation of these strategies.

Future research could contemplate the use of optimization models to select the stakeholders and the type of aid and resources needed to minimize operations costs. A limitation of this work is the lack of available data to develop an information system that contains complete information regarding the available resources of possible stakeholders.

References

Altay, N., & Green, W. G. (2006). OR/MS research in disaster operations management. *European Journal of Operational Research, 175*(1), 475–493.

Angeles, R., & Nath, R. (2001). Partner congruence in electronic data interchange (EDI) enabled relationships. *Journal of Business Logistics, 22*(2), 109–127.

Balcik, B., Beamon, B. M., Krejci, C. C., Muramatsu, K. M., & Ramírez, M. (2010). Coordination in humanitarian relief chains: Practices, challenges and opportunities. *International Journal of Production Economics, 126*(1), 22–34.

Besiou, M., Pedraza-Martínez, A. J., & Van Wassenhove, L. N. (2014). Vehicle supply chains in humanitarian operations: Decentralization, operational mix, and earmarked funding. *Production and Operations Management, 23*(11), 1950–1965.

Blecken, A. (2010). Supply chain process modelling for humanitarian organizations. *International Journal of Physical Distribution & Logistics Management, 40*(8–9), 675–692.

Cagliano, R., Caniato, F., & Spina, G. (2003). E-business strategy: How companies are shaping their supply chain through the Internet. *International Journal of Operations Management, 23*(10), 1142–1162.

Cao, M., & Zhang, Q. (2011). Supply chain collaboration: Impact on collaborative advantage and firm performance. *Journal of Operations Management, 29*(3), 163–180.

Carroll, A., & Neu, J. (2009). Volatility, unpredictability and asymmetry: An organising framework for humanitarian logistics operations? *Management Research News, 32*(11), 1024–1037.

Chandes, J., & Paché, G. (2009). Pensar la acción colectiva en el contexto de la logística humanitaria: Las lecciones del sismo de Pisco. *Journal of Economics, Finance and Administrative Science, 14*, 47–62.

Charles, A., & Lauras, M. (2011). An enterprise modelling approach for better optimisation modelling: Application to the humanitarian relief chain coordination problem. *OR Spectrum, 33*(3), 815–841.

Costa, S. R. A. Da, Campos, V. B. G., & Bandeira, R. A. De M. (2012). Supply chains in humanitarian operations: Cases and analysis. *Procedia—Social and Behavioral Sciences, 54*, 598–607.

Cozzolino, A., Rossi, S., & Conforti, A. (2012). Agile and lean principles in the humanitarian supply chain: The case of the United Nations World Food Programme. *Journal of Humanitarian Logistics and Supply Chain Management, 2*(1), 16–33.

Dobson, M. S. (2004). *The triple constraints in project management*. Oakland, CA: Berrett-Koehler Publishers.

Dorasamy, M., Raman, M., & Kaliannan, M. (2013). Knowledge management systems in support of disasters management: A two decade review. *Technological Forecasting and Social Change, 80*(9), 1834–1853.

Ertem, M. A., Buyurgan, N., & Rossetti, M. D. (2010). Multiple-buyer procurement auctions framework for humanitarian supply chain management. *International Journal of Physical Distribution & Logistics Management, 40*(3), 202–227.

Eßig, M., & Tandler, S. (2010). Disaster response supply chain management (SCM): Integration of humanitarian and defence logistics by means of SCM. In W. Feichtinger, M. Gauster, & F. Tanner (Eds.), *Economic impacts of crisis response operations—An underestimated factor in external engagement* (pp. 283–310). Vienna, Austria: Landesverteidigungsakademie (LVAk)/ Institut für Friedenssicherung und Konfliktmanagement (IFK).

Falasca, M., & Zobel, C. W. (2011). A two-stage procurement model for humanitarian relief supply chains. *Journal of Humanitarian Logistics and Supply Chain Management, 1*(2), 151–169.

Federal Emergency Management Agency. (2008). *Emergency support function annexes: Introduction.* Washington, DC: FEMA.

Fondo de Prevención y Atención de Emergencias, & Alcaldía Mayor de Bogotá D.C. (Emergency Prevention and Response Fund, & Bogotá D.C. Mayor's Office). (2008). *Plan de emergencias de Bogotá.* Bogotá, DC, Colombia: FOPAE.

González Forero, M. C. (2013). *Análisis de la relación entre políticas de asignación de recursos en la atención de desastres y la mortalidad por medio de la metodología integral y dinámica.* Master's thesis, Facultad de Ingeniería, Universidad de La Sabana, Chía, Colombia.

González Rodríguez, L. J., Kalenatic, D., Rueda Velasco, F. J., & López Bello, C. A. (2012). Potencial uso de la logística focalizada en sistemas logísticos de atención de desastres. Un análisis conceptual. *Revista Facultad de Ingeniería, 62,* 44–54.

González Rodríguez, L. J., Kalenatic, D., Rueda Velasco, F. J., & Sarmiento, A. (2013). Caracterización del sistema logístico de ayuda humanitaria y de los modelos matemáticos asociados. In D. Kalenatic (Ed.), *Logística focalizada: Una respuesta ante ambientes de asimetría, incertidumbre y volatilidad* (pp. 69–85). Chía, Colombia: Universidad de La Sabana.

Harland, C. M., Zheng, J., Jhonsen, T. E., & Lamming, R. C. (2004). A conceptual model for researching the creation and operation of supply networks. *British Journal of Management, 15*(1), 1–21.

Holguín-Veras, J., Jaller, M., Aros-Vera, F., Amaya, J., Enarnación, T., & Wachtendorf, T. (2016). Disaster response logistics: Chief findings of fieldwork research. In C. W. Zobel, N. Altay, & M. P. Haselkorn (Eds.), *Advances in managing humanitarian operations* (pp. 33–57). Cham, Switzerland: Springer International Publishing.

Holguín-Veras, J., Jaller, M., Van Wassenhove, L. N., Pérez, N., & Wachtendorf, T. (2014). Material convergence: Important and understudied disaster phenomenon. *Natural Hazards Review, 15*(1), 1–12.

Holguín-Veras, J., Jaller, M., & Wachtendorf, T. (2012). Comparative performance of alternative humanitarian logistic structures after the Port-au-Prince earthquake: ACEs, PIEs, and CANs. *Transportation Research Part A: Policy and Practice, 46*(10), 1623–1640.

Kalwani, M. U., & Narayandas, N. (1995). Long-term manufacturer-supplier relationships: Do they pay off for supplier firms? *Journal of Marketing, 59*(1), 1–16.

Klein, R. (2000). *Scheduling of resource-constrained projects*. New York, NY: Springer US.

Kovács, G., & Spens, K. M. (2007). Humanitarian logistics in disaster relief operations. *International Journal of Physical Distribution & Logistics Management, 37*(2), 99–114.

Kovács, G., & Spens, K. M. (2009). Identifying challenges in humanitarian logistics. *International Journal of Physical Distribution & Logistics Management, 39*(6), 506–528.

Kunz, N. (2012). A meta-analysis of humanitarian logistics research. *Journal of Humanitarian Logistics and Supply Chain Management, 2*(2), 116–147.

Lester, A. (2006). *Project management, planning and control: Managing engineering, construction and manufacturing projects to PMI, APM and BSI standards* (5th ed.). Oxford: Butterworth-Heinemann.

Long, D. (1997). Logistics for disaster relief: Engineering on the run. *IIE Solutions, 29*(6), 26–29.

Ludema, M. W., & Roos, H. B. (2000). Military and civil logistic support of humanitarian relief operations. In *Proceedings of the 10th Annual International Symposium—International Council on Systems Engineering (INCOSE)* (pp. 143–152). Minneapolis, MN: British Library Document Supply Centre Inside Serials & Conference Proceedings.

Malhotra, A., Gosain, S., & El Sawy, O. A. (2005). Absorptive capacity configurations in supply chains: Gearing for partner-enabled market knowledge creation. *MIS Quarterly, 29*(1), 145–187.

Maon, F., Lindgreen, A., & Vanhamme, J. (2009). Developing supply chains in disaster relief operations through cross-sector socially oriented collaborations: A theoretical model. *Supply Chain Management: An International Journal, 14*(2), 149–164.

Mentzer, J. T., Foggin, J. H., & Golicic, S. L. (2000). Collaboration: The enablers, impediments, and benefits. *Supply Chain Management Review, 4*(4), 52–58.

Ministerio del Interior y Justicia, & Dirección de Gestión del Riesgo (Ministry of Interior and Justice, & Risk Management Authority). (2010). *Guía metodológica para la formulación del Plan local de emergencia y contingencias (PLEC's)* (2nd ed.). SNPAD/DGR: Bogotá, DC, Colombia.

Moreno Valbuena, K. V., & González Rodríguez, L. J. (2011). Relación entre recursos, eficiencia y tiempo de respuesta del sistema logístico de atención humanitaria desde un enfoque sistémico. In *Proceedings of the 9° Encuentro Colombiano de Dinámica de Sistemas*. Bogotá, DC, Colombia: Universidad del Rosario.

Oloruntoba, R., & Gray, R. (2006). Humanitarian aid: An agile supply chain? *Supply Chain Management: An International Journal, 11*(2), 115–120.

Pan American Health Organization. (2001). *Humanitarian supply management and logistics in the health sector*. Washington, DC: PAHO.

Park, N. K., Mezias, J. M., & Song, J. (2004). A resource-based view of strategic alliances and firm value in the electronic marketplace. *Journal of Management, 30*(1), 7–27.

Pettit, S. J., & Beresford, A. K. C. (2006). *Modelling humanitarian aid supply chains*. Paper presented at the Logistics Research Network Conference, Newcastle upon Tyne, UK.

Richey, R. G., Adams, F. G., & Dalela, V. (2012). Technology and flexibility: Enablers of collaboration and time-based logistics quality. *Journal of Business Logistics, 33*(1), 34–49.

Safran, P. (2003). *A strategic approach for disaster and emergency assistance*. Paper presented at the 5th Asian Disaster Reduction Center International Meeting and the 2nd UN-ISDR Asian Meeting, Kobe, Japan.

Sheu, C., Yen, H. R., & Chae, B. (2006). Determinants of supplier-retailer collaboration: Evidence from an international study. *International Journal of Operations & Production Management, 26*(1), 24–49.

Simatupang, T. M., & Sridharan, R. (2002). The collaborative supply chain. *The International Journal of Logistics Management, 13*(1), 15–30.

Sistema Nacional para la Prevención y Atención de Desastres, & Dirección de Prevención y Atención de Desastres (National System for Prevention and Response to Natural Disasters, & Disaster Prevention and Response Authority). (2006). *Guía de actuación y protocolos de alto gobierno en caso de un desastre súbito de cobertura nacional*. Bogotá, DC, Colombia: DPAD.

Slack, N., Chambers, S., & Johnston, R. (2010). *Operations management* (6th ed.). Harlow, UK and New York, NY: Financial Times/Prentice Hall.

Thomas, A. S., & Kopczak, L. R. (2005). From logistics to supply chain management: The path forward in the humanitarian sector. *White Paper*, Fritz Institute, San Francisco, CA.

Unidad Nacional para la Gestión del Riesgo de Desastres (National Disaster Management Unit). (2013). *Estandarización de ayuda humanitaria de Colombia*. Bogotá, DC, Colombia: UNGDR.

Unidad Nacional para la Gestión del Riesgo de Desastres (National Disaster Management Unit). (2016). *Guía de funcionamiento sala de crisis nacional* (2nd ed.). Bogotá, DC, Colombia: UNGDR.

US Department of Defense. (2000). *Joint Vision 2020*. Washington, DC: US Government Printing Office.

Van Wassenhove, L. N. (2006). Humanitarian aid logistics: Supply chain management in high gear. *Journal of the Operational Research Society, 57*(5), 475–489.

Váncza, J., Monostori, L., Lutters, D., Kumara, S. R., Tseng, M., Valckenaers, P., & Van Brussel, H. (2011). Cooperative and responsive manufacturing enterprises. *CIRP Annals, 60*(2), 797–820.

12

Agent-Based Modeling in Humanitarian Operations

Luisa Díez-Echavarría, Karthik Sankaranarayanan, and Sebastián Villa

12.1 Introduction

Humanitarian operations are considered complex adaptive systems due to their uncertainties and the involvement of multiple decision-makers such as humanitarian organizations, military, governmental, and non-governmental agencies, etc. These operations encompass facility processes such as location, supply chain design, distribution planning, and inventory planning (Zobel, Altay, & Haselkorn, 2016). When a humanitarian

L. Díez-Echavarría (✉)
Facultad de Ciencias Económicas y Administrativas, Instituto Tecnológico Metropolitano, Medellín, Colombia
e-mail: luisadiez@itm.edu.co

K. Sankaranarayanan
Faculty of Business and Information Technology, University of Ontario, Oshawa, ON, Canada
e-mail: Karthik.Sankaranarayanan@uoit.ca

S. Villa
School of Management, Universidad de los Andes, Bogotá, Colombia
e-mail: s.villab@uniandes.edu.co

crisis occurs, organizations need to coordinate their operations to provide relief to the most vulnerable people. However, coordination is difficult and uncertain for two main reasons. First, it is not easy to obtain comprehensive information regarding the affected population's distribution of needs and the total relief capacity. This makes it challenging for the organizations to effectively coordinate their efforts to satisfy the needs of the affected population (Stauffer, Pedraza-Martinez, & Van Wassenhove, 2016; Tomasini & Van Wassenhove, 2009). Second, the presence and interaction of multiple (and different) agents affects the coordination among organizations aiming to deliver aid, and those looking for media visibility (Balcik, Beamon, Krejci, Muramatsu, & Ramirez, 2010; Besiou, Pedraza-Martinez, & Van Wassenhove, 2012; Dolinskaya, Shi, Smilowitz, & Ross, 2011; Ergun, Karakus, Keskinocak, Swann, & Villarreal, 2010; Lindenberg & Bryant, 2001; Van Wassenhove, 2006). The heterogeneity of actors in the humanitarian setting is challenging because different agents come with "different political agendas, ideologies and religious beliefs" (Van Wassenhove, 2006) and this misalignment of actors' agendas leads to inefficiencies at the aggregate level of the response (Ergun et al., 2010).

Organizations involved in a disaster are autonomous entities that redefine their operational strategies based on the behavior of other organizations, the people in need, and the environment (Altay & Pal, 2014). Given the challenges faced by the humanitarian sector in having to coordinate different actors with separate goals, we use Agent-Based Modeling (ABM) as a methodology to understand the effect of individual organizational actions on the overall performance of a response. ABM enhances the understanding of the different factors affecting the overall operational performance of a system (Urrea, Besiou, & Pedraza-Martinez, 2018), meaning that it can be used as a methodology to analyze the emerging behavior of a system composed of the interactions among different actors with conflicting interests (Van Wassenhove, 2006; Ergun et al., 2010; Dolinskaya et al., 2011), limited information sharing (Oloruntoba & Gray, 2006), and tradeoffs in allocating resources (Dolinskaya et al., 2011).

In this chapter, we explain what ABM is, how it works, and how it can be applied to study humanitarian operations. We define ABM as a bottom-up approach that models individual interactions and reveals the system behavior that emerges because of those interactions (Sankaranarayanan, 2011; Sankaranarayanan, Delgado, van Ackere, & Larsen, 2014). ABM allows us to represent systems made up of different types of agents and study decision-making rules under different conditions. Agents (e.g. humans, organizations, or systems) can be heterogeneous in their preferences and skills, and are programmed to follow defined behavioral rules in this disaggregated approach. Moreover, ABM allows us to run different simulation scenarios to study the effects of different (and extreme) factors on performance.

ABM has been used to solve and understand a variety of problems that include the prediction of the spread of epidemics, population dynamics, agent behavior in stock markets and traffic congestion, and consumer behavior in marketing (Macal, 2016). However, ABM can be extended to study situations similar to the challenges faced by humanitarian organizations regarding competition for scarce resources and coordination, where the collective goal could be overlooked due to the prevalence of individual goals. Therefore, in this book chapter, we show how existing agent-based decision-making models can be fine-tuned for humanitarian operations (Sankaranarayanan, Castañeda, & Villa, 2017).

This chapter is organized as follows: Sect. 12.2 introduces the main concepts of ABM, its advantages and disadvantages, and the process to build an agent-based model. Section 12.3 describes the applications of ABM for decision-making. Four sub-sections discuss opportunities for ABM in providing support for humanitarian operations. The chapter ends with a conclusion section that emphasizes the key takeaways.

12.2 Agent-Based Modeling

ABM made its appearance in the 1990s as a response to the need to analyze implications of agent interactions within social structures. It was implemented during that period thanks to the growth of high performance computing (Epstein, 1999) as an interdisciplinary "bottom-up" technique for modeling dynamic systems of *agents* that interact with each other and with their *environment*, following a set of *rules* (Bonabeau,

2002; Macal & North, 2010). These interactions occur in discrete time steps, and generate behavior and patterns in the system at the aggregate level. This is known as the emergent behavior of the system (Bonabeau, 2002). Three fundamental parts of an ABM are then recognized: agents, environment, and rules.

An *agent*—also called entity—can be defined as an autonomous individual element with specific properties and actions (Epstein, 1999; Jennings, 2000) (Epstein, 1999; Jennings, 2000). An agent can represent animate and inanimate objects, such as people, animals, and institutions. These agents must satisfy some basic characteristics: (i) *autonomy* regarding the control over their actions and internal states; (ii) *social ability* when communicating with other agents and adopting behaviors such as coordination, cooperation, and competition; (iii) *reactivity* when perceiving their environment and responding to the changes; (iv) *goal-directed* when taking the initiative to follow a specific objective (Šalamon, 2011; Wooldridge & Jennings, 1995).

The *environment* is the virtual space or world in which the agents are located and act. Three of the most popular types of environments are: *spatial location*, which may be used to provide information relative to other agents, such as the space in which a flock of birds moves. The environment may also provide a rich set of *geographic information* through the use of geographic information systems (GIS). Or it can represent a *network*, where the interactions are determined by the links or relationships between the agents, such as a group of friends (Macal & North, 2010; Sankaranarayanan et al., 2014).

The behavior or interactions of the agents are described by a set of *rules*, which can range from the simplistic "if-then" to complex behaviors modeled by adaptive techniques (Bonabeau, 2002; Macal & North, 2010). Interactions can occur in multiple ways: agents can interact among themselves, with other agents or with the environment. For example, in a predator-prey model (Reisman, 2006; Wilensky & Reisman, 1998), wolves and sheep (agents) are spatially located (environment). If wolves see a sheep nearby, they move toward it to hunt it (interaction).

After knowing the three fundamental parts of an ABM, a natural question arises: When is it appropriate to use ABM? Here, we present some characteristics of systems where this methodology is relevant:

(i) heterogeneity in the agents of the system; (ii) decisions and behaviors defined discretely; (iii) adaptation and learning of agents; (iv) environment that influences the system interactions and behavior; and (v) important relationship between agents and their environment (Bonabeau, 2002; Macal & North, 2006). Clearly, the more of these features a system has, the more likely it is for an ABM to provide a good way to model and analyze it. In Sections 12.2.1 and 12.2.2, we discuss some of the advantages and disadvantages of using ABM, and the main process involved in building an agent-based model.

12.2.1 Advantages and Disadvantages of Agent-Based Modeling

The use of ABM as a tool for modeling and understanding complex systems has three main advantages (Vogel, 2009). First, ABM provides a highly intuitive method to model a system by describing the actions agents should execute, instead of formulating dynamic equations that govern the system they form (Bonabeau, 2002). For example, it is more natural to describe how people evacuate a building than to come up with the equations that explain that behavior. Second, ABM captures emergent behavior that results from the interactions between agents and the environment according to the defined rules. This behavior cannot be reduced to the sum of the system's parts (Epstein, 1999). One of the clearest examples is a traffic jam, which results from the interactions between individual vehicle drivers. However, the traffic jam may be moving in the opposite direction to that of the cars that cause it (Bonabeau, 2002). Third, ABM is very flexible, i.e., it has the ability to change levels of description and aggregation. For example, it is easy to add or remove agents or rules in the model (Bonabeau, 2002).

In addition to the main advantages, we should also consider the three main disadvantages of this methodology. First, ABM requires a much larger amount of information than other methodologies to properly calibrate the model (Gilbert & Terna, 2000; Gilbert & Troitzsch, 2005; Šalamon, 2011). However, information is not always easy to obtain and it is necessary to describe the system and the agents in detail. For example, in the previous case of the traffic jam, it is necessary to specify the average number of cars in a lapse of time, their speed and acceleration, the average distance between them, and the available space where they can move. The second disadvantage is related to the computational cost to run the simulations (Bonabeau 2002; Šalamon, 2011). It is not the same to calculate the solution of equations as it is to recreate the environment, simulating the necessary actions and interactions of individual agents. ABM requires proper storage of all the data that is generated from the simulation (Bonabeau, 2002). The third disadvantage is related to the robustness and generalization of the findings (Mollona, 2008). Due to the particularity of each case and the data itself, extrapolations should be avoided unless new data is adjusted and a validation process is performed.

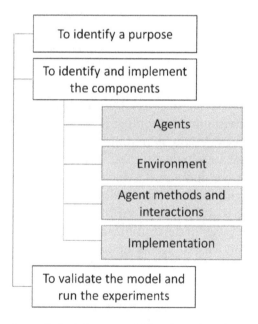

Fig. 12.1 General steps in building an AMB [Authors, based on Macal and North (2006)]

12.2.2 How to Build an Agent-Based Model

There are three main steps that are commonly used for the creation of a simulation model (see white boxes in Fig. 12.1). The first step is to identify a clear purpose, the questions the model is intended to answer, and the hypotheses. For example, in the well-known predator-prey model (Reisman, 2006; Wilensky & Reisman, 1998), the objective is to explore the populational stability of predator-prey ecosystems. The second step is to identify components, interactions, and relevant data sources that allow us to codify the model; i.e., it is necessary to define what the agents are, and how and with whom they interact. The final step is to run the "what-if" experiments by systematically varying parameters based on the hypotheses, and to understand the robustness of the model and its results by using validation techniques (Macal & North, 2006).

The fundamental difference of an ABM with respect to other modeling techniques is in the second step, in which one must assume an agent perspective instead of a process-based perspective, as is the case in other simulation techniques (Macal & North, 2006). Therefore, we need to divide the second step into four different stages (see gray boxes in Fig. 12.1): (i) identify the agent types and their attributes; (ii) define the environment in which agents will thrive and interact; (iii) define the methods by which agents' attributes are updated in response to either agent-to-agent or agent-to-environment interactions, and include the methods that control when, how, and which agents interact over the simulation; and (iv) select a computational software to implement the agent model (Macal & North, 2010).

To facilitate the building and implementation of the model, we can use specialized ABM toolkits. There are more than 50 available ABM toolkits based on the object-oriented paradigm, which are as diverse as the community of people who use them (Nikolai & Madey, 2009). Some of the most frequently used ABM toolkits are Swarm, Repast Ascape, Mason, and NetLogo. Similarly, traditional programming languages such as Python, C, and R can also be used to create agent-based models. However, the development of a language from scratch is extremely expensive and specialized (Macal & North, 2010). The selection of the software will be dictated by the affinity of the modelers and the needs of the problem (for further information regarding the advantages and disadvantages of the most frequently used ABM toolkits see Allan, 2010).

12.3 Applications in the Humanitarian Sector

In terms of ABM applications, there is a broad spectrum of sizes and intentions. Some of the models are small, but well designed. These models include only the basic characteristics of a system of interest and are useful in developing insights about the system behavior (Macal & North, 2010). Other models are developed in great detail and the results are intended to aid in policy development and decision-making processes (Macal & North, 2010). The areas in which ABM has been applied are very broad, including biology, ecology, physics, computer sciences, social sciences, and economics. Some of the most popular topics are: supply chains (Macal, 2004), spread of epidemics (Bagni, Berchi, & Cariello, 2002; Linard, Ponçon, Fontenille, & Lambin, 2009), business and consumer purchasing behavior (North & Macal, 2007), and innovation diffusion (Kiesling, Günther, Stummer, & Wakolbinger, 2012). These examples illustrate the interdisciplinary nature of ABM applications.

One additional field of ABM application that has attracted the attention of researchers is the humanitarian sector. Even if this methodology has not been widely used in humanitarian applications, in recent years, ABM has raised the attention of researchers, positioning itself as a promising technique to study interactions in the humanitarian sector (Altay & Pal, 2014; Crooks & Wise, 2013; Das & Hanaoka, 2014; Menth & Heier Stamm, 2015).

Following are a few of the noteworthy studies that discuss the use of ABM. Menth and Heier Stamm (2015) talk about the need for humanitarian decision support tools and show how ABM helps to capture complexities in humanitarian operations and helps improve coordination efforts. Das (2014) uses ABM to study resource allocation issues and concludes by saying that ABM offers flexibility when compared to traditional methods such as linear programming and dynamic linear programming.

Altay and Pal (2014) use ABM to study information exchange within the United Nations' cluster approach to disaster management. Oliveira, Lima, and Montevechi (2016) state that ABM addresses the limitations of traditional methods such as discrete-event simulation and system dynamics by taking a bottom-up approach. All of the above-mentioned papers bring in the behavioral perspective in humanitarian operations, and they show how ABM can help understand the inherent complexities observed in the humanitarian context. In this section, we provide some insights on how ABM can be used to study operations within the humanitarian sector. The following sub-sections elucidate four examples taken from closely related fields to show how ABM can be extended to the humanitarian context.

12.3.1 Humanitarian Relief Operations

ABM can be used in a humanitarian setting to describe a system in which organizations face several obstacles in distributing aid to the right person, at the right time, and at the right location (Das & Hanaoka, 2014). An agent-based model requires the definition of organizations and the people in need as two different types of agents, which are defined within a spatial location in which needs are distributed. Organizations need to define their strategies in an uncertain environment. On the one hand, they cannot predict where the disaster will occur, its magnitude, or the type of aid required (demand side). On the other hand, they are not sure of their own capacity, the generosity of donors, or the effect of the media (supply side). One mechanism, which can be used to cushion this uncertainty, is coordination. Coordination improves the efficiency in the process, reduces the duplication of efforts, and leads to better outcomes for the beneficiaries (Menth & Heier Stamm, 2015). An ABM enhances the evaluation of different strategies created to foster better coordination among organizations. Some possible objectives of the simulation are to evaluate the effect of centralization (pre-established partnerships) and organizational capacity on the level of suffering, duplication of efforts, and average response time.

The role of the media is also important in a humanitarian setting. Media can increase an organization's visibility, which also increases donors' attention and donations. This increase in donations can be translated into higher organizational capacity. An ABM allows the evaluation of different organizational actions in a setting in which media plays an important role in the decision-making process. Running different simulations, we can test strategies such as whether organizations should operate individually or form partnerships, whether the aid they provide is in a disaster area that is closely covered by the media or not, and decide on how to allocate the available resources to the affected population.

12.3.2 Emergency Department

Hospitals' emergency departments constitute a highly complex system and hospital administrators constantly struggle to find a balance between quality of service and operational efficiency. It is complex because patient arrivals are uncertain, and the treatment path followed by patients depends on numerous factors such as urgency and resource availability. In addition, multiple decision-makers (staff, nurses, and doctors) make the emergency department a highly complex and connected system. Liu, Epelde, and Luque (2017) use ABM to capture these complexities in collaboration with a hospital in Spain. The authors create a generic ABM model that can help hospital administrators to make informed decisions regarding resource utilization for scheduling and allocation policies, to understand the correlation between individual decision-making and system behavior, and to test the robustness of the system during uncertainties (e.g. spread of infectious diseases).

In a similar vein, researchers in humanitarian operations can use this agent-based model as a foundation to build such a generic simulator to capture the complexities observed in humanitarian operations. Transportation and logistics in humanitarian operations is one avenue where such a generic simulator would be helpful. Transportation is critical irrespective of the nature of crisis, whether it is relief or development. If transportation is required for relief operations then optimizing response time is the focus; whereas, if it is required for development, then operational efficiency is important (Sankaranarayanan, Laite, & Portman, 2017). An agent-based model can be designed to include entities such as distribution centers, shelters, environmental factors, and road conditions to better strategize and reduce lead-time during humanitarian response. Relief workers and managers of distribution centers should be included in this model to see how individual decision-making affects system performance. Real-time data collected from previous studies could be used to model the characteristics of agents in this system and study emergent behavior. This helps decision-makers strategize on how to manage transportation under various conditions and test the robustness of the current system when the next humanitarian crisis strikes.

12.3.3 Coordination and Collaboration

People and agencies (both governmental and non-governmental) are an integral part of humanitarian operations. Partnerships between various stakeholders are paramount to providing aid during a crisis, which, in turn, has made coordination and collaboration a major challenge. Coles, Zhang, and Zhuang (2016) use an experimental approach to build a decision model to study how agencies' partnership decisions affect humanitarian operational efficiency. The authors run six experiments to understand biases in decision-making when agencies engage in partnerships. Coles et al. (2016) then use this data to build decision models to predict agencies' behavior during relief operations. Research participants were asked to make decisions of resource allocation and utilization, and acceptance or rejection of partnerships among others, as a part of this experimental work. The literature available on this issue is scant. Coles et al. (2016) conclude by saying that it is critical to test their model in an agent-based simulation (as a validation methodology) to examine additional dimensions in crisis coordination. This is another avenue for the use of the agent-based model to design a system with multiple partners with various characteristics and to see how individual decision-making leads to operational efficiency. This allows humanitarian organizations to identify various approaches to strategize the humanitarian aid action plan that best suits their organizational goals.

12.3.4 Aid Planning during Humanitarian Operations

Harold Hotelling, in his paper "Stability in Competition" (Hotelling, 1929), examines facility location and pricing of goods in facilities that aim to maximize profits. Ottino, Stonedahl, and Wilensky (2009) extend Hotelling's work by exploring consumer decision-making in choosing a facility based on its distance from them and the price of its goods. In this model, consumers are intelligent agents who choose a facility based on their distance from each store and the price of the goods in those stores (the lowest sum of distance and price equates to best location). In this model, the facility can be moved randomly to see if this move can result in a better market share. The price of goods in each facility can be varied to see if this results in greater profits.

An analogy exists in humanitarian operations where experimental work has been carried out to study biases in inventory decisions when prepositioning emergency supplies during the preparedness phase. Facility location is crucial, and Menth and Heier Stamm (2015) use ABM to study the facility location problem by using data collected from the 2015 Nepal earthquake. The study looks at location; i.e., inventory management in humanitarian aid and coordination efforts that provide equity in aid distribution. The Hotelling model along with other ABM models can help bring together the facility location problem, and coordination and cooperation research in humanitarian operations.

12.4 Conclusion

This chapter provides an overview of ABM as a tool to study decision-making in humanitarian operations. We discuss the main concepts of ABM, its advantages and disadvantages, and the process to build an agent-based model. In addition, we use four examples to provide some initial research ideas to researchers who would like to delve into the use of ABM within the humanitarian sector. Researchers can use the examples to build foundational pieces, which can then be brought together to create a decision-aid toolkit.

Hybrid modeling approaches can be envisioned in which ABM is used with neural networks to study decision-making in choosing a service facility (Laite, Portman, & Sankaranarayanan, 2016; Sankaranarayanan, 2011; Sankaranarayanan, Laite, et al., 2017). The authors use data collected via experimental methods (participants were asked to decide on a service facility based on their expectations and experiences) to train the neural network and test the predictive capability of the model. This is in line with Dr. Charles Macal's statement at the 2016 Winter Simulation Conference, in which he talked about linking agent-based models with system dynamics models; the former providing micro features (i.e. individual behavioral rules and characteristics) and the latter, supplying macro variables.

References

Allan, R. (2010). *Survey of agent based modelling and simulation tools*. Retrieved January 2018, from http://www.citeulike.org/user/allyharp/article/5092191

Altay, N., & Pal, R. (2014). Information diffusion among agents: Implications for humanitarian operations. *Production and Operations Management, 23*(6), 1015–1027.

Bagni, R., Berchi, R., & Cariello, P. (2002). A comparison of simulation models applied to epidemics. *Journal of Artificial Societies and Social Simulation, 5*(3). Retrieved January 2018, from http://jasss.soc.surrey.ac.uk/5/3/5.html

Balcik, B., Beamon, B. M., Krejci, C. C., Muramatsu, K. M., & Ramirez, M. (2010). Coordination in humanitarian relief chains: Practices, challenges and opportunities. *International Journal of Production Economics, 126*(1), 22–34.

Besiou, M., Pedraza-Martinez, A. J., & van Wassenhove, L. N. (2012). The effect of earmarked funding on fleet management for relief and development. *INSEAD Working Paper No. 2012/10/TOM/INSEAD Social Innovation Centre*.

Bonabeau, E. (2002). Agent-based modeling: Methods and techniques for simulating human systems. *Proceedings of the National Academy of Sciences of the United States of America, 99*(Suppl. 3), 7280–7287.

Coles, J., Zhang, J., & Zhuang, J. (2016). Experiments on partnership and decision making in a disaster environment. *International Journal of Disaster Risk Reduction, 18*, 181–196.

Crooks, A., & Wise, S. (2013). GIS and agent-based models for humanitarian assistance. *Computers, Environment and Urban Systems, 41*, 100–111.

Das, R. (2014). *Advancement on uncertainty modeling in humanitarian logistics for earthquake response*. Tokyo Institute of Technology. Retrieved January 2018, from http://transport-titech.jp/thesis/TSU-DC2014-007.pdf

Das, R., & Hanaoka, S. (2014). An agent-based model for resource allocation during relief distribution. *Journal of Humanitarian Logistics and Supply Chain Management, 4*(2), 265–285.

Dolinskaya, I. S., Shi, Z. E., Smilowitz, K. R., & Ross, M. (2011). Decentralized approaches to logistics coordination in humanitarian relief. In *Proceedings of 2011 Industrial Engineering Research Conference*, Reno, NV.

Epstein, J. M. (1999). Agent-based computational models and generative social science. *Generative Social Science: Studies in Agent-Based Computational Modeling, 4*(5), 41–60.

Ergun, O., Karakus, G., Keskinocak, P., Swann, J., & Villarreal, M. (2010). Operations research to improve disaster supply chain management. In *Wiley encyclopedia of operations research and management science*. Hoboken, NJ: Wiley.

Gilbert, N., & Terna, P. (2000). How to build and use agent-based models in social science. *Mind & Society, 1*(1), 57–72. Retrieved January 2018, from https://link.springer.com/article/10.1007/BF02512229

Gilbert, N., & Troitzsch, K. (2005). *Simulation for the social scientist (Second Edition)* (p. 295). New York: McGraw-Hill Education.

Hotelling, H. (1929). Stability in competition. *The Economic Journal, 39*(153), 41. https://doi.org/10.2307/2224214

Jennings, N. R. (2000). On agent-based software engineering. *Artificial Intelligence, 117*(2), 277–296.

Kiesling, E., Günther, M., Stummer, C., & Wakolbinger, L. M. (2012). Agent-based simulation of innovation diffusion: A review. *CEJOR, 20*, 183–230.

Laite, R., Portman, N., & Sankaranarayanan, K. (2016). Behavioral analysis of agent based service channel design using neural networks. In *2016 Winter Simulation Conference (WSC)* (pp. 3694–3695). IEEE.

Linard, C., Ponçon, N., Fontenille, D., & Lambin, E. F. (2009). A multi-agent simulation to assess the risk of malaria re-emergence in southern France. *Ecological Modelling, 220*(2), 160–174.

Lindenberg, M., & Bryant, C. (2001). *Going global: Transforming relief and development NGOs*. Bloomfield, CT: Kumarian Press.

Liu, Z., Rexachs, D., Epelde, F., & Luque, E. (2017). An agent-based model for quantitatively analyzing and predicting the complex behavior of emergency departments. *Journal of Computational Science, 21*, 11–23.

Macal, C. (2004). Emergent structures from trust relationships in supply chains. In C. Macal, D. Sallach, & M. North (Eds.), *Proceedings of Agent 2004: Conference on social dynamics: Interaction, reflexivity and emergence* (pp. 743–760). Chicago: Argonne National Laboratory.

Macal, C. (2016). Everything you need to know about agent-based modelling and simulation. *Journal of Simulation, 10*(2), 144–156.

Macal, C., & North, M. (2006). Tutorial on agent-based modeling and simulation part 2: How to model with agents. In L. F. Perrone, F. P. Wieland, J. Liu, B. G. Lawson, D. M. Nicol, & R. M. Fujimoto (Eds.), *Proceedings of the 2006 Winter Simulation Conference* (pp. 73–83). Monterey, CA.

Macal, C., & North, M. (2010). Tutorial on agent-based modelling and simulation. *Journal of Simulation, 4*(3), 151–162.

Menth, M., & Heier Stamm, J. (2015). An agent-based modeling approach to improve coordination between humanitarian relief providers. In L. Yilmaz, W. K. V. Chan, I. Moon, T. M. K. Roeder, C. Macal, & M. D. Rossetti (Eds.), *Proceedings of the 2015 Winter Simulation Conference* (pp. 3116–3117). IEEE.

Mollona, E. (2008). Computer simulation in social sciences. *Journal of Management & Governance, 12*(2), 205–211.

Nikolai, C., & Madey, G. (2009). Tools of the trade: A survey of various agent based modeling platforms. *Journal of Artificial Societies and Social Simulation, 12*(2), 1–37.

North, M., & Macal, C. (2007). *Managing business complexity: Discovering strategic solutions with agent-based modeling and simulation*. Oxford University Press.

Oliveira, J. B., Lima, R. S., & Montevechi, J. A. B. (2016). Perspectives and relationships in supply chain simulation: A systematic literature review. *Simulation Modelling Practice and Theory, 62*, 166–191.

Oloruntoba, R., & Gray, R. (2006). Humanitarian aid: An agile supply chain? *Supply Chain Management: An International Journal, 11*(2), 115–120.

Ottino, B., Stonedahl, F., & Wilensky, U. (2009). NetLogo Hotelling's Law model. Retrieved January 2018, from http://ccl.northwestern.edu/netlogo/models/Hotelling'sLaw

Reisman, K. (2006). Thinking like a wolf, a sheep or a firefly: Learning biology through constructing and testing computational theories—An embodied modeling approach. *Cognition and Instruction, 24*(2), 171–209.

Šalamon, T. (2011). *Design of agent-based models, developing computer simulations for a better understanding of social processes*. Academic series. Repin, Czech Republic: Thomas Bruckner.

Sankaranarayanan, K. (2011). *Study on behavioral patterns in queuing: Agent based modeling and experimental approach.* Università della Svizzera italiana. Retrieved December 2017, from https://doc.rero.ch/record/27284/files/2011ECO006.pdf

Sankaranarayanan, K., Castañeda, J. A., & Villa, S. (2017). Future research in humanitarian operations: A behavioral operations perspective. In G. Kovács, K. Spens, & M. Moshtari (Eds.), *Handbook of humanitarian logistics and supply chain management.* London, UK: Palgrave Macmillan.

Sankaranarayanan, K., Delgado, C., van Ackere, A., & Larsen, E. R. (2014). The micro-dynamics of queuing: Understanding the formation of queues. *Journal of Simulation, 8*(4), 304–313.

Sankaranarayanan, K., Laite, R., & Portman, N. (2017). Neural network analysis of behavioral agent based service channel data. In *Proceedings of the 2017 IEEE Industrial Engineering and Engineering Management Conference*, Singapore.

Stauffer, J. M., Pedraza-Martinez, A. J., & Van Wassenhove, L. N. (2016). Temporary hubs for the global vehicle supply chain in humanitarian operations. *Production and Operations Management, 25*(2), 192–209.

Tomasini, R., & van Wassenhove, L. N. (2009). *Humanitarian logistics* (Vol. 20, 1st ed.). London, UK: Palgrave Macmillan.

Urrea, G., Besiou, M., & Pedraza-Martinez, A. J. (2018). *Volunteer management in charity storehouses: Volunteer experience, congestion and operational performance.* Bloomington.

van Wassenhove, L. N. (2006). Humanitarian aid logistics: Supply chain management in high gear. *Journal of the Operational Research Society, 57*(1), 475–489.

Vogel, M. P. (2009). Understanding emergent social phenomena comparatively: The need for computational simulation. *European Journal of Social Sciences, 7*(4), 84–92.

Wilensky, U., & Reisman, K. (1998). Connected science: Learning biology through constructing and testing computational theories—An embodied modeling approach. *International Journal of Complex Systems, 234*, 1–12.

Wooldridge, M., & Jennings, N. R. (1995). Intelligent agents: Theory and practice. *The Knowledge Engineering Review, 10*(2), 115–152.

Zobel, C. W., Altay, N., & Haselkorn, M. P. (Eds.). (2016). *Advances in managing humanitarian operations.* Cham: Springer International Publishing.

13

Effects of Wholesale Competition in Supply Chains: An Analysis with Heterogeneous Decision-Makers

Yuly Arboleda and Santiago Arango-Aramburo

13.1 Introduction

Currently, firms compete throughout their supply chain to satisfy final customer demand (Gigola, 2001; Hwarng & Xie, 2008; Wu, Gan, & Wei, 2011). These supply chains consist of a network of manufacturers, suppliers, distribution centers and customers, as well as the respective relationships between them. In these networks, operations that comprise the production, supply, and distribution of goods are carried out, generating flows of products and information (Ponte, Sierra, de la Fuente, & Lozano, 2017; Rúa, 2008).

Supply chains are complex dynamic systems which contain feedback, non-linearity, delays (Hwarng & Xie, 2008), demand and delivery uncertainty (Wu et al., 2011) and involve the participation of multiple agents with implications on system behavior, as well as decision-making on when and how much to stock. It is important to comprehend the

---

Y. Arboleda (✉) • S. Arango-Aramburo
Decision Sciences Group, Universidad Nacional de Colombia, Faculty of Mines, Medellín, Colombia
e-mail: yaarbole@unal.edu.co; saarango@unal.edu.co

complexity of the supply chain and the rationality of the decision-making processes of agents in order to enhance the system's productivity and lessen possible impacts on society (Villa, 2011).

In a humanitarian aid context, the primary task of the supply chain is to deliver the right supplies to the right people, in the right place, at the right time and in the right amounts (Stephenson, 1993). In this context, the supply chain is a complex and interlinked network in which different actors, processes, decisions and information are combined to serve the needs of victims in a catastrophe. The effective management of aid determines the number of lives that can be saved (Cuervo, Diaz, Namen, Palacio, & Sierra, 2010). Therefore, in a disaster, receipt, transportation, storage and delivery of necessary goods become difficult tasks that require the mobilization of a great amount of resources (Cuervo et al., 2010). Disaster relief largely depends on logistics, so improvements in this area have major impacts on the three performance dimensions of relief operations: effectiveness (quality), responsiveness (time), and efficiency (cost) (Charles, Lauras, Van Wassenhove, & Dupont, 2016).

One of the most frequent and costly issues in supply chains is known as the Bullwhip Effect (Armony & Plambeck, 2005). The term "Bullwhip" describes the effect wherein order fluctuation increases as the orders move higher up the supply chain (Croson & Donohue, 2002; Wang & Disney, 2016). The Bullwhip Effect indicates an asynchronization among supply chain agents, since a small variation in the final customer demand generates fluctuations in the production of the suppliers at the other end of the chain. In times of increasing (or decreasing) demand, links lower down the chain will increase (or reduce) the orders (Buchmeister, Pavlinjek, Palcic, & Polajnar, 2008). In this situation, the supplier takes the decision to increase production capacity according to perceived demand (Cachon & Lariviere, 1999). However, once the supplier has enough capacity to satisfy the perceived demand, and the last customers stop ordering, the supplier retains installations for a high production capacity (Villa, 2011). The difference between the final customer demand and the supplier's surplus production capacity generates a speculative bubble of demand.

The causes of the Bullwhip Effect are operational and behavioral (Lee, Padmanabhan, & Whang, 1997a). Operational causes are structural characteristics that allow the agent to amplify demand variation (Croson,

Donohue, Katok, & Sterman, 2014). According to Lee et al. (1997a, 1997b) the variability in orders happens as a result of four causes: (i) batch orders, (ii) price fluctuations, (iii) capacity deficit which leads to rationing by the supplier, and (iv) demand signal processing. Behavioral causes are attributed to the cognitive limitations (bounded rationality) of the decision-makers, and are mainly due to insufficient consideration being given to feedback and delay cycles (Croson et al., 2014; Sterman, 1989). These cognitive limitations trigger a surplus of capital investment, excess or inadequate stock, the hiring and firing of workforce, difficulties with demand forecasting and manufacturing programming, as well as delivery delays and impacts on competitiveness (Armony & Plambeck, 2005; Lee et al., 1997a; Nienhaus, Ziegenbein, & Duijts, 2006; Sterman, 2000; Wang & Disney, 2016). In general, the Bullwhip Effect makes management and efficient operation of the system difficult, since available resources are not used efficiently (Kaminsky & Simchi-Levi, 1998). Different industries around the world have felt the impact of the Bullwhip Effect, for example, Pampers diapers (Croson & Donohue, 2002; Lee et al., 1997a; Wang & Disney, 2016), General Electric in 1958, Motorola in 1993, Cisco in 2000, and Tesco in 2007 to name just a few. However, these events have not been sufficient to gain a complete understanding of the Bullwhip Effect due to the heterogeneity of the agents involved, the way they behave in a competitive environment and the possible existence of multiple decision rules, as observed by Delgado, van Ackere, Larsen, and Arango (2017). Ponte et al. (2017) found that the efficiency of each inventory model depends on not only on the external environment but also on the decisions of the other links in the chain.

This more comprehensive understanding of the Bullwhip Effect is in line with the current requirements for humanitarian logistics, where there is a call for more integrated models that require better comprehension of the problem (Özdamara & Alp Ertemb, 2015). In response, demand in the context of humanitarian logistics has been empirically studied (e.g. van der Laan, van Dalen, Rohrmoser, & Simpson, 2018) and in this investigation, we focus on the effect of demand in humanitarian logistics through the use of modeling and laboratory experiments.

We proposed an experiment that would test demand for a scarce product in a competitive environment, with a supply chain characterized by multiple wholesale customers and a unique supplier. In this chapter, we develop a strategy which allows the identification of agents' typical behaviors when presented with the management of a specific echelon in a supply chain, through an agent-based simulation model with System Dynamics and a pilot decision-making laboratory experiment in a network. This strategy will permit us to determine the basic elements that allow for the definition of better supply, manufacturing and distribution policies in a supply chain.

In the case of supply chains in the humanitarian sector, once a disaster has occurred, the supply needs (the demand for medicines, products and other items) of the affected population must be assessed. The needs of the affected population are assessed by distribution centers, which are then responsible for requesting the necessary items to meet the needs of the population. The organizations must do this in a complex and competitive sector, where the supply chain structure is, in some cases, similar to the structure that we deal with in this chapter. The organizations are often highly diverse, with many differences in their functions and operations, and so can be interpreted as heterogeneous agents.

This chapter starts by describing the methodology implemented. Then, the mathematical model is proposed and the results are developed and analyzed. Next, building on the concepts of experimental economics, we use our mathematical model to run a behavioral experiment (a pilot) in order to understand the impact of the delays in the participant's performance, taking into account that they are heterogeneous agents. Finally, the conclusions and recommendations for future studies are presented.

13.2 Methodology

The operational and behavioral factors that generate the Bullwhip Effect are studied using simulation and laboratory experiment methodologies. Simulation methodologies consist of System Dynamics and agent-based modeling that allow both the understanding of the structure of the system and the modeling of the decision rules of the different agents. The simulation starts with the construction of a model that reproduces a certain global problematic behavior through the interrelated functioning of its multiple variables (Cassar & Friendman, 2004). Consequently, this tool allows for the evaluation of the impact of different strategies on the variables of interest, as well as for the proposal of strategies to solve different types of problems (Garayalde & Rodriguez, 1985).

A causal diagram is constructed to find the main causes that lead people to adopt certain behaviors (Sterman, 2000). Likewise, a mathematical model based on differential equations is developed which allows the global problematic behavior to be reproduced (Cassar & Friendman, 2004). As stated above, the model combines System Dynamics and agent-based simulation methodologies. The former allows us to model the supply chain characterized by feedback cycles, delays, nonlinear relationships and accumulation and flow processes, while the latter allows us to model wholesalers as heterogeneous agents with their respective decision rules.

The behavioral factors of the Bullwhip Effect have been studied through laboratory experiments, demonstrating that this phenomenon persists even in idealized supply chains, in which the operational factors are eliminated (Croson & Donohue, 2002). In this study, a pilot experiment was developed within a network that allowed people's behavior when making decisions to be determined (Friendman & Sunder, 1994), through the control of information and dynamic complexity (Arango, Castañeda, & Olaya, 2012), assuming the role of wholesale customers in a supply chain characterized by having a single supplier selling a unique and irreplaceable product to several wholesale customers. The experiment is developed in a realistic environment that takes into consideration a continuous time step, limited capacity, endogenous and variable delays, perceptions of system behavior and delays in adjustment. For further research on Humanitarian Operations from a behavioral operations perspective, see Sankaranarayanan, Castañeda, and Villa (2018).

In general, the Bullwhip Effect is formulated using System Dynamics and Agent-Based simulation to study the formal dimension of the supplier-customer relationship in a supply chain. The mathematical model is based on the formulation of the decision-making experiment. The orders of the decisions made by agents on the supply chain, assuming the role as the wholesale customer, are researched through laboratory experiments. Finally, the results are presented using the mathematical model.

13.3 Model Design

In this section, the mathematics of simulation using both the System Dynamics and Agent-Based model methods are presented in order to study the formal relation between supplier and customer in the supply chain. The System Dynamics model is adapted following the instructions in Villa, Gonçalves, and Arango (2015). In this model, the wholesale customer's decision-making process is modified. While the System Dynamics formulation uses a single decision rule, we incorporate a number of different decision rules which represent agents with heterogeneous behavior. This consideration becomes the component called the Agent-Based Simulation, where the agents are humanitarian logisticians competing for a scarce resource. Then, we formulate the model based on Grimm et al. (2006, 2010).

13.3.1 General Vision

The aim is to design a model of the basic structure of a supply chain, including the different wholesale customer decision-making processes. The supply chain is characterized by having a unique supplier who sells a unique and irreplaceable product to five wholesale customers in a competitive environment. In this scenario, Villa et al. (2015) suggests that the wholesale customer increases their orders when considering the proportional difference between the assigned supply and the final demand. The model simulates weekly periods, taking into account weekly orders to the supplier by the wholesale customers.

The main expected result of the model is to show how the Bullwhip Effect typically behaves in the presence of the variability of the wholesale customer's orders. To achieve it, we carried out laboratory experiments where we studied the results of a 20% increase in the final demand. This allowed us to show to what extent variability in orders impacts the suppliers' production capacity. These behaviors stem from the use of different decision rules by wholesale customers when placing product orders. Here, the wholesale customer's goal is to minimize their total costs during the simulation. Total costs are the sum of both ordering costs and stock or deficit costs. The main model outputs are the wholesale customer's orders and the resulting change in producer capacity, which are necessary to be able to see the dynamics of the system.

The wholesale customer adjusts the supply line to the desired levels, while the capacity adjustment carried out by the supplier seeks to balance the effect of the system's positive cycle through the variation in capacity. Meanwhile, in a scenario without competition, the wholesale customers change their orders with the purpose of adjusting the supply line, taking into account the perceived delays in the delivery. In the scenario that includes competition, the wholesale customers tend to overcompensate for the increased delays in delivery by ordering a lot of what they need in advance. The wholesale customer's desire to have greater stock security, which makes it necessary to increase orders to the supplier, thus increasing orders received and, therefore, future delays. Since wholesale customers think that they will receive only a part of their total orders as a result of the competition for a scarce product, they exaggerate orders with the expectation of getting what they want. However, this implies an increase in the accumulated orders and desired stock. Finally, wholesale customers order more than needed to compensate for the unreliability generated by receiving part of the order and because they know they are in competition for a scarce product. Thus, the model explores the typical behavior of the Bullwhip Effect, representing an increase and decrease in the orders as the wholesale customers respond to a deficit in the supply.

13.3.2 Mathematical Model

The mathematical model builds on the model discussed by Villa (2011) and Villa et al. (2015). The supply line is expressed as follows:

$$PO = P - E,$$

where

PO: pending orders to deliver
P: wholesale customer orders
E: delivery

The wholesale customer adjusts the orders, taking into consideration the final customer demand (D), the adjustment term of the Desired Level of Pending Orders (PO*) and the supplier's real pending orders (PO) in a delivery time (τ_E).

$$P = \text{Max}\left(0, D + \frac{PO^* - PO}{\tau_E}\right)$$

In turn, PO* depends on the final customer demand (D), and the expected delays of the delivery function $f(x)$ capturing the adjustment made by wholesale customers in response to the real delays. The expected delays in deliveries are determined based on a real delays function $g(y)$, while those real delays are the relation between PO and E.

$$PO^* = D \times f(\text{expected delays})$$

$$PO^* = D \times g(\text{real delays})$$

$$PO^* = D \times g\left(\frac{PO}{\text{deliveries}}\right)$$

On the other hand, the supplier's production capacity (C) is limited, thus, this determines the E flow. Therefore, the desired production capacity (C*) depends on the PO and the desired delivery time $\left(\tau_E^*\right)$:

$$E = C; \quad C^* = \frac{OP}{\tau_E^*}$$

The supplier can adjust C, considering that C* will respond to the wholesale customer's orders, C and the time needed to build the new capacity (τ_c):

$$\Delta C = \frac{C^* - C}{\tau_c}$$

This model assumes that wholesale customers adapt their expected delays to each of the three decision rules (T) that they are following, according to Villa (2011) and Villa et al. (2015):

T1: Wholesale customers make the adjustment for the expected delays proportionally to the real delays perceived by the supplier.

$$f(\text{expected delays}) = \alpha \times g(\text{Real delays}), \text{ where } \alpha \geq 1,$$

where α is the linear coefficient, which shows the wholesale customers' aggression when making orders to the supplier.

T2: Wholesale customers make the adjustment for expected delays as an average between the desired delivery time and the real delays of the supplier.

$$f(\text{expected delays}) = \text{average}(\text{Desired delivery time, real delays})$$

T3: The wholesale customers' expected delays are equal to the supplier's real delays.

$$f(\text{expected deylays}) = \text{real delays}$$

T4: This decision rule is composed of the T1, T2, and T3 and it is an interaction between the decision rules. In T4, wholesale customers 1 and 2 follow the decision rule T1, wholesale customers 3 and 4 follow T2, and the wholesale customer 5 follows T5.

Finally, stock variables used for cumulative shipments and demand are included which is useful in calculating the costs by stock or deficit.

$$D_{\mathrm{CF}} = d$$
$$E_{\mathrm{Total}} = E$$

The supplier can adjust production capacity assuming a delay in the supply to wholesale customers. The supplier does not have decision rules as to how and when to build capacity, they can only increase or decrease it in response to the perceived demand of wholesale customers. The model includes five wholesale customers who order from the same supplier. The order decisions are regulated by the wholesale customers' delays adjustment. Thus they behave according to decision rules that are considered heterogeneous.

The validation of a System Dynamics model is a process of establishing confidence in the model in order to evaluate if the model's representation corresponds to reality, checking not only structure but also behavior (Barlas, 1996). The model considered here has been widely verified by Villa (2011) and Villa et al. (2015).

13.4 Simulation Result

Based on the model, simulation exercises are carried out during a period of 25 weeks. Simulations allow the Bullwhip effect's behavior to show itself in the supply chain proposed. The simulation targets observe the wholesale customers' response to an increase in the final demand of 20% (see Fig. 13.1a). In the first four periods, the final demand is established at 20 units per week. Then the demand grows to at 24 units per week. Considering the final demand, the increase seeks to represent periods of exhaustion in the system and the resulting order decisions with regard to the supplier's production capacity.

Under the four decision rules simulated, we observe that increasing the final demand pushes agents and wholesale customers to increase their orders to the supplier, even placing much larger orders (twice the demand) in comparison to the perceived demand. This behavior is explained by the belief that the demand will continue increasing over time. For this reason, the wholesale customer increases their orders and places them in

Effects of Wholesale Competition in Supply Chains... 301

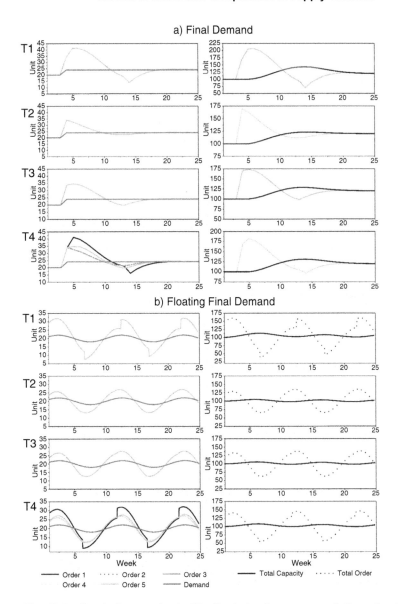

Fig. 13.1 Simulation results. In T1 all wholesale customers follow the decision rule T1; and the same applies to T2 and T3, respectively. T4 is an interaction of decision rules where wholesale customers 1 and 2 follow T1; wholesale customers 3 and 4 follow T2, and wholesale customer 5 follows T3. Wholesale customer's behavior (left) and supplier's behavior (right)

advance with the intention of stocking up and satisfying the final demand that they hope will increase in the meantime. On the supplier's side, we observe an adjustment of the production capacity in response to the total orders made by the wholesale customer agents.

The second decision rule can be explained by the fact that the change in the capacity of the supplier is less extreme than in the rest of the cases. This can be explained by the order decisions of wholesale customers, which are more aggressive at the moment they perceive the change in demand, as well as the way in which wholesale customers place large orders to ensure supply.

Finally, in the four decision rules, the typical behavior of the Bullwhip Effect appears when the wholesale customer increases the orders beyond the final demand perceived, and in response, the supplier reacts by increasing its production capacity.

13.4.1 Floating Demand

Figure 13.1b analyzes the supply chain behavior with a final floating demand. We suppose that the demand variation follows a sinusoidal wave pattern with minimum values of 18 units and a maximum of 22 units over 25 weeks.

Regarding the four decision rules, we observe the amplification of orders to the supplier in comparison with the perceived demand. Although the final customer demand follows a sinusoidal behavior, it is possible to see that orders behave similarly, only greatly amplified. Once the final customer demand increases again, the wholesale customer amplifies the orders, thus sending the supplier an erroneous demand signal. With regard to capacity build-up, even though the orders placed by the wholesale customers are far superior to the final customers' orders, the supplier does not experiment a dramatic change in production capacity. This behavior can be explained by the delays that are considered part of the model. These delays allow the supplier to avoid having to immediately build the capacity necessary to satisfy the orders that have been observed.

13.5 Toward a Network Experiment

With the purpose of analyzing the Bullwhip Effect, a pilot experiment is initially proposed. It allows for the exploration of the decisions of five competing wholesale customers and a unique supplier in a supply chain network. The pilot experiment seeks to analyze the influence of two basic characteristics of the supply chain, identified previously by Gonçalves and Arango (2010) and evaluated by Villa (2011). These two characteristics consist of: (i) Delays from the moment the wholesale customer places an order to the moment the order is received by the supplier; and (ii) Delays in the supplier's capacity development. The new component of the experiment considers that instead of one-single-player that represents the aggregated behavior of the system, we add more realism by considering five players in a network game that represent different agents, as described below.

The proposed experiment takes place over 35 periods. Each period represents a week in which each participant or wholesale customer decides the number of units that will be ordered from the supplier in order to cover customer demand. The goal of the experiment is not communicated to the participants of the experiment so as to avoid biases that could trigger an exaggerated order or suborder. The period is longer than the simulations to avoid unusual end-of-game behavior.

Order decisions made by the five wholesale customers are received by a unique supplier, two or three periods after the order is made, and they are accumulated in the pending orders. The supplier behavior is simulated by a computer, with its initial production capacity at 100 units per week. However, the supplier has the ability to change in response to the wholesale customer's total orders. The construction time of the supplier's capacity is one to three weeks, depending on the treatment to which the participants are subjected. In total, there are four treatments due to the crossover between the supplier's delay in investing in capacity and the decision delays of wholesale customers. If the supplier does not have enough capacity to satisfy the needs of the wholesale customer, they begin to experience delays in the delivery of orders, which are assigned to the wholesale customer in proportion to the orders placed by each one. Once the wholesale customer perceives the failure to deliver, they will also default on their final customers, incurring high costs due to order decisions, deficit or stock.

The model calculates the participant's performance through total accumulated costs. Participant costs per week have two components.

- Order costs (OC):

$$OC = \frac{1 \times (\text{Order decision})^2}{1.000}$$

- Deficit/stock costs (DC):

$$DC = \frac{2 \times (\text{Order decision})^2}{1.000}$$

- The total accumulated costs (TCA) by the wholesale customers are given as follow:

$$TCA = \sum_{t=1}^{T} (OC_t + DC_t)$$

In the first three weeks the wholesale customers order 20 units per week. Afterwards, the participants make the decision to order a certain number of units from the supplier in order to satisfy the final customers' demand. Meanwhile, demand is constant for the first four weeks, then the demand increases by 20%, and then remains constant at this new level. In this way, the participants play as wholesale customers and confront a sudden demand increase, trying to satisfy the demand while trying to minimize total costs throughout the entire experiment.

13.5.1 Experimental Method

The pilot experiment developed follows the methodology and protocol used in the experimental economy (Cassar & Friendman, 2004; Friendman & Sunder, 1994). We followed standard protocol, which is not reported here since it is a pilot. The validity of the results of the experiment is supported by the findings of the experiment conducted by Croson and Donohue (2006). The authors concluded that the results from the professional groups are consistent with the results obtained in the experiments with students.

The experiments were conducted in the same Powersim simulation software in which the experimental model was designed, allowing orders of wholesale customers to be made in real time to the same supplier (server) using different computers. In the computer room, the four treatments were simulated at the same time so that the wholesale customers did not know who their direct competitors were. Each experimental treatment corresponded to a market consisting of 5 participants, who were asked to write order decisions on a sheet of paper along with the total costs incurred. This was done in order to have physical evidence of the decisions made and a record of participants' performance in order to pay out the rewards.

Croson and Donohue (2006) argue that a monetary reward is of great importance since it acts as an incentive for the participants in the experiment to minimize the costs in the game. In this way, the participants of the experiment were paid for their participation according to the performance attained, according to the estimate created by Villa (2011):

$$\text{Reward}[\$] = 1000 \times R_{max} \times \frac{1}{1 + R_{min}^{-TCA}},$$

where:

R_{max} and R_{min}: maximum and minimum reward for developing the experiment.
TCA: total accumulated costs of each participant (wholesale customer).

13.5.2 Pilot Experiment Results

Numerical results are preliminary indications of possible results, and they are useful as a fundamental step toward a formal experiment. It is worth highlighting that, for this pilot, an experiment was performed for each of the experimental treatments. In this way, the order behaviors of the participants are shown without exception after statistical analysis. Figure 13.2 describes the order decisions for each treatment of the laboratory experiment (right) and the average orders (left).

The four treatments present a wholesale customer's average expected behavior based on simulation results. Once participants perceive that the final demand increases to 24 units, they exaggerate their orders beyond this level. In treatments 1 and 4, the increase reaches 26 units, equivalent to 106%, while treatment 2 reaches 40 units, 166%. When the supplier satisfies the demand, we observe that the order decisions of wholesale customers decrease in order to use up stocks and reduce costs. Nevertheless, orders increase again during the following periods in order to stock up, since the previous low orders were not sufficient to satisfy the final demand.

The average orders of the third treatment do not present the expected increase at the beginning of the experiment. On the contrary, it was not until the eighth week of the simulation that the orders reached 36 units, with the orders below final customer demand. This behavior is shown in the low order decisions of decision-makers 3 and 5. The first decision-maker orders below demand during periods 4–7, then increases their orders and then reduces them. In the learning period, 20 units per week are ordered. Decision-maker five orders zero units after the three learning periods then increases the orders above demand from the eighth week on.

Finally, with regard to the ordering decisions of each participant in the different treatments, it is not possible to demonstrate the effect of the delays present in these experimental treatments, where treatments three and four present greater delays. The third treatment shows the greatest instability, while in the fourth treatment it is not possible to attribute instability to greater delays in the wholesale customer system.

Effects of Wholesale Competition in Supply Chains... 307

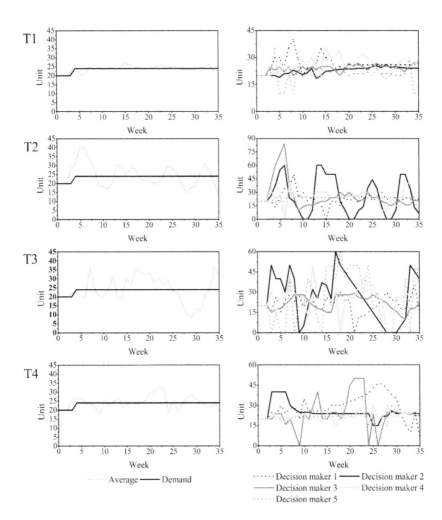

Fig. 13.2 Economic experiment results. In T1 all wholesale customers follow the decision rule T1; and the same applies to T2 and T3, respectively. T4 is an interaction of decision rules where wholesale customers 1 and 2 follow T1; wholesale customers 3 and 4 follow T2, and wholesale customer 5 follows T3. Treatments of the laboratory experiment (right) and the average orders (left)

13.6 Conclusions

To analyze the supply chain, we developed a simulation model based on previous behavioral studies. This model was proposed in order to complement the homogeneity problem in the wholesale customer decision rule, using the heterogeneity rules. The model combined both Agent-Based Simulation and System Dynamics. This study is presented in the context of humanitarian logistics, with the aim of improving the delivery of supplies to the right people, in the right place, at the right time and in the right amounts, as desired (Stephenson, 1993); therefore, we advance toward more effective management where humanitarian logistics is required. In this particular case, we improved understanding of the Bullwhip Effect resulting from the agents' heterogeneity, modeling the way humanitarian agents behave when competing for a scarce first-need item and there is the possible existence of multiple decision rules.

Simulation results show the typical behavior of the Bullwhip Effect when facing a demand increase. Therefore, simulation results are coherent as they show the final customer demand with sinusoidal behavior, as shown in previous literature and in line with the expected behavior of the Bullwhip Effect.

We implemented the decision-making experiment to understand and capture the behavior of the agents (wholesale customers) in a supply chain and to test the results obtained in the simulation model with System Dynamics. Indicatively and without being conclusive, the pilot experiment shows consistency with model assumptions. In general, when participants are confronted with changing demand, they tend to exaggerate the number of orders beyond the real final customer demand in order to satisfy the perceived demand, obliging the supplier to invest in capacity.

Thus, in this investigation we observed that the development of hybrid models using System Dynamics and Agent-Based Simulation act as a methodological approximation that allows for the study of the way in which the wholesale customer makes decisions that trigger the Bullwhip Effect. Further, the experimental economy allows for the assessment of the participants' behavior when taking on the wholesale customer's role and making orders to the supplier when faced with an increase in demand and competition at the same echelon.

For further research, we recommend including other elements in the model, such as the order decisions behavior of the wholesale customer when faced with greater production scarcity from the supplier as well as adding another set of parameters in the decision-making of the wholesale customer. We also suggest running formal experiments with different treatments that have delays in order to analyze the effects on order decisions and on the order amplifications made by wholesale customers, using the data to explore a new heuristic for the wholesale customer decision rules. Additionally, experiments could also include real humanitarian logistics agents and be framed in a humanitarian context, in order to capture the rationality of the decision-making in a humanitarian context.

References

Arango, S., Castañeda, A., & Olaya, Y. (2012). Laboratory experiments in the system dynamics field. *System Dynamics Review, 28*(1), 94–106.

Armony, M., & Plambeck, E. L. (2005). The impact of duplicate orders on demand estimation and capacity investment. *Management Science, 51*(10), 1505–1518.

Barlas, Y. (1996). Formal aspects of model validity and validation in system dynamics. *System Dynamics Review, 12*(3), 183–210.

Buchmeister, B., Pavlinjek, J., Palcic, I., & Polajnar, A. (2008). Bullwhip effect problem in supply chains. *Advances in Production Engineering and Management, 3*(1), 45–55.

Cachon, G. P., & Lariviere, M. (1999). Capacity allocation using past sales: When to turn-and-earn. *Management Science, 45*(5), 685–703.

Cassar, A., & Friendman, D. (2004). *Economics Lab: An intensive course in experimental economics*. Routledge Advances in Experimental and Computable Economics.

Charles, A., Lauras, M., Van Wassenhove, L. N., & Dupont, L. (2016). Designing an efficient humanitarian supply network. *Journal of Operations Management, 47*(48), 58–70.

Croson, R., & Donohue, K. (2002). Experimental economics and supply-chain management. *Interfaces, 32*(5), 74–82.

Croson, R., & Donohue, K. (2006). Behavioral causes of the bullwhip effect and the observed value of inventory information. *Management Science, 52*(3), 323–336.

Croson, R., Donohue, K., Katok, E., & Sterman, J. (2014). Order stability in supply chains: Coordination risk and the role of coordination stock. *Production and Operations Management, 23*(2), 176–196.

Cuervo, R., Diaz, F., Namen, I., Palacio, C., & Sierra, C. (2010). Humanitarian crisis: When supply chains really matter. In *The 28th International Conference of the System Dynamics Society* (Vol. 1 of 4, pp. 818–854). Red Hook, NY: Currant Associates, Inc.

Delgado, C. A., van Ackere, A., Larsen, E. R., & Arango, S. (2017). Managing capacity at a service facility: An experimental approach. *European Journal of Operational Research, 259*(1), 216–228.

Friendman, D., & Sunder, S. (1994). *Experimental methods: A primer for economists*. Cambridge University Press.

Garayalde, I., & Rodriguez, L. (1985). Perspectivas del mercado de trabajo en la C.A.P.V.: Aplicación de un modelo de simulación ad hoc [Perspectives of the job market in the C.A.P.V. using ad hoc simulation]. *Ekonomiaz: Revista Vasca de Economía, 1*, 169–194.

Gigola, C. (2001). Bullwhip effect. Los efectos de una mala sincronización de la Cadena de Suministro [Bullwhip effect: The effects of wrong sinchronization in supply chains]. *Escuela de Negocios. Instituto Tecnológico Autónomo de Mexico, 5*(ITAM).

Gonçalves, P., & Arango, S. (2010). Supplier capacity decisions under retailer competition and delays: Theoretical and experimental results supplier capacity decisions under retailer competition and delays: Theoretical and experimental results. In *Proceedings of the 28th International Conference of the System Dynamics Society* (pp. 1–28).

Grimm, V., Berger, U., Bastiansen, F., Eliassen, S., Ginot, V., Giske, J., ... DeAngelis, D. L. (2006). A standard protocol for describing individual-based and agent-based models. *Ecological Modelling, 198*(1–2), 115–126.

Grimm, V., Berger, U., DeAngelis, D. L., Polhill, J. G., Giske, J., & Railsback, S. F. (2010). The ODD protocol: A review and first update. *Ecological Modelling, 221*(23), 2760–2768.

Hwarng, H. B., & Xie, N. (2008). Understanding supply chain dynamics: A chaos perspective. *European Journal of Operational Research, 184*(3), 1163–1178.

Kaminsky, P., & Simchi-Levi, D. (1998). A new computerized beer game: A tool for teaching the value of integrated supply chain management. *Global Supply Chain and Technology Management. POMS Series in Technology and Operations Management, 1*, 216–225.

Lee, H. L., Padmanabhan, V., & Whang, S. (1997a). Information distortion in a supply chain: The bullwhip effect. *Management Science, 43*(4), 546–558.

Lee, H. L., Padmanabhan, V., & Whang, S. (1997b). The bullwhip effect in supply chains. *Sloan Management Review, 38*(3), 93–102.

Nienhaus, J., Ziegenbein, A., & Duijts, C. (2006). How human behaviour amplifies the bullwhip effect—A study based on the beer distribution game online. *Production Planning & Control, 17*(6), 547–557.

Özdamara, L., & Alp Ertemb, M. (2015). Models, solutions and enabling technologies in humanitarian logistics. *European Journal of Operational Research, 244*(1), 55–65.

Ponte, B., Sierra, E., de la Fuente, D., & Lozano, J. (2017, September). Exploring the interaction of inventory policies across the supply chain: An agent-based approach. *Computers and Operations Research, 78*(2016), 335–348.

Rúa, G. (2008). *Modelación de una cadena de suministro considerando múltiples objetivos y múltiples parámetros bajo incertidumbre*. Universidad Nacional de Colombia.

Sankaranarayanan, K., Castañeda, J. A., & Villa, S. (2018). Future research in humanitarian operations: A behavioral operations perspective. In G. Kovács, K. Spens, & M. Moshtari (Eds.), *The Palgrave handbook of humanitarian logistics and supply chain management*. London: Palgrave Macmillan.

Stephenson, R. (1993). UNDP/UNDRO Disaster Management Training Programme. *Logistics*. Geneva, Switzerland.

Sterman, J. D. (1989). Misperceptions of feedback in dynamic decision making. *Organizational Behavior and Human Decision Processes, 43*(3), 301–335.

Sterman, J. D. (2000). *Business dynamics systems thinking and modeling for a complex world*. Chicago, IL: Irwin/McGraw-Hill.

van der Laan, E., van Dalen, J., Rohrmoser, M., & Simpson, R. (2018). Demand forecasting and order planning for humanitarian logistics: An empirical assessment. *Journal of Operations Management, 45*, 114–122.

Villa, S. (2011). *Efecto de las Decisiones de Pedidos de Clientes Mayoristas en Cadenas de Abastecimiento: Un análisis experimental* [Effect on orders' decisions on wholesale clients in supply chains: An experimental study]. Master's thesis, School of Mines, Universidad Nacional de Colombia, Medellín, Antioquia, Colombia.

Villa, S., Gonçalves, P., & Arango, S. (2015). Exploring retailers' ordering decisions under delays. *System Dynamics Review, 31*(1–2), 1–27.

Wang, X., & Disney, S. M. (2016). The bullwhip effect: Progress, trends and directions. *European Journal of Operational Research, 250*(3), 691–701.

Wu, S., Gan, W., & Wei, F. (2011). Analysis of bullwhip effect based on ABMS. *Procedia Engineering, 15*, 4276–4281.

Index[1]

A
Advance purchase discount (APD), 160
Agent, 277, 278
Agent-Based Modeling (ABM), 277–282
Aid planning, 286
Anchoring, 133, 136
Asian disease problem, 196, 211
Attribute framing, 198, 209, 212, 214
Aversion to leftovers, 134, 136

B
Bangladesh, 81, 92–93
Basic relief items, 9
Beer Game (BG), 152–153
Behavioral experiments (BeExs), 127–130, 216
Behavioral forecasters, 138–142
Behavioral newsvendors, 131–138
Behavioral operations (BeOps), 127
Bonus contract, 207
Bounded rationality, 148
Bullwhip effect, 152–153
Buyback contract, 159

C
Cash donations, 33, 42–44
Causal loop diagrams (CLDs), 233
Change, 138, 140
Change-to-noise ratio, 138
Choice shift, 198
Climate change, 79–82

---

[1] Note: Page numbers followed by 'n' refer to notes.

Index

Climate change adaptation (CCA), 85
Climate information, 77–96
Cognitive biases, 149
Collaboration, 250, 285
Competition, 157–159
Confounding variables, 129
Contract, 159
Control, 129
Convergence, 46
Coordination, 156, 158, 285
Credit scheme, 204, 213
Crowdfunding, 43

D

Data-driven newsvendor, 142
De-biasing, 131, 136
Decision frame, 195
Decision frequency, 132
Demand, 138, 142
Demand forecasting, 138, 140, 141
Disaster management cycle (DMC), 32, 37–42
Disaster-risk reduction (DRR), 85
Distribution-free newsvendor, 138
Disutility of leftovers, 134
Disutility of shortages, 134, 136
Dominance, 129
Donations, 32
Donor identification, 35
Dynamic hypothesis, 233
Dzud, 93–95

E

Earmarking, 33, 42
Emergency department, 284–285

Emergency items catalogue, 9
Emergency Response Unit (ERU), 4
Employee effort allocation, 207
Employee productivity, 213
Environment, 128, 277, 278
Experiments, 147
Exponential smoothing, 138, 139
External validity, 136, 141
Extrinsic incentives, 35

F

Fairness, 186
Feedback, 232
Feedback interventions, 132
Field Assessment Coordination Team (FACT), 4
Financial incentives, 214
Floods, 92–93
Forecast-based actions, 86–95
Forecast-based financing (FbF), 88
Forecast error, 138
Forgone payoffs, 132
Forgone profits, 135
Forgone savings, 135
Framing effects, 194, 196, 198, 199
Fundamental attribution error, 149
Fundraising activities, 36

G

Goal framing, 199, 209, 212
Greenhouse gases, 80

H

Hardship and danger pays, 214
Heuristics, 149

Horizontal coordination, 154–157
Humanitarian operations (HuOps), 127, 150–152

Induced valuation, 129–130
In-kind donations, 8, 33, 46–47
Innovation, 87–89
Institution, 128
Institutional donors, 32
Interdependent preferences, 35
International Committee of the Red Cross (ICRC), 4
International Federation of Red Cross and Red Crescent Societies (IFRC), 4, 7
Intrinsic motivations, 34
Intrinsic motivator, 214

Knowledge exploitation, 69n1
Knowledge exploration, 69n1
Knowledge management, 55–69
Knowledge retention, 69n1

Labor assignment, 45
Learning, 131
Level bias, 131, 135, 139–141
Lives saved/lives lost framing, 211–213
Loan scheme, 204, 213
Long-term actions, 85–86
Loss aversion, 195, 200, 208

Matching forecast, 89
Material convergence, 213
Mental accounting, 187
Mitigation, 41
Monetary rewards, 35
Mongolia, 93–95
Monotonicity, 129
Motivation, 149
Motivations to donate, 34–36
Multi-agent supply chains, 152–159
Multinomial logit choice model, 173, 174, 176

Negative frame, 198, 199, 201, 203, 210
Negative utility frame, 205
Negativity bias, 200
Newsvendor experiments, 131, 132, 139
Newsvendor problem, 131
Noise, 138
Non-governmental organizations (NGO), 7

Observed behavior, 128
Operational transparency, 44
Opportunity cost, 202, 210, 211
Ordering behavior, 201–204
Outcome feedback frequency, 133
Overconfidence, 139, 141
Over-precision, 139–141
Overreaction to noise, 139, 140

P

Paris Agreement, 81
Payment schemes, 204, 213
Penalty contract, 207
Penalty cost, 202, 210, 211
Performance evaluation, 214
Performance targets, 214
Permanent shocks, 138
Positive frame, 198, 199, 201, 203, 210
Positive utility frame, 205
Post-trigger, 90
Preference reversal, 197, 198
Preparedness, 37, 77–96
Prepositioning, 4, 135, 141, 156
Prepositioning problem, 210, 212
Privacy, 129
Private donations, 31–49
Private donors, 32
Prospect theory, 185, 187, 195
Punishment frame, 208
Purchasing transactions, 204

R

Randomization, 130
Red Cross Red Crescent movement, 88, 91
Reference dependence, 134, 136
Refugee pathways, 100
Rehabilitation, 41
Relief operations, 283–284
Response, 37
Return periods, 80
Revenue-sharing contract, 160
Reward frame, 208
Risky choice framing, 197, 212
Rules, 277, 278

S

Saliency, 129
Seed capital, 35
Shortage costs, 202
Short-term actions, 86–91
Simulation model, 281
SL emphasis, 135, 136, 140, 141
Social capital, 57
Sphere standards, 6
Standard scheme, 213
Stock and flow (S&F), 233
Strategy, 55–69
Strong network ties, 58
System Dynamics (SD), 223

T

Task decomposition, 139, 141
Temporary shocks, 138
Time donations, 33, 44–46
Training, 133
Transshipments, 154
Trigger, 89

U

Underreaction to change, 139, 140
United Nations High Commissioner for Refugees (UNHCR), 9
Unsolicited donations, 47

V

Vertical coordination, 159–162
Volunteer convergence, 46
Volunteering, 44
Volunteer management, 44, 216
Volunteer satisfaction, 45
Volunteer skills and experience, 44

W

Warm glow, 34
Weak internal network ties, 58
Weather-related disasters, 77
Wholesale-price contract, 159
Worker productivity, 208
World Food Program (WFP), 9

CPSIA information can be obtained
at www.ICGtesting.com
Printed in the USA
LVHW080314301118
598754LV00010B/117/P